Medbh
McGuckian

CONTEMPORARY **IRISH** WRITERS

a Bucknell series

Series Editor:
John Rickard

Irish studies is currently undergoing a renewal, not only in connection to major figures such as James Joyce and W. B. Yeats, but also within a larger framework, with particular attention to women's issues, nationalism, Northern Ireland and its writers, the Irish language, and the fiction, poetry, drama and film of contemporary Ireland.

These short monographs bring newer, more theoretically informed perspectives to a consideration of the work and lives of single authors, and they provide a general discussion of interpretive issues and strategies for understanding this work. These books will appeal to a sophisticated but not solely professorial audience—that is, advanced undergraduates, graduate students, and independent readers and scholars as well as professors of Irish literature and culture.

Titles in the Series

Richard R. Russell on Bernard MacLaverty

Jody Allen Randolph on Eavan Boland

Borbála Faragó on Medbh McGuckian

www.bucknell.edu/universitypress

CONTEMPORARY IRISH WRITERS

Medbh McGuckian

Borbála Faragó

CORK UNIVERSITY PRESS

Published in 2014 by
Cork University Press
Youngline Industrial Estate
Pouladuff Road, Togher
Cork, Ireland

First published in the United States by Bucknell University Press
This edition is published by arrangement with The Rowman & Littlefield Publishing Group Inc.
4501 Forbes Boulevard, Suite 200, Lanham, Maryland 20706
www.rowman.com

British Library Cataloguing in Publication Data
A CIP catalogue record for this book is available from the British Library.

ISBN: 978-1-78205-088-9

Printed in Malta by Gutenberg Press

To Tadhg

CONTENTS

ACKNOWLEDGMENTS

I WOULD LIKE TO THANK AND ACKNOWLEDGE the financial support provided by the European Commission Seventh Framework Programme Marie Curie Actions (Intra-European Fellowships [IEF], Acronym MIGLIT, Contract number 299613, at http://ec.europa.eu/research/mariecurieactions). Thanks are also due to the Central European University, Budapest, Department of Gender Studies that hosted me for the duration of the Marie Curie project. The writing of this book was made possible by a postdoctoral fellowship awarded by the Irish Research Council (IRCHSS), which I gratefully acknowledge. In addition I would like to express my thanks to University College Dublin Humanities Institute and especially Marc Caball and its current director, Gerardine Meaney, for institutional support. Poems in the book were reproduced by kind permission from Medbh McGuckian, The Gallery Press, and Wake Forest University Press, for which I am very grateful. Some of the writing in this book is based on the following articles and essays I published previously: "'Self-Portrait in the Act of Painting a Self-Portrait': Tropes of Inspiration in Medbh McGuckian's *Shelmalier*," *Études Britanniques Contemporaines* 25 (December 2003): 31–45; "'The Meeting of Two Tidal Roads': Tradition and Identity in Medbh McGuckian's *The Face of the Earth* and Eiléan Ní Chuilleanáin's *The Girl Who Married the Reindeer*," *Hungarian Journal of English and American Studies* 10, nos. 1–2 (Spring–Fall 2004): 331–41; "Origin and Oblivion: Representations of Death in the Poetry of Medbh McGuckian and Eiléan Ní Chuilleanáin," in *Ireland: Space, Text, Time*, ed. Yvonne Whelan, Patrick Crotty, and Liam Harte (Dublin: Liffey Press, 2005), 67–76; "Medbh McGuckian: The Angel in Two Parts," *European English Messenger* 13, no. 2 (Autumn 2004): 47–55; and "'They Come into It': The Muses of Medbh McGuckian," in *The Poetry of Medbh McGuckian: The Interior of Word*, ed. Shane Alcobia-Murphy and Richard Kirkland, (Cork: Cork University Press, 2010), 162–76.

ACKNOWLEDGMENTS

There are many people who supported me throughout this project with scholarly guidance, kindness, and good humor. I am very grateful to Anne Fogarty and Guinn Batten for their encouragement, to the director of the press, Greg Clingham, and series editor John Rickard for giving me the opportunity to write this monograph, to Shane Alcobia-Murphy for his astute insights and assistance, and to Sam Brawand for her invaluable assistance with the copyediting process. I also wish to thank my friends and colleagues Luz Mar González-Arias, Lucy Collins, Kathryn Kirkpatrick, Michaela Schrage-Früh, Hedwig Schwall, Philip Coleman, Eva Bourke, and Zsófia Balla for all things poetical, and Jasmina Lukic for her generosity and kindness. My friends and extended family, as always, have stood by me and held my hand when necessary. Many thanks to Maureen McAuley and Ali Carey for bringing out a different side of me, to Zsuzsa Mátrai and all the others who cared for my children with so much love, to László Varga and the whole big Nagy family for friendship that goes beyond words, to my Irish family, to my father and brother, and to my mother, who is always a shining beacon in my eyes.

I also wish to say a special thanks to Medbh McGuckian, who never lost patience with me and replied to every single email I harassed her with. I am very grateful for her friendship and trust, and for the wonderful poetic universe she has created.

Finally I would like to thank my inexpressibly brilliant children, Lorka, Liadh, and Imre, who are everything to me. This book is dedicated with love and gratitude to the light of my life, Tadhg. Grá mo chroí go deo thú.

ABBREVIATIONS

The poetry collections of Medbh McGuckian:

BTA	*The Book of the Angel* (Oldcastle, Ireland: Gallery Press, 2004).
CL	*Captain Lavender* (Oldcastle, Ireland: Gallery Press, 1994).
CRNH	*The Currach Requires No Harbours* (Oldcastle, Ireland: Gallery Press, 2006).
DB	*Drawing Ballerinas* (Oldcastle, Ireland: Gallery Press, 2001).
FM	*The Flower Master and Other Poems* (Oldcastle, Ireland: Gallery Press, 1993).
FOE	*The Face of the Earth* (Oldcastle, Ireland: Gallery Press, 2002).
HCC	*The High Caul Cap* (Oldcastle, Ireland: Gallery Press, 2012).
HTL	*Had I a Thousand Lives* (Oldcastle, Ireland: Gallery Press, 2003).
MC	*Marconi's Cottage* (Oldcastle, Ireland: Gallery Press, 1991).
MLFI	*My Love Has Fared Inland* (Oldcastle, Ireland: Gallery Press, 2008).
OBB	*On Ballycastle Beach* (Oldcastle, Ireland: Gallery Press, 1995).
SHEL	*Shelmalier* (Oldcastle, Ireland: Gallery Press, 1998).
VR	*Venus and the Rain* (Oldcastle, Ireland: Gallery Press, 1994).

INTRODUCTION

In 1979, Jean Fisher won the National Poetry Competition Prize with three submitted poems, "The Flitting," "Tulips," and "McGregor's Garden." The prize money was £1,000, and since this was a well-publicized, important national competition, the media went to the house of Jean Fisher to broadcast the event. When they arrived, six-month-pregnant Medbh McGuckian, a Catholic schoolteacher and housewife from Belfast, opened the door and let them know she was Jean Fisher. Soon after this interview the competition authority decided to redistribute the prize money, and gave McGuckian only half of the original amount.

The *Times Literary Supplement* later ran an editorial about the event. Sidestepping the quite astonishing decision to withhold the prize money, "Poetic Initiatives" remarked that

> the Poetry Society's initiative has not, however, been without its controversial aspects. Some critics have attacked the basic notion of the competition, believing that the large prizes encourage "mercenary" attitudes; others object to the elevation of "single poems": should not a larger body of work be the proper focus of attention? This year there has been more specific grounds for complaint: the award of first prize to a young Belfast poet Medbh McGuckian. The quality of Ms. McGuckian's poem, "The Flitting" is not at issue; on the contrary, the poem is generally agreed to be a fine one, and there has been surprise that the three judges—Craig Raine, Brian Patten, and Anne Stevenson—decided to withhold the £1000 they could have given it, and award only £500 instead. The more important question, though, is how they managed to overlook the fact that the poem was longer than the competition allowed: a limit of thirty-two lines was stipulated, but "The Flitting" had thirty-five.[1]

The following week Brian G. Mitchell from the Poetry Society responded to the editorial, saying,

> The judges of the 1979 National Poetry Competition were well aware, that the winning poem "The Flitting" by Medbh McGuckian, exceeded the stated maximum 32 lines. They decided that any of the three poems entered by Medbh deserved first prize, but marginally preferred "The Flitting" and did not wish to exclude such a fine poem on the grounds that it had 3 lines too many. . . . it is [also] ironic that the competition judges should be criticised for awarding only a £500 first prize; last year's judges were criticised for awarding £1000 prize as excessive for any single poem. In this case the judges simply wished to award several other entrants with a major prize and so redistributed the total prize money.[2]

Although Mitchell brushes aside any notion of an ulterior motive behind the decision, the suspicion had lingered that the prize money was cut in half because the winner was a woman, or because Medbh McGuckian was an uncomfortably Irish-sounding name compared to Jean Fisher, or even because she was pregnant and unknown. In any case, in the political milieu of 1970s Northern Ireland, Medbh McGuckian consciously and cautiously planned her entry into this competition. In an interview she recalls how she

> sent away for the previous year's winners and saw they liked narrative poems of about forty lines—it had to be substantial and to flitter about the place. I wrote three poems in this style and submitted them under a pseudonym, and I won. . . . They assumed that I was a male pretending to be a woman. They couldn't believe I was six months pregnant when they came over with their cameras. The big thing about it was that a well-known literary figure came second to me, and they rearranged the prize money so that I got less and he got more. I didn't care. I was pregnant, and I had won this.[3]

It is hard to know in hindsight whether it was winning the competition or the ensuing publicity or her Northern Irish background which created a momentum for McGuckian. She herself mentions that although, regrettably, the media fuss diverted attention from reading the poems, the phones kept ringing, and soon Oxford offered to publish her first major collection, *The Flower Master*, which appeared in 1982.[4]

Although many critics have argued that McGuckian's poetry divorces itself from direct political engagement, an incident of this kind perfectly demonstrates the impossibility of ignoring the fact that she comes from the peculiar political and literary milieu of Northern Ireland. When asked about her poetic formation she remarked:

> Why do I write? Out of the helplessness of the human condition—the only kind of control I can muster over the incoherence and apparent senselessness of it. Also to communicate and diagnose and express what cannot otherwise be expressed; to be a voice or give a voice to things that have been oppressed and repressed in my peculiar culture; to find an emotional valve for the deepest joys and sorrows.[5]

Throughout her poetry McGuckian strives to use her voice as an "emotional valve" for poetic expression. Relatively little can be found in McGuckian's oeuvre in the way of autobiography: her poems seldom speak directly about her childhood or upbringing. However, the little we know from interviews does shed an informative light on her poetic formation. Born in 1950 as Maeve McCaughan, the third of six children in a Catholic family in Belfast, from a very early age political and sectarian tensions left their mark on her development. McGuckian attended the local Holy Family Primary School, where her father was vice principal, and later went to Dominican Convent, Fortwilliam, for her grammar-school education. At this time a sense of religious vocation mingled with the poetic: McGuckian talks about how it was in this school that she decided "not to be a nun but a poet." She reached adulthood as the political temperature in Northern Ireland began to heat significantly, as attempted reforms by Terrence O'Neill stimulated a more assertive attempt by Northern Catholics to gain equality and the anxieties of Loyalist extremists became increasingly exacerbated.[6] This process found its culmination in the Civil Rights marches in Northern Ireland in 1968 and 1969 and the ensuing bloodshed and civil conflicts of the Troubles. McGuckian went to Queen's University Belfast to study English in 1968, which evidently came as something of a culture-shock: it certainly threw her identity-politics into sharp relief. The only woman poet among her noted contemporaries, Paul Muldoon, Ciaran Carson, and Frank Ormsby, her poetic identity was scrutinized, questioned and pressurized. It is of little wonder that she said she began to write poetry "so that nobody would read it. Nobody. Even the ones who read it would not understand it, and certainly no other poet would understand it."[7] Meeting Seamus Heaney and the poetry circle he set up proved crucial in the development of McGuckian's confidence in herself as a poet. As she describes: "He was the first person who didn't make me feel that poetry was a closed shop. I got up the courage to say that I would like to be a poet, and although I hadn't yet put pen to paper he invited me to the group and Paul Muldoon was there. There was this openness and friendliness that I trusted."[8] McGuckian graduated in 1972, the year she met Heaney, and went on to do a master's in the same institution. Her thesis, "Gothic Influence on Nineteenth-Century Anglo-Irish Fiction," dealing with the Banims, Maria Edgeworth, and William Carleton, was received very well and is also indicative of her early thematic interests. After graduation McGuckian went on to teach English in a grammar school for boys, St Patrick's College, Knock, and in her own Dominican alma mater. Her first poem, "Marriage," appeared in *The Honest Ulsterman* in 1975. Two years later she married John McGuckian, a geography teacher, and by the time her first volume, *Portrait of Joanna,* was published in 1980, McGuckian had already won one of the most important poetry competitions and had given birth to her first son, Liam.

The 1980s, however, were fraught with difficulties. Although *The Flower Master*, which was published by Oxford in 1982, won three awards, within a few years McGuckian had to juggle four children and a full-time teaching job with her writing work. Also, significantly, she suffered from severe postnatal depression and was advised to stop writing poetry.[9] A move to Northern Belfast, where sectarian tensions were more manifest and going outside was often dangerous meant that the poet and her family were more or less housebound. Finally, in 1985 McGuckian was offered the job of writer in residence in Queen's University, becoming the first woman ever to be awarded this position. She immediately left her grammar-school teaching job and spent three years between 1985 and 1988 taking up invitations to read abroad and further developing her work. However, as the poet remembers, travelling around put a lot of pressure on her husband and children, and eventually in 1991 she had to cut short a visit to the University of California, Berkeley, because of domestic difficulties.[10] After the retirement of her husband from his teaching job matters eased somewhat; however, this in turn put pressure on McGuckian as the sole breadwinner of the family. Nevertheless, the 1990s were prolific years: the poet published three further volumes and a *Selected Poems* and received two more awards. Between 1994 and 1997, at the time of the IRA ceasefires, she became writer in residence at the University of Ulster, Coleraine, and she also spent a term in Trinity College, Dublin, in 2000. The following year McGuckian took up a part-time creative writing post at Queen's University Belfast, which, before and after it turned into a full-time post with the opening of the Seamus Heaney

Centre for Poetry in 2003, was an ideal situation for the poet. Despite the pressure of earning a living and writing poetry amidst heavy teaching and administrative duties, McGuckian has published six volumes of poetry since 2000, making her one of the most prolific contemporary Irish writers.

Critical Reception

Medbh McGuckian's publishing record is indeed impressive: since 1982 she has produced fifteen volumes, including an American edition and a *Selected Poems*.[11] However, critical responses have been somewhat sluggish in their engagement with her work. In 1984 an early reviewer tagged her work a "half-coherent . . . disorientating experience,"[12] and five years later her third collection did not fare better when Patrick Williams wrote it off as "inane," "boring," and a testimony to the "author's terminal egoism."[13] Although Catherine Byron swiftly came to McGuckian's defense, claiming that her "yoking together of disparate worlds" is "rooted in the body" and should be seen as "prophetic,"[14] reviewers were reluctant to recognize the intellectual power of her poetry and preferred to see her work as a "landscape of metonymic consciousness" that "can strain meaning."[15] In the early nineties, *Marconi's Cottage* got a more generous reception and a consensus developed with regard to the quality of her work. However, her work was still seen as "difficult," albeit containing "insights, rhythms, phrases and images" pleasing to the ear.[16] Damningly, her work was described as "a kind of literary autism" that fails to communicate with the reader.[17]

Thomas Docherty's "Postmodern McGuckian" was among the first essays to position McGuckian's work within a postmodernist theoretical context. Although Docherty also struggled with the search for meaning (suggesting that "the language is at odds with the mouth speaking it"),[18] he acknowledged the poet's skill and phenomenological intellect. However, as was (and still is) the case with several other male critics of McGuckian, Docherty remained eager to position McGuckian within a literary canon recognizable to a male audience. Thus, he pondered that "if one were to look for predecessors, it would be an error to search among the Irish poets of the twentieth century,"[19] even if, in Docherty's view, Clarke, Kavanagh, Yeats, Joyce, Beckett, and Heaney are all discernible influences (needless to say, no female writers make it to the pantheon of "Irish poets" in Docherty's search for poetic predecessors). Docherty concluded that McGuckian has "more in common with both nineteenth-century decadence and with twentieth-century surrealism,"[20] which, materialized as "linguistic internationalism," explains the "instability" and "alienation" in her work.[21]

With the emergence of more feminist criticism McGuckian has gained greater recognition. Clair Wills's influential book *Improprieties: Politics and Sexuality in Northern Irish Poetry*[22] paved the way for a more coherent and theoretically based wave of criticism, which positioned McGuckian within a feminist and politicized school of thought. Wills's argument, that "McGuckian self-consciously thematises the issues of the obscurity of her work and the relationship between personal and public reference"[23] has lifted the critical discourse from a continuous search for meaning toward a more intellectually elevated discussion about the semantic relevance of impenetrability within her work. Moreover, Wills's positioning of the poet within a politicized narrative allowed for an analysis of McGuckian's work outside the constraints of "feminine experience" that had been commonly imposed on her work up to that point. Wills convincingly argued that the historical material in the poet's work is "muted, radically 'privatized,' and filtered through the screen of poetic tradition, and of maternal and familial experience."[24] This does not mean, however, that McGuckian uses sexuality as a metaphor for cultural conditions, but rather, as Wills puts it, that "the body itself becomes a historical document."[25] As I will argue in chapter 2, McGuckian's political aesthetic is represented in a circuitous way, and her poems resist direct political decoding. However, McGuckian's historical awareness, precisely as Wills argued, is deeply ingrained in her representation of the private and familial.

In the mid-1990s, critics, even those who enjoyed McGuckian's poetry, still thought she was "odd," and "[didn't] know what she [was] saying."[26] Anne Fogarty's essay "Fault Lines" investigated the reception of contemporary women's poetry in the Irish literary establishment and argued that the "discriminatory ghettoising of creative talent" has marginalized and "almost entirely obliterated" these works.[27] In this context, she emphasized McGuckian's ability to "adequately describe female experience,"[28] and rightfully concluded, that "their [Irish women's] poetry makes us aware not of women as other or different but of the pleasurable differences of women's voices."[29] Fogarty's essay has paved the way for feminist literary critics who boldly assert that "[McGuckian's] poetic voice is distinctly feminist"[30] and "her subject is almost always the relationship between the different facets of a woman's life."[31] Although this present book argues for a more rounded approach to McGuckian's work, one that considers her poetry within theoretical frameworks stretching the boundaries of what Haberstroh terms "women's multiple lives,"[32] nevertheless the significance and relevance of these issues in relation to McGuckian's oeuvre are indisputable.

More recent critical works on McGuckian emphasize a wider array of theoretical considerations. Robert Brazeau has considered McGuckian's poetry in relation to avant-garde poetics,[33] and this present book often engages with his ideas concerning what he terms McGuckian's "non-representational language."[34] Employing, among others, Butler's theory of gender performativity, Brazeau maintains that "McGuckian's poetry offers a sense of the viability of not necessarily performing identity but of staging a series of linguistic and avant-garde disruptions that trouble familiar social and ideological categories."[35] This has proved a helpful argument when considering McGuckian's identity-politics as presented in her poems and interviews. Guinn Batten's enlightening comparative study of McGuckian and Thomas Kinsella argues for a fundamental rethinking of gender within their work.[36] Convincingly, she contends that "representational readings" of McGuckian's poetry, those that are eager to delineate the "Western, middle-class, and heterosexual woman's domestic life"[37] within her work, are inevitably misrepresenting a poet "whose deconstructiveness also disrupts the spaces of maternal sustenance."[38] Batten makes a cogent case for how, in fact, it was McGuckian's "psychic collapse" during her postpartum depression that triggered her creative impulse, and how, subsequently, death and negativity (the "muse of the minus") have become central tropes in her poetry.[39] Batten's sensitive analysis of absence and negative space in "No Streets, No Numbers"[40] successfully ties together disparate concepts of fertility and futility and opens up strikingly innovative critical perspectives on McGuckian's work. One of these entails a reconsideration of the figure of the muse in her poetry, not as a representation of feminine authority, but rather, as a "creative maternity that has been banished to the perimeters of ordinary language."[41] This muse, a "soundless, broken idol,"[42] by confounding distinctions between absence and presence, fundamentally disrupts feminized readings of her work that seek comfort in her presumed domesticity.

Leontia Flynn's coherent and comprehensive 2004 study[43] offers detailed commentary on all but the last three of McGuckian's volumes. Flynn interrogates McGuckian's work from a feminist point of view, and yet she also offers substantially divergent arguments from established feminist critics. Thus, in her critique of Eavan Boland's poetry, for example, (one of her chapters cross-compares the work of Boland and McGuckian) Flynn argues against the "representative authority and categorical certainties suggested by the term 'woman poet,'" and instead calls for an appreciation of the "feminist subversions" that appear in McGuckian's work.[44] In particular, Flynn's reading of McGuckian's political poetry has been highly illuminating. Her assertion that McGuckian's poetry "foregrounds interpretation of political narratives, rather than engaging with the narratives themselves"[45] has crystallized the direction of the readings of the political poetry in the present study.

Elin Holmsten's 2006 article offers a hermeneutical and phenomenological reading of the dialogical relation between desire and otherness in McGuckian's poetry. In an insightful analysis Holmsten describes the encounter with otherness as a spiritual experience, characterized by an "existential desire to be" within McGuckian's work.[46] Catriona Clutterbuck has also investigated issues relating to the self and otherness. Her work's primary focus is self-representation and the question of authority from a gendered perspective within the context of contemporary Irish literature and politics.[47] Michaela Schrage-Früh's astute analysis of the poet's engagement with Northern Irish politics and her representation of women in her work have informed some of the present book's methodology, in particular with regards to discussing the mythical within the poet's work.[48]

Arguably McGuckian's most influential critic has been Shane Alcobia-Murphy. Alcobia-Murphy has published numerous essays, coedited a volume dedicated to McGuckian's work, assigned a large section of a monograph to the analysis of her poetry, and in 2012 published an introductory volume on her work. Not only is he the most prolific among McGuckian's critics, but he is also the one who has fundamentally changed the course of criticism on the poet's work. In 1996 Murphy published an essay discussing the obliquity within the work of Paul Muldoon and Medbh McGuckian. In this comparative analysis he claimed that while Muldoon's "intertextual references are neither arbitrary nor meaningless," McGuckian's method of "borrowing," "palimpsestic double-writing" hints at plagiarism and witnesses her "obvious concern with the anxiety of influence."[49] Alcobia-Murphy's painstaking research of McGuckian's notebooks at Emory University unearthed textual sources within the poet's work which are unacknowledged within the publications. In his essays Alcobia-Murphy queried the legitimacy of McGuckian's writing methodology and consequently cast a shadow on the poet's reputation. Although in later years he acknowledged "the naive excesses"[50] of his early work and has done a great service to McGuckian's readers through his unrelenting interest and advocacy of McGuckian's poetry, his basic reading methodology remains focused on intertextual analysis. Several critics have followed in his footsteps and created what could be best described as a school of "genetic criticisms" of McGuckian's work. These scholars base their analysis on the McGuckian notebooks held in Emory University, and offer readings of poems alongside with the source materials, thus highlighting their "genetic" origins. The usefulness of this critical methodology is debated among scholars. While there is undoubted value in discovering McGuckian's sources (if for nothing else than for getting a better view of what she is reading) interpreting her work solely on intertextual grounds threatens to limit understanding of her creative impetus. However, with the appearance of Google it has become relatively easy to trace McGuckian's sources, which has opened up the field for a more integrative scholarship that recognizes, but does not center its ideology around, intertextual detective work.

This brief overview of the existing criticism of McGuckian's work highlights the lacunae that prevail in relation to some of the issues that this book intends to explore. The two major lines of inquiry, one that explores "meaning," and the other that considers issues of femininity and feminism, permeate critical studies. However, literary performance has not hitherto been a subject of detailed investigation. The current study offers an in-depth, thematic study of McGuckian's poetry, investigating her creative performance, diverse muse-figures, gender, politics, and spirituality across all her published work. While the eagerness of Docherty, and later Shane Alcobia-Murphy, to pinpoint literary sources in McGuckian's work has stimulated my interest in the poet's methodology of interweaving multivalent voices together, and in particular her conceptualization of the muse as "influence," the methodology of this analysis differs sharply from their approach. Close reading of her poetry is something from which, for reasons of obliquity, many of her critics still shy away.[51] However, despite recent theoretical reluctance in this regard, the present study hopes to demonstrate that tracing her *modus operandi* becomes liberating for any reader who seeks to encounter "meaning" in her poetic texts.[52] McGuckian herself does not offer too much assistance in the interpretative process. Asked about poetical language, she once remarked: "What I do with language is, it is the sense of the sentence. I couldn't have a sentence without some kind of a bump in it. It has to be like a wavy sea, everything contradicting."[53] Thus, she remains one of the most complex poets to read and classify within any particular category. This guarantees that those readers of McGuckian who are drawn to her poems become fractions of the creative palimpsest themselves and are left with a desire to read more.[54]

Therefore, the close readings of poetry offered in this work eventually unsettle as many presuppositions as they confirm. My theoretical intention remains to "read" the texts as "writings," in the verbalized, present-continuous sense of the word. Also, methodologically, the close reading of poetry which is provided in this study has itself been vitally influenced by my theoretical concentration on the performativity of creativity.[55] Throughout the book, the reading of poetry concentrates on poems in their entirety, an approach not necessarily prevalent in the existing secondary literature on Medbh McGuckian, nor indeed in contemporary Irish criticism in general. This is reflected in the structure of the book, which is divided into five chapters, following the chronological publications of her volumes.

Chapter 1 begins the detailed close readings that form the bulk of this study. Opening with McGuckian's first volume, *The Flower Master*, the chapter discusses the formation of the creative self in her first four collections. The chapter's main thesis is that at the early stages of her career literary performance, and the methodology of writing, was at the center of the poet's attention, accompanied by musings on gender and motherhood. There is a marked shift toward the political from the fifth volume onward, which I discuss in chapter 2, which is devoted to McGuckian's politicized aesthetic. The three volumes discussed in this chapter ponder upon history and the politics of violence, with particular attention to the poet's circuitous approach to this subject. Chapter 3 looks at three volumes published between 2002 and 2004, her most prolific years so far. The poems in these collections address death and spirituality, and religious influences are particularly noticeable. Chapter 4 considers McGuckian's latest three volumes, published in 2006, 2008, and 2012, respectively, which take an inward retrospective journey toward the poetic psyche. The final chapter offers a theoretical discussion of the prevalent themes and reading methodologies of Medbh McGuckian's work.

Notes

1. "Poetic Initiatives," *Times Literary Supplement*, January 25, 1980, 89.

2. Brian G. Mitchell, "Letter to the Editor," *Times Literary Supplement*, February 1, 1980, 117.

3. Laura O'Connor, "*Combrá*: Conversation between Medbh McGuckian and Nuala Ní Dhomhnaill," *Southern Review* 31, no. 3 (Summer 1995): 592.

4. Medbh McGuckian, *The Flower Master* (Oxford: Oxford University Press, 1982). This volume, with the addition of some newer poems, was revised and republished as *The Flower Master and Other Poems* (Oldcastle, Ireland: Gallery Press, 1993). Citations are to the Gallery Press edition (hereafter cited as *FM*).

5. Medbh McGuckian, "Author Statement," British Council Literature, n.d., http://literature.britishcouncil.org/medbh-mcguckian (accessed October 19, 2013).

6. Ed Moloney, *A Secret History of the IRA* (New York: W. W. Norton, 2002), 60–73.

7. L. O'Connor, "*Combrá*," 590.

8. Ibid., 592.

9. She talks about this experience in ibid., 595.

10. Medbh McGuckian, e-mail message to author, October 6, 2011.

11. McGuckian, *The Flower Master*, 1982; and *FM*; *Venus and the Rain* (Oxford, Oxford University Press, 1984), repr. (Oldcastle, Ireland: Gallery Press, 1994); *On Ballycastle Beach* (Oxford: Oxford University Press, 1988), repr. (Oldcastle, Ireland: Gallery Press, 1995); *Marconi's Cottage* (Oldcastle, Ireland: Gallery Press, 1991); *Captain Lavender* (Oldcastle, Ireland: Gallery Press, 1994); *Selected Poems* (Oldcastle, Ireland: Gallery Press, 1991), repr. as *Selected Poems: 1978–1994,* selected and edited by Peter Fallon, 1997; *Shelmalier* (Oldcastle, Ireland: Gallery Press, 1994), repr. 1998; *Drawing Ballerinas* (Oldcastle, Ireland: Gallery Press, 2001); *The Soldiers of Year II*, with afterword by Guinn Batten (Winston-Salem, NC: Wake Forest University Press, 2002), repr. 2003; *The Face of the Earth* (Oldcastle, Ireland: Gallery Press, 2002); *Had I a Thousand Lives* (Oldcastle, Ireland: Gallery Press, 2003); *The Book of the Angel* (Oldcastle, Ireland: Gallery Press, 2004); *The Currach Requires No Harbours* (Oldcastle, Ireland: Gallery Press, 2006); *My Love Has Fared Inland* (Oldcastle, Ireland: Gallery Press, 2008); and *The High Caul Cap* (Oldcastle, Ireland: Gallery Press, 2012).

12. Michael Allen, "Barbaric Yawp, Gibbous Voice," review of *Venus and the Rain*, by Medbh McGuckian, *Honest Ulsterman* 77 (Winter 1984): 59 and 64.

13. Patrick Williams, "Spare That Tree!" review of *On Ballycastle Beach*, by Medbh McGuckian, *Honest Ulsterman* 86 (Spring–Summer 1989): 49.

14. Catherine Byron, "Such Declarations Are Routine in the McGuckian Household—A Response to Patrick Williams's Review of *On Ballycastle Beach*," *Honest Ulsterman* 87 (Summer–Autumn 1989): 89.

15. William A. Wilson, "A Dream—without the Pronoun 'I,'" review of *On Ballycastle Beach*, by Medbh McGuckian, *Irish Literary Supplement* (Spring 1989): 17.

16. Leon McAuley, "Wuthering Depths," review of *Marconi's Cottage*, by Medbh McGuckian, *Honest Ulsterman* 93 (1992): 65.

17. Mary O'Donnell "Responsibility and Narcosis," review of *What's What*, by Julie O'Callaghan; *Marconi's Cottage*, by Medbh McGuckian, *Poetry Ireland Review* 35 (Summer 1992): 111.

18. Thomas Docherty, "Initiations, Tempers, Seductions: Postmodern McGuckian," in *The Chosen Ground: Essays on the Contemporary Poetry of Northern Ireland*, ed. Neil Corcoran (Bridgend: Seren Books; Chester Springs, PA: Dufour Editions, 1992), 208.

19. Ibid., 207.

20. Ibid.

21. Ibid., 208.

22. Clair Wills, *Improprieties: Politics and Sexuality in Northern Irish Poetry* (Oxford: Clarendon Press, 1993).

23. Ibid., 158.

24. Ibid., 192.

25. Ibid.

26. Eileen Cahill, "'Because I Never Garden': Medbh McGuckian's Solitary Way," *Irish University Review: Journal of Irish Studies* 24, no. 2 (Fall–Winter 1994): 264–65.

27. Anne Fogarty, "Fault Lines," *Graph* 2, no. 1 (1995): 18.

28. Ibid., 23.

29. Ibid., 25.

30. Kimberly S. Bohman, "Borders or Frontiers?: Gender Roles and Gender Politics in McGuckian's Unconscious Realm," *Irish Journal of Feminist Studies* 1, no. 1 (March 1996): 119.

31. Patricia Boyle Haberstroh, *Women Creating Women: Contemporary Irish Women Poets* (Dublin: Attic Press, 1996), 157.

32. Ibid.

33. Robert Brazeau, "Troubling Language: Avant-Garde Strategies in the Poetry of Medbh McGuckian," *Mosaic: Journal for the Interdisciplinary Study of Literature* 37, no. 2 (June 2004): 127–44.

34. Ibid., 128.

35. Ibid., 137.

36. Guinn Batten, "'The More with Which We Are Connected': The Muse of the Minus in the Poetry of McGuckian and Kinsella," in *Gender and Sexuality in Modern Ireland*, ed. Anthony Bradley and Maryann Gialanella Valiulis (Amherst: University of Massachusetts Press, 1997), 212–44.

37. Ibid., 216.

38. Ibid., 239.

39. Ibid., 218.

40. The poem "No Streets, No Numbers" can be found in *Marconi's Cottage*, 39–41.

41. Batten, "The More," 232.

42. Ibid., 233.

43. Leontia Flynn, "Reading Medbh McGuckian," PhD diss., Queen's University Belfast, 2004.

44. Ibid., ii.

45. Ibid., 204.

46. Elin Holmsten, "'Like a Wished-For Body': Dialogues of Desire in the Poetry of Medbh McGuckian," in *The Body and Desire in Contemporary Irish Poetry*, ed. Irene Gilsenan Nordin (Dublin: Irish Academic Press, 2006), 165.

47. Catriona M. Clutterbuck, "Self-Representation and the Politics of Authority in Contemporary Irish Poetry: Eavan Boland and Medbh McGuckian," PhD diss., University of Oxford, 1996.

48. Michaela Schrage-Früh, *Emerging Identities: Myth, Nation and Gender in the Poetry of Eavan Boland, Nuala Ni Dhomhnaill and Medbh McGuckian*. Trier: WVT, Wissenschaftlicher Verlag Trier, 2004.

49. Shane Murphy, "Obliquity in the Poetry of Paul Muldoon and Medbh McGuckian," *Éire-Ireland: Journal of Irish Studies* 31, nos. 3–4 (Fall–Winter 1996): 76–101. Shane Murphy's later publications appear under the name Shane Alcobia-Murphy.

50. Shane Alcobia-Murphy and Richard Kirkland, eds., *The Poetry of Medbh McGuckian: The Interior of Words* (Cork: Cork University Press, 2010), 19.

51. Shane Murphy for example argues that McGuckian's intertextual technique "places a heavy burden on the reader" and that she "has chosen her intertexts more for their aural effect than for any semantic value." Murphy, "Obliquity in the Poetry," 88; 92.

52. In his polemical essay, Valentine Cunningham, although arguably overstressing the importance of a sentimental relationship between text and reader, makes a cogent case for the rediscovery of meaning in texts: "Textual instability, even extreme instability, is not a nothing. Far from it. The problem of textual variants isn't that they generate absence of meaning, but rather that they produce an excess of it." Valentine Cunningham, *Reading after Theory* (Oxford: Blackwell, 2002), 74.

53. Deirdre Murphy, "Interview with Medbh McGuckian," *Irish Literary Supplement* 16, no. 1 (Spring 1997): 21–23.

54. The emphasis is on the emotional attitude of the reader. Derrida argues: "To deconstruct a text is to disclose how it functions as desire. . . . One cannot read without opening oneself to the desire of language, to the search for that which remains absent and other than oneself. Without a certain love of the text no reading would be possible. In every reading there is a *corps-á-corps* between reader and text, an in-corporation of the reader's desire into the desire of the text." Jacques Derrida, "Deconstruction and the Other: An Interview with Jacques Derrida," in *Dialogues with Contemporary Continental Thinkers*, ed. Richard Kearney (Manchester, UK: Manchester University Press, 1984), 126.

55. For a more detailed explanation of this study's interpretation of the performativity of creativity and literary performance, see chapter 5.

1

Literary Performance in Medbh McGuckian's Early Volumes: *The Flower Master*, *Venus and the Rain*, *On Ballycastle Beach*, and *Marconi's Cottage*

BETWEEN 1982 AND 1991 MEDBH MCGUCKIAN PUBLISHED four volumes, which are the subject of this chapter. Although her career took off after winning the National Poetry Competition, her publishing history was less unproblematic. *The Flower Master* and the next two volumes were first brought out by Oxford University Press in their Oxford Poets series, but in the following years the relationship between poet and publisher soured. As McGuckian recounts in an email:

> I was invited to publish with Oxford after I won the National Poetry Award in 1979. My first three books were theirs but then they began to complain that I was becoming too esoteric and obscure. They wanted too many changes made to the poems that eventually ended up in Marconi's Cottage. Peter [Fallon of the Gallery Press] corresponded with them and firstly was to co-publish with them but finally took me over. I published with Bloodaxe as well for that book. Wake Forest also took me on in North Carolina. It was a very traumatic time but I felt Peter then was more willing to give me the benefit of the doubt.[1]

Eventually McGuckian moved her work over to The Gallery Press in 1991 where she republished the *The Flower Master*, *Venus and the Rain*, and *On Ballycastle Beach* more or less unchanged, with the addition of some new poems. For the sake of clarity and continuity this chapter follows the Gallery editions. The 1980s, when McGuckian was still with Oxford, were also fraught with violence and political upheaval in Northern Ireland: the decade began with the hunger strikes at the Maze Prison, particularly significant bombing incidents took place in Brighton and Enniskillen (in 1984 and 1987 respectively), Ian Paisley delivered his famous "Ulster Says No" speech in November

1985 at Belfast City Hall, and the Gibraltar Three were shot in 1988, which provoked further killings in the coming weeks. During this time McGuckian's career was on an upward trajectory: these were extremely prolific years, with several poetry awards (Cheltenham Prize 1989, Bass Ireland Award 1991, Helen Waddell Award 1992) and an important residency in Queen's University Belfast (1985–1988), the first given to a woman. However, with young children to look after, and in the midst of a seemingly hopeless political situation, McGuckian's poetic voice was far from jubilatory. There are overtones of postnatal depression in *The Flower Master* and *Venus and the Rain*, and *On Ballycastle Beach* and *Marconi's Cottage* both convey a kind of passive resistance to any hint of optimism. This chapter traces the development of McGuckian's creative voice in these volumes through a close reading of both her creative performance and the varied sources of inspiration she calls into being. The chapter's structure is simultaneously chronological and thematic: it concentrates on the first four volumes published by the poet with The Gallery Press,[2] which are thematically distinguished by a meditation on the creation of self in relation to poetic performance.

The Seed-Work Performance of *The Flower Master*

In her first full volume published by Oxford University Press and then later republished by The Gallery Press,[3] Medbh McGuckian situates her work in the context of natural phenomena. Her poems reflect on writing as growth and natural maturing, and her creative self is implied in most of these pieces as an involuntary facilitator and observer. The writing performance is therefore conceptualized as a passive process, which disregards the will of the creative mind. Ideas of disruption and natural growth signify the poet's reflection on her creative process, making this volume the first to introduce her seed-work technique of self-reflection. For thematic coherence the page numbers given follow the Gallery edition, with some notes on changes implemented by the poet.

"The Sofa," a poem that appears in both the Oxford and Gallery editions,[4] introduces the subject of writing. The poem is written in an imaginary epistolary form, insofar as it charts the narrator's intention to respond to a letter:

Do not be angry if I tell you
Your letter stayed unopened on my table
For several days. If you were friend enough
To believe me, I was about to start writing
At any moment; my mind was savagely made up,
Like a serious sofa moved
Under a north window. (*FM*, 25)

Writing the letter, however, becomes a creative act that reflects on the source and process of production. The second stanza describes the sites of creativity that the poet might reach out to: the heart ("not the calmest of places"), the books ("seem real enough to me"), and past experiences ("my disasters, my surrenders, all my loss"). Readerly expectation is also evoked with an interesting twist:

Since I was child enough to forget
That you loathe poetry, you ask for some—
About nature, greenery, insects, and, of course,
The sun—surely that would be to open
An already open window? (*FM*, 25)

Although the addressee of this poem is the writer of the "unopened" letter, these lines can be read as reflections on the wider issue of expectations directed at female authors. The bucolic subjects of "nature, greenery, insects" and "sun" are at odds with the type of poetry the narrator intends to write, and, in addition, their validity as suitable subject matter is queried in the above quoted last two lines, which hint at their futility and clichéd character ("to open an already open window"). Instead, the poetic voice offers an alternative subject matter, one which positions her in an interpersonal nexus:

. . . If I could
Interest you instead on his large, gentle stares,
How his soft shirt is the inside of pleasure
To me, why I must wear white for him (*FM*, 25)

These lines might surprise a reader who expects politicized feminist poetry from McGuckian. However, the poetic emphasis here is not on power relations, but rather, the relational context of love. As the ending of the poem demonstrates, the subject matter of love is not sentimental, and it also cannot be restricted and constricted into definable topics or value judgments ("Imagine he no longer trembles // When I approach, no longer buys me / Flowers for my name day"). The poetic persona is thus positioned outside expectations and definitions:

> . . . But I spread
> On like a house, I begin to scatter
> To a tiny to-and-fro at odds
> With the wear on my threshold. Somewhere
> A curtain rising wonders where I am,
> My books sleep, pretending to forget me. (*FM*, 25)

The poetic self therefore seems to be a passive participant in the writing process, scattered and forgotten, outside the canonical heritage that books can offer. However, in a typical McGuckianesque fashion, the subject of the poem contradicts its existence: although the lines chart the dissolution and scattering of a poetic voice, the poem as a whole demonstrates the coherence and strength of it. In Elim Holmsten's convincing reading "The Sofa" "draws attention to the difficulty of expressing the self in language, since the effect is shown to be a dislocation of the self."[5] This is certainly true on the level of creative content: the desired subject matter never meets the intended content. Rather, a poetic encounter seems to be taking place on a more subconscious level where "books sleep" and emotionality (but not sentimentality) is allowed to surface.[6]

"The 'Singer,'"[7] (*FM*, 14) a relatively straightforward, simple poem, plays on the double meaning of the sewing machine's brand name, to imply the speaker's identification of the creative process with the workings of the machine:

> Pressing my feet occasionally
> Up and down on the treadle
> As though I were going somewhere
> I had never been. (*FM*, 14)

The atmospheric description of the room where the speaker spends the evening studying for exams is reminiscent of romantic notions of inspiring quietude and calm. However, McGuckian introduces a simple twist into this process and portrays the production of work not as result, but as a failed attempt:

> . . . There were nights
> I sent the disconnected wheel
> Spinning madly round and round
> Till the empty bobbin rattled in its case. (*FM*, 14)

The finished poem stands witness to its own process. Writing is the performance of the portrayal of futility, and the poem's birth is the deconstruction of the normal functionality of a machine. In other words, the failure of production, represented by the "empty bobbin" (*FM*, 14) of the sewing machine, becomes the eventual output of the creative process.[8]

"The Soil-Map"[9] (*FM*, 36–37) returns to the question of female authorship. The title refers to ordinary maps that outline soil quality in certain geographical areas. Significantly, these maps make qualitative as well as quantitative distinctions in their markings, hinting at the author's intention of reproducing this within a creative context. The poem addresses a building, engaging with its features emotively, rather than descriptively:

> . . . I will not
> Take you in hardness, for all the dark cage
> Of my dreaming over your splendid fenestration,
> Your moulded sills, your slender purlins,
> The secret woe of your gutters. (*FM*, 36–37)

The resistance of the speaker to go inside creates an inverse image where the act of entering seems to become a suffered violation. Gender roles are partly reversed ("I am not a woman's man" as the speaker states in the first line of the poem), partly confused (entering has strong male sexual connotations, and yet in this instance the house possesses the phallic "hardness"). McGuckian, as she states in an interview, addresses this poem to the new house she was moving into, which was situated in a Protestant area and was previously owned by a Protestant family.[10] The house is "soiled," run-down in an area of past affluence that is politically heavily charged. The metaphorical significance of the image of the house is undeniable in several interpretative contexts. In terms of feminine authorship traditional interpretations, where the domestic environment of the house is regarded as the primary site of work and self-expression for women, McGuckian's description of a building that is being violated and talked to hints at subversion. In Scott Brewster's careful reading of "The Soil Map" the "house and the woman stand in for the motherland, as each is already colonised by representation."[11] This is a house that has already been lived in, entered into, and occupied. In terms of female authorship it is akin to a conventional masculinized poetic canon that prescribes sites of representation and simultaneously questions feminine creativity and originality. The last stanza reflects on this issue by listing houses with female names, inheritance of a somewhat patronizing tradition that endowed buildings with diminutive girls' names, signaling perhaps the dwellings' homeliness, cuteness, and societal insignificance. The speaker of the poem acknowledges this tradition, but instead of entering into a linguistic polemic ("some disease / of language") she/he renames the buildings with a new terminology that acknowledges precisely their originality and singularity:

> I have found the places on the soil-map,
> Proving it possible once more to call
> Houses by their names, Annsgift or Mavisbank,
> Mount Juliet or Bettysgrove: they should not
> Lie with the gloom of disputes to interrupt them
> Every other year, like some disease
> Of language making humorous the friendship
> Of the thighs. I drink to you as Hymenstown,
> (My touch of fantasy) or First Fruits,
> Impatient for my power as a bride. (*FM*, 36–37)

These virginal buildings manage to overstep the political binaries of nationality, gender, and creativity that burden the description of the house at the start of the poem. The real and unique names of the houses on the soil map qualitatively acknowledge the singularity of the female voice, accepting its "power as a bride."[12]

"Chopping," a short but poignant poem, also identifies an object, in this case an onion, to metaphorize artistic output.[13] The site of the creative process is the feminized space of the kitchen, and the performance of writing is associated with the peeling of the onion:[14]

> Close your eyes
> Unwinding the bitter onion—
> Its layers of uncertainty are limited. (*FM*, 17)

The deconstructive gesture of "unwinding" reveals a core of emotional turbulence and self-exposure, and the process of literary production is reversed to become scattering and self-inflicted violence:

> Today I am feeling up to it:
> I bend my throat aside—
> There is no pain, only the soft entrances[15]
> Again, again, the vegetable's
> Finely numbered bones. (*FM*, 17)

The image of the disseminated bones (maybe referencing Sylvia Plath's poem "Cut"[16]) corresponds to the overriding sense of failure, which permeates this poem. However, the resulting success is implied in the process of the poem's own creation. The images of the sewing machine, house, and onion highlight a concern with the mechanics of writing that imply failure in success and collapse in completion. This emphasizes the sense of loneliness of the creative self permeating this volume. As a first collection, *The Flower Master* shows a remarkable awareness of its own compositional development. In one poem, "The Long Engagement," the focus is shifted from the process of writing to its facilitator, the creative mind:

> In my all-weather loneliness I am like a sparrow
> Picking leftovers of rice in a mortar,
> A dark cicada clinging to a branch,
> The empty space created by your kiss. (*FM*, 18)

The site of composition, "the empty space," simultaneously signifies the potential of creative output and its futility. (The emptiness is already a product of creation by the kiss.) Timothy Clark argues that the image of the "blank page" (or empty space) is

> a virtual space whose locus is neither in the psyche of the writer nor yet outside it. It is a space of mediation in which what I write, no matter what intention or fantasy it may seem designed to express, is echoed back to me transformed. It may be even an experience of historical alienation, the manifestation in my "inmost" speech of the social within or behind the individual. This effect is all the stronger given that literature, unlike some of the fine arts, has an irreducible referential dimension, one necessary even to the most concrete of concrete poems. The two-dimensional space of the page takes on inevitably and at once a "three-dimensional" effect.[17]

This virtual space, the in-between text, acts as a site of interference, the third dimension of the reader's input. In this context therefore the invoked "you" of the first stanza potentially positions him/herself in the reader's psyche so that the deposited kiss relocates its origin onto the reader's lips. The "kiss" therefore becomes the enabling empty space of composition, the archetypal kiss of the muse, and it is in this context that "you" (in this reading the reader) are asked, like a true goddess of fate, to "make a thread from the fibres of the five signs / Leading to the eight valleys, my lush palace gate" (*FM*, 18).[18]

The force of the encounter between the imaginary faculties of the poetic mind underscores the creative energies of the poem, and the serene atmosphere of the first part is followed by another, more intimate quietude.

However, the physical blank space between parts one and two conceals the violence implied in inspiration, and we see the poetic self lying down "thirsty from the thunderstorm, / Visualising first this book, the objects on the tray" (*FM,* 18). The rest of the poem unfolds and explores the delicate and threatening relationship between the reader-muse and the poetic self. From the point of view of the performance of writing, however, "The Long Engagement" is a significant template for most of McGuckian's later poems, insofar as it introduces the concept of the empty space as a site of creative futility and possibility.

An example for a poem that presents the concept of death as a creative agency in the process of composition is "The Seed-Picture," which describes the composition of a portrait through embroidery and arranging seeds. The image of the dead seeds which creates this female portrait is characterized as "beautiful . . . / with no immediate application" (*FM*, 28), allowing for its own subliminal consciousness to surface. Because the sense of conscious poetic agency is denied, the "seed-work" opens up "new spectrums of activity" and, eventually

> The seeds dictate their own vocabulary,
> Their dusty colours capture
> More than we can plan,
> The mould on walls, or jumbled garages,
> Dead flower heads where insects shack. . . . (*FM*, 28)

Significantly the images "captured" by the seeds depict decay ("mould," "dead flower heads") alongside a promise of existence implied by the insects and architectural compositions (and also the fact that biologically seeds die in order to bring forth new life). McGuckian elaborates on an organic sense of growth as linguistic creation in this poem and replaces the lack of conscious agency with the representation of vegetative self-arrangement:

> I only guide them not by guesswork
> In their necessary numbers,
> And attach them by the spine to a perfect bedding,
> Woody orange pips, and tear-drop apple. (*FM*, 28)

The creative act of the poetic consciousness is likened to "bonding all the seeds in one continuous skin" (*FM*, 28), where the seeds are allowed to mature into words. The creative performance is involuntary and transposed to the created composition. The death of the seeds generates their own creation, following the stereotypical implications of their imagery. Another aspect of this poem, as Shane Alcobia-Murphy points out, is its reference to origin and continuation, archetype and copy.[19] The originality of female craft and handiwork is often queried, as images are traditionally passed on and copied among women. Similarly, this poem's intention is to produce a "portrait" of Joanna, and not to bring to life the original person. This also has connotations with regard to the interpretation of the role of Joanna in this work. Hers is an alternative voice in this poem that belongs to an enigmatic female, who "makes women / Feel their age, and sigh for liberation" (*FM*, 28). Embodying both the organic death of words and a facilitating poetic consciousness, the figure of this woman can be read as a muse, who smoothes the progress of creation and yet simultaneously becomes captured by it.

Traditionally, the imagined "other" of the creative process has most commonly, and most conveniently, materialized in the body of a woman. Conveniently that is because for the male poetic imagination the female simultaneously represents comfort and enticement. The urge to create surfaces as sexual and, indeed sometimes filial, desire and gains fulfillment in the creative output of representing this desire. The muse, this beautiful, inert, and distant woman embodies the maternal origin and sexual target of the male poetic imagination. However, for the female creative mind she is neither straightforwardly maternal nor (simply) erotic. In fact, in McGuckian's poetry, if she is a woman, she is complicated, moody, and never inert.

For a woman writer, engaging with the female muse involves an exploration of feminine agency. The individualized, embodied subject of the female muse disrupts conventional identity categories open to women within the context of poetry writing. McGuckian's poetic liberation of the restricting figure of the muse reinforces a linguistic reimagining of a female poetic self. The figure of the muse retains her emblematic characteristics, insofar as her direct influence on the performance of writing is explicitly acknowledged. What McGuckian questions and reformulates are the poetic and social attitudes surrounding and forming the muse. In this context, the explicit appearance and naming of the muse in McGuckian's poetry cannot be considered as a progressive utilization of a cultural "icon" in her work, but rather, as a means by which the poet is enabled to question and circumnavigate cultural expectations surrounding her role as a poet. This explains the linguistic abandon with which the figure of the female muse is evoked. Unlike the romantic muse, she rarely stands alone and distant, and her role and position in the creative process are exposed to continuous challenge and an occasional *coup d'état*.

In the poem under discussion, "The Seed Picture" (*FM*, 28), Joanna is portrayed as the separated partner of a relationship, who has left behind poems, the "children" of the liaison:

> This is my portrait of Joanna—since the split
> The children come to me like a dumb-waiter,
> And I wonder where to put them, beautiful seeds
> With no immediate application. . . . (*FM*, 28)

Although Joanna, in this reading the muse, has withdrawn from the relationship with the poetic self, her absence continues to have a profound effect on the poet's creative performance, albeit a negative one. Distanced from the muse, the work takes on a life of its own and detaches itself from all authorial influence: "The seeds dictate their own vocabulary" (*FM*, 28). The second part of the poem attempts to explain why the "split" has happened. Here we get a glimpse of a more conventional positioning of the muse:

> Was it such self-indulgence to enclose her
> In the border of a grandmother's sampler,
> Bonding all the seeds in one continuous skin,
> The sky resolved to a cloud the length of a man? (*FM*, 28)

The answer is implied in the question: it seems that it is, in fact, the "self-indulgence" of "enclosing" the muse, which leads to her abandonment. However, this is not to say that poetic creation cannot happen without her. On the contrary, "The Seed-Picture" paints the muse in her absence and develops the "split" as the backdrop against which the poem is written. In other words, this poem is "unwriting" the stereotypical set-up of a presumed distance between poet and muse. Although separated, what is emphasized is the relational context in which muse and poet operate. The male poetic imagination seems to be unperturbed by the muse: she has no input into his work, and her only function is to reflect or absorb the creative performance. The muse of the woman poet, on the other hand, is an intrinsic participant in the creative process who refuses to be ignored.

"The Seed-Picture" focuses on the creative possibilities inherent in the death of seeds and their organic arrangement acts as the future image of the muse. However, "The Truth Room" considers the full cycle of natural growth and describes a tree, which exists in the conditional composition of the poetic consciousness:

> If I were to plant a tree in my handkerchief
> Of a garden, it would be a tree of heaven

> Which will grow in ash or gravel—like the jewelweed,
> Its roots will travel stone, its seeds
> Fall fast in a still room. (*FM*, 50)

However, the distance between the seeds and the creative mind, which is characteristic of the previous poem, is surpassed here when the speaker claims "there would be no danger / In our paths crossing, it will never come / To resemble me, my cousin of a touch-me-not" (*FM,* 50). The threatening sense of attraction between creator and created disrupts a presupposed continuum of the compositional process. The production of the poem implies its threat of backfiring harm and the careful treading of words creates their own undoing:

> . . . From some secret place
> Where colour troubles me, I shake a yellow dust.
> And yet the very heart of a tree is dead,
> Its life is all on the surface, if air reaches it
> It leaves the centre hollow. (*FM*, 50)

The "surface," understood here as the two-dimensional scope of the page, carries all that is left of the words' "truth." The "air," if read as a metaphor of inspiration,[20] touches the words but fails to reach their center. However, the poem implies that although "external" forces are ineffectual in shaping the creative process, it is in fact "this death that supports" the composition. In other words, by doing away with the idea of external influence, the poem is allowed to "grow" and eventually it "wills itself to sleep, / Turning inside out, inventing its own sweetness" (*FM*, 50). McGuckian diverts the reader's attention from the exposure of a presupposed meaningfulness in the creative process and, instead, she exemplifies her individual compositional strategy. Death serves as a central symbolic origin of "work," the ultimate source of transgression. The symbolic "tree" (of life? of work?) incorporates its own destruction and "starts / asserting itself," carefully dodging interventions from author and reader alike. However, the "fruit" of this creation cannot take ownership of its own construction, and at the end the narrating "I" is reinvited to thematically reinstate an intervening poetic consciousness:

> But unless the purpose of fruit is just
> To distance itself, or be crushed, one must wait
> Four seasons to see a place, how leaf-fall sums it up.
> Then I would call my house 'Falling Water',
> Like a truth room where my symptoms feel at home. (*FM*, 50)

The "truth room" uncovers the representation of linguistic creativity, which allows for the cohabitation of the apparently incompatible fractions of the compositional process, signified in this poem by the clashing images of "fruit" and "death."[21] Consolidating the paradoxical "symptoms" of the writing process, the poetic consciousness arrives at a "freedom" which "I thought I had averted stir within me" to find "blue as God intended" (*FM*, 50). The materialization of God in the penultimate line of the poem signifies both the aim and lack of divine presence in the composition. The color "blue" therefore is symbolic of the dualities functioning in the inspirational process: the blue of the sky ("with its streets of seeding cloud") is simultaneously representative of the "createdness" of the universe and its vast emptiness. "Blue as God intended" is a typical McGuckian "joke": a presence which is an absence, a lack which is not a lack, an uncreated creation and a created nothing.

"The Mast Year" also uses arboreal imagery to discuss creativity. Mast year denotes a year in which an abundance of fruit is produced by forest trees. Leontia Flynn offers a reading of this poem where the trees stand for "a mysterious sense of specifically maternal power and powerlessness."[22] Although the maternal perspective is never far from McGuckian's poetic thinking, I believe "The Mast Year" further develops the idea of reproduction to incorporate poetic creativity. The poem describes a variety of forest trees and their ecosystems:

> Some kinds of trees are ever eager
> To populate new ground, the oak, or pine,
> Though beech can thrive on many soils
> And carve itself an empire, its vocation
> Is gentler; it casts a shade for wildflowers
> Adapted to the gloom, which feed
> Like fungus on its rot of bedstraw leaves. (*FM*, 58)

The symbiosis between the undergrowth and the trees indeed hints at a type of maternal thinking, where worth is not measured by success but by strength of attachment. In poetic terms, a somewhat didactic interpretation of these lines would suggest that the poem is speaking up for poetry that is outside the canon and the canonical. Whether this denotes women's poetry in a feminist reading, or McGuckian's own poetic language, is less important. What is emphasized in this allegory is the organic sense of creativity McGuckian posits on the one hand, and on the other her petition to the readers to read poetry in a new light, looking not only at the magnificent trees but also their symbiotic undergrowth and "the thickening of their dreams."

By giving agency to the written word, *The Flower Master* exposes one of the most significant characteristics of Medbh McGuckian's compositional technique.[23] The grammatical and syntactical ambiguities gain significance as precise manifestations of a conscious acknowledgment of the inherent tautology of the writing process (by creating the word, the word is created, which repeatedly creates the word). Decoding McGuckian's transgression of grammar as a conscious strategy of self-exposure *and* concealment, the reader is given more confidence in delving into the disruptive chaos of her next volume, *Venus and the Rain.*

Chaos Retouched: *Venus and the Rain*

After the playful and ambiguous self-exposure and simultaneous concealment of *The Flower Master*, chaos and negation are the defining characteristics of McGuckian's second collection, *Venus and the Rain.*[24] This is true not only on the level of syntax and vocabulary but also as a transcendental opacity which permeates the poems. Written as a reflection on postpartum depression suffered after the birth of her first child in 1980, *Venus and the Rain* tackles issues of pain, abandonment, and feelings of insularity. The theme of creativity is dealt with in a similar manner, and poems, which reflect on their composition, convey an overriding sense of chaos and futility. *Venus and the Rain* was not particularly well received. After its initial publication in 1984, Michael Allen, in his review, for example, although admitting that "something good is happening in nearly all of them"[25] discussed the poems as "disorientating—particularly for the male reader"[26] and regarded the collection as a quirky and odd volume, written from a very feminine point of view.[27] Although McGuckian's overriding sense of displacement within a predominantly male poetic tradition is reflected in many of the poems of *Venus and the Rain,* the main theme of the book remains focused on the creative process.

"Scattering," a somewhat eerie poem, considers visual creation as a means of manifestation of the compositional process. Opening in the conditional, the first two lines set the scene of confusion and disarray: "If you had walked in, the room / Would have broken up into questions" (*VR*, 21). The "room," as in the poem "The Truth Room" from the previous collection, can aptly be considered as a representation of the poetic psyche, which becomes suffused with confusion following the appearance of a purposeful consciousness. As the "room" breaks into "questions," its occupants, (who might be "thoughts" or "ideas") represented by "such-and-such a pear," are dislocated and "no longer nourished / By its old bad-tempered roots" (*VR*, 21). In other words, the creative process is halted at the source, and the idea of progress is denied from the outset. However, the poem goes on, and its own process of creation is unfaltered by its self-implied incapacity. This seeming paradox is appropriately acknowledged by the hesitation and ambivalence of the second stanza:

> For in one minute the moon
> Can move the distance of her body,
> With all the calm of a pietà,
> From a mouth that matches hers, so that
> A state of good repair still clings
> To Venus putting on her sandals
> Abstemiously in the pre-dawn hours. (*VR*, 21)

The light of the moon, sweeping over the female body, creates it. The relationship between desire and language is discernible in the context of the creative process. McGuckian's language is the desire which generates desire. In other words, she articulates simultaneously the subject and object of desire, by symbolically identifying with the "moon" and the female body of Venus, the agency of creation and its artifact. As Moynagh Sullivan argues:

> Desire in McGuckian's poetry is not always *for* the child/reader, but is for objects we do not often recognise or which are obscured from our understanding and our view, objects of desire which are veiled, making explicit the woman as a *subject of desire* who actively chooses to reveal (or not) *objects of her desire*, as opposed to a structural object which, after Nietzsche and Derrida, is seen to veil and unveil *herself*. For McGuckian not only knows what she is saying, she knows, more importantly, *how* she is saying it.[28]

The crucial point here, I believe, is that McGuckian is also aware of the *process* of "saying it." As a "state of good repair still clings / To Venus" (*VR*, 21), her words carry within them their own composition, their arbitrary arrangement on the white page, their "abstemious" construction.

"Scattering" concludes with the reinstatement of the poetic self through the image of light on "my edge-to-edge bolero" (*VR*, 21). Light, in fact, takes central stage as the agency of composition, and after denying the "genuine daylight" of reason, it is transformed into a negative scattering of a "dark effect." The poem's progress is circular and futile: from the broken-up image of the room the reader is led to the confusion of darkness, and the lines chart a mental journey of (de)composition. However, this construction of chaos retains a symbolic significance, where the diffusion of syntactic sense is transformed into a completed artifact, the poem.

"Moonshots" (*VR*, 24), on the other hand, in this context considers the reader as subject, and as such, it constitutes a direct challenge of interpretation:

> . . . and if
> You stumble into me as a great meal,
> You may learn how cold a man will feel
> In the interior of the moon. (*VR*, 24)

McGuckian delineates the reader's contribution as necessarily male and also accidental and possessive. This masculinized imagination of appropriation (devouring) and reason (learning) is delegitimized and transposed onto a conventionally female attribution, "feeling." The crude juxtaposition of an Enlightenment "male" reason to a Romantic "female" sensitivity is dependent on the conditional "if" in the poem, and is duly deconstructed in the second stanza:

> Yet I hold you fast there, your
> Rudimentary impression of leaves and stalks,
> Like the spin of false suns, or
> The doubtful weight of morning,
> Preparing to sail away again. (*VR*, 24)

The temporal proximity of reader and writer allows for a mutual performance of creativity, before the poetic consciousness "sail(s) away again." The poem highlights the vulnerability, and yet the importance, of reader participation. Although conceived of as initially hostile and male, the reader's consciousness is allowed a fleeting moment of "rudimentary impression," without which the composition would fail. Derek Attridge, writing about literary performance, argues that

> the temporality of creation, as a retrospectively constituted element in interpretation, is part of our understanding of any literary work. And yet the writtenness of the work remains unrealised until it is read, read in a singular enactment of its potential that puts into play many (but never all) the possibilities encoded within it.[29]

The subversive effect of this particular poem, however, is that its process of creation entangles the reader in her/his process of interpretative performance. Simultaneously rebuffing and seducing the reader, the performance of reading is overtaken by the "writtenness" of the poem. In other words, it is not the reader's act of reading which "puts into play" the poem, but rather, it is the process of the poem's composition *of* the reader which allows for a temporary moment of interpretation. Attridge argues that "if I am responding creatively to a work being performed before me, if I am doing justice to its singularity, alterity, and inventiveness, I am still active in performing it—which is also to say I am caught up in, and partly constituted as a subject by, the event of performance."[30] However, a poem like "Moonshots" disrupts the assumed continuity between writing and reading, and therefore precedes and also rejects the reader's performative act. Significantly, understanding is portrayed as provisional and fragile, represented by the incredible and syntactically challenging "spin of false suns" and "the doubtful weight of morning" (*VR*, 24). "Moonshots" eventually leaves the reader behind, offering no more than a glimpse, a "shot," of its creation.

"Isba Song" employs a different technique and takes the reader deep inside the creative consciousness:

> Beyond the edge of the desk, The Victorian dark
> Inhabits childhood, youth-seeking, death-seeking,
> Bringing almost too much meaning to my life. (*VR*, 26)

The interior, like a pregnant womb, carries the poetic mind as "its mournful locus . . . requiring to be renamed." This preverbal terrain is depicted as the origin of both the corporeality and mentality of the poetic self. Here the maternal voice is re-created and its agency restored. However, the inescapable division, which follows birth, is surpassed here with a gentle readjustment of the maternal back into the womb:

> . . . I have heard
> In it the sound of another woman's voice,
> Which I believed was the sound of my own,
> The sound the first-timeness of things we remember
> Must make inside. And although she was eager
> To divide her song, from her I took nothing
> But the first syllable of her name, so the effect
> Was of a gentler terrain within a wilder one. (*VR*, 26)

Moynagh Sullivan sees this "inside" terrain as the "material origin of language,"[31] the language of the mother, which is (re)discovered by the speaker in the concluding lines of the poem:

> . . . Otherwise I might have well
> Ignored the ground that shone for me, that did enough
> To make itself rebound from me, out of which I was made. (*VR*, 26)

She argues that "the 'inside' is inside of the mother, the ground of the other woman that the speaker might very well have 'ignored' in erasing the mother by thinking that the ground only shone for her (and not in itself). Instead the difference of the other woman is inscribed and connected to a corporeality."[32] Sullivan sees the maternal voice as a facilitator and originator of the speaker's identity. However, the maternal in "Isba Song" is consciously created and positioned within the imaginary womb of the poetic consciousness. In other words, the daughter creates the mother to create the daughter, and thus the acknowledgement of a maternal presence is also, simultaneously, a recognition of the poetic mind's own capacity to (re)create. The poem, and the "poet" with it, are "made" out of the gentle cohabitation of mother and child, without the necessarily implied severance of the two. The process of composition within "Isba Song" linguistically and symbolically erases the corporeal and mental consequences of creation, and instead of dividing mother from daughter, work from reader, it serves as an instigation of a combined performance. Attridge has postulated a definition of creation as a "mental activity involved in [a] transition from non-being to being."[33] However, in "Isba Song" McGuckian defies this account by composing the *site* of creation (the womb), rather than its produce. Put differently, the mental transition of creation in this poem is not from nonbeing to being, but from nonbeing to a *potential of being*, which is always contingent on the joint performances of writer and reader.

This line of thought is developed further in "Lime Trees in Winter, Retouched," where the act of creation produces a definitive negative: waste. The opening lines set the site of composition in the destructive backdrop of the color "black," which swallows up the visible contours of creation:[34]

> Black is my continuum, my black wheat ripens
> From peach black, vine black, to the resins
> Of darkness. That is how good a picture
> Should be, oil abetting, light disturbing,
> Hoisted between two windows like the soul
> Of modesty, constantly straightening against them. (*VR*, 49)

The compositional product, the "picture," remains conditioned by its dimensions as a visible, tangible invention. The "soul of modesty," which legitimizes its existence, is reminiscent of Victorian attributes of women. McGuckian subverts her positioning as the female artist and directs her attention to a conventionally very "unwomanly" subject, excrement:

> But I am agitated less by glass or apertures
> Than moisture trapped like a stain or white

> Secretion, an old swab I was confident
> Had broken down to paste, or was ingrained
> In the next meconium, my intent and cherished waste. (*VR*, 49)

Moynagh Sullivan rightfully observes the significance of this event when she remarks that "McGuckian cherishes the 'waste' with which woman has been identified and the cherishing of the abjected body[35] signals the birth of a different poetical relation to matter."[36] McGuckian's consideration of the body and its secretions is undoubtedly noteworthy and radical, indicating an acute awareness of feminist concerns relating to embodiment. However, "Lime Trees in Winter, Retouched," once more directs the reader's attention to issues of creative production. Because what is excrement, if not a symbol of production? Arguably, waste is the ultimate negation of invention, being as it is the by-product of that which is important. It is a nonbeing created out of nonbeing, if you sideline the fortuitous matter of "being" (that which is "important") deposited somewhere along the process.[37] This negation, or chaos, is symbolized by the leaking bodily fluids, which as meconium signals our entrance to the world.[38] On a textual level, this leakage is an essential component in the production of meaning, allowing for a fluid mixing of authorial intention and the reader's interpretative performance. This is what ultimately gives meaning to the idea of an "intent and cherished waste": it is the authorial gesture, which invites the reader to recycle and recover the original nonbeing of the poetic idea. The title, "Lime Trees in Winter, Retouched," already hints at this intention. The dead winter trees, like the waste at the end of the poem, are "retouched," their image awaiting the recycling signal of the reader's gaze.

Looking at literary performance from a different perspective, we find poems in this volume mapping out McGuckian's representation of the female muse. As introduced earlier, the figure of the female muse is less a reconfiguring of a traditional, romanticized icon than a means by which McGuckian queries and rewrites her conceived role as a female poet. One of the first poems in the volume, "Ode to a Poetess," (*VR*, 13) is especially instructive in describing and summarizing the poet's methodology of rewriting the female muse. The title suggests that this poem is self-reflexive and will present a more or less straightforward imaginary construct of the speaking subject. In other words, the reader expects this to be a poem written either to another female poet or to the poet herself. However, the relational context set out in the first part of the poem complicates this assumption:

> What survives of our garden is held together
> By the influence of water, as if we could only live

In the shelter of each other, and just leave the matter
Where we must leave all the doors that matter.
How clear and beautiful and hard to bear,
The shutters of these full delaying months,
Like a window not made to open, or a house
That has been too long to let, my dark woman's
Slope. (*VR*, 13)

If there is a distance between two separate entities here—as a prerequisite of intersubjective communication—this is more like the distance that Robert Brazeau (paraphrasing Susan Friedman) calls "self-difference" visited upon a woman as a result of pregnancy.[39] The speaker and the addressed self can only exist "in the shelter of each other." The suggestive pregnant imagery of "the full delaying months" and of the "house let too long" implicitly deals with the sense of "self-othering" experienced by a woman through pregnancy.[40] In terms of poetry, where childbirth becomes poem-birth, the split sense of self within the poetic persona corresponds to the imaginary presence of a contributing participant, a kind of midwife-muse, who, as the other half, "half" shares in the pangs of creative labor:

. . . Half real, half-dreamed,
Untouched, untouchable, the yet-to-be-born weather,
Distempering me as lips disturb the vespered worlds
Of grapes, this onset of a poetess and her
Persuasive bones sending me and my life away. (*VR*, 13)

The "onset of the poetess," recalling the onset of labor, simultaneously becomes the poetic performance and its instigator. The speaking subject persistently blurs with the "spoken" subject, maintaining a tension within the female poetic self. This becomes explicitly registered at the beginning of the second part of the poem where the (compound) speaker says, "I will not write her name although I know it" (*VR*, 13). The act of naming would inevitably bring about separation and dissociation, which would eliminate the creative frustration inherent in this union. However, the poem suddenly destabilizes the parameters of speaker-within-speaker (the "I" talking about the "she" inside) by directly addressing the muse:

Now you are in a poem of your own cold
Making, on your second fret, your life knit
Like a bird's, when amid the singing
Of the Sparrow Hills you yourself could not sing. (*VR*, 13)

The muse's agency lies in her own creation. Similar to the pre-Platonic muses, she is the giver of language that makes her come alive. She cannot sing, but gives the song which sings her. However, the speaker-subject reflects on the pain and frustration inherent in this process. Lacking in the erotic gratification often experienced by male poets when relating to their muse, "Ode to a Poetess" focuses on the dissatisfying self-distancing and self-othering the female poetic speaker undergoes. The female muse of a female poet has a profound effect on the construction of poetic self, and the collusion of the two is often portrayed as a threat to self-coherence. "Ode to a Poetess" aptly captures this sense of danger when it surmises about the muses that "what they ask of women is less their bed . . . than to be almost gone" (*VR*, 13).

In another example of a muse poem, "The Sitting" (*VR*, 18), the female figure is named as "my half sister." That leaves no doubt about her personal relationship to the poet. With only one parent shared, the half-sister is an apt representation of an intimate, but somewhat problematized, association. In the first line of the poem the half-sister arrives to be painted by the painter-poet.[41] She is posing for a picture in, and of, the poem, but she resists representation. First she is seen "posing furtively, like a letter being / Pushed under the door" and then the painting begins:

> . . . Yet her coppery
> Head is as bright as a net of lemons. I am
> Painting it hair by hair as if she had not
> Disowned it, or forsaken those unsparkling
> eyes as blue may be sifted from the surface
> Of a cloud. (*VR*, 18)

However, before the painting could be completed, the half-sister, in this reading a muse, steps into the poem, questioning its progress and methodology:

> . . . and she questions my brisk
> Brushwork, the note of positive red
> In the kissed mouth I have given her,
> As a woman's touch makes curtains blossom
> Permanently in a house: she calls it
> Wishfulness, the failure of the tampering rain
> To go right into the mountain, she prefers
> My sea-studies, and will not sit for me
> Again. (*VR*, 18)

McGuckian pictures the desire to possess and understand her female muse through the metaphorical act of painting but what really interests her is the tension of never achieving unification. This also explains the sense of fragmentation implied by naming her a "half-sister" and describing the sitting as "something half-opened" (*VR*, 18). The symbolic use of the color "red" reveals a similar message. The "dull-rose dress" of the half-sister transforms into a "note of positive red" in the painting, much to the muse's dislike, and the poem culminates in "a soiled red-letter day" (*VR*, 18). When interpreted as an image of the creative performance, the use of red charts the ambivalence inherent in artistic representation, demonstrating its implied failure.[42]

The emotional frustration of an unsuccessful encounter between a reluctant muse and her painter returns in a somewhat more violent manner in "The Rising Out" (*VR*, 36). The "half-sister" becomes a "dream-sister" who arrives not to pose but to murder:

> My dream sister has gone into my blood
> To kill the poet in me before Easter. (*VR*, 36)

In the pre-Platonic era challenging the Muses was an act that symbolized confronting the self. The inevitable failure of this venture led to self-destruction. In this poem, however, if we follow a reading where the "dream sister" represents the muse, she poses a direct threat to the "poet" within. Her "tender visit" precipitates a "split in two"; yet, she does not produce the expected violence. Rather, she seems content and untroubled by the pain of the creative process experienced by the speaker:

> She gentles me by passing weatherly remarks
> That hover over my skin with an expectant summer
> Irony, soliloquies that rise out of sleep,
> And quite enjoy saying, "Rather a poor year." (*VR*, 36)

On the other hand, the poet is painfully at work completing the poem which is centered around the muse:

> I continue meanwhile working on my arm-long
> "Venus Tying the Wings of Love," hoping
> She will recede with all my heroes, dark
> Or fair, if my body can hold her bone to term. (*VR*, 36)

Ann Beer has remarked on the apparent conflict between the "physical and artistic motherhood"[43] represented in "The Rising Out." The intense tension between these different forms of mothering creates the violence of the poem. The metaphysical muse clashes with the corporeal woman within the poetic self, yearning to gain the advantage to create. It is only in the actual performance of writing the poem that the tension dissolves. With this, however, the distinction between the two females blurs. Entering the body of the poet the "dream sister" dissolves into the "other" Alice (a reference that takes its origin from a Mary Cassatt painting but no doubt brings to mind Lewis Carroll's Alice going through the looking glass[44]):

> In my mind,
> I try and try to separate one Alice
> From the other, by their manner of moving,
> The familiar closing of the unseen room,
> The importunate rhythm of flowers. (*VR*, 36)

The unsettling desire of creativity becomes self-reflexive and manifests itself as a desire for separation. Thus by the end of the poem it is unclear who is meant by the pronoun "she":

> If she had died suddenly I would have heard
> Blood stretched on the frame, though her dream
> Is the same seed that lifted me out of my clothes
> And carried me till it saw itself as fruit. (*VR*, 36)

Whether it is the muse or the "poet" within, the slow death of "her" becomes the gradual process of writing the poem, the appearing "fruit." Although this muse (because of her aggression) is markedly different to the pre-Platonic muses, her metaphorical representation as the "spectral other" in the creative performance makes sense. Because McGuckian gives her authorial agency, her immediate and physical challenge to the poetic self produces "fruit" and not destruction.

Venus and the Rain is undoubtedly a dark volume, where harsh imagery is coupled with stark psychological themes to produce an overriding sense of chaos and futility.[45] The creation of the self is questioned and impeded from the inside and remains contingent on accidental circumstance. The collection toys with the idea of potentiality but ultimately leaves it to the reader to trace the outlines of a coherent writing self within the transcendental murkiness of the poems.

On Ballycastle Beach: Crawling into Words

McGuckian's next volume, *On Ballycastle Beach*, first published in 1988 by Oxford University Press and republished in 1995 by The Gallery Press,[46] continues in a similar vein and further develops the theme of involuntary creation through images of leakage, melting, and escape. Ideas of progress and development are thwarted at the outset, and most of the poems in the collection focus on the involuntary "happening" of the creative process.

"Apple Flesh" revisits the metaphor of "the room" as a site of the poetic psyche. However, unlike in previous examples, this room does not accommodate certain aspects and sediments of the compositional process, but in itself it becomes representative of creative alteration:

> The room getting lighter and darker
> Is a kind of travel also.
> No dream could find its way in here,
> Up the now weak stairs,
> Where my body tasted like apple flesh
> The day and night of fifteen countries,
> Or we sat about, unsmiling,
> In a long, twisting sunset of 1910. (*OBB*, 11)

Significantly, the poetic consciousness is not conceived of as the disseminator of creative ideas, but rather, as the single creative idea itself, which remains trapped in its own interior. The "weak stairs," signaling the inward collapse of the poetic construction, lead to a dehumanized, transcendental body, which, stripped of its corporeality (like a peeled apple), exists only in the perception of an imagined other. Whether interpreted as the physicality of the written page "tasted" by its readers, or an authorial presence impressed on the poem, "apple flesh" signifies the remains of a broken and violated entity. The image of the "room," inhabited by tangible damage, is a hostile environment for the fragile "dreams" of the imagination. The second stanza further reinforces the sense of isolation and hurt when it describes past memories:

> . . . I remembered
> White pictures of birds and sun-healed
> Water—birds that had lost
> Their ability to shiver
> And died in the brainwashed sea. (*OBB*, 11)

The pictorial "birds," symbolic of the creative "flight" of composition, are stripped of their ontological quality of progress. As creations of the mind, they die in a "brainwashed sea," like an unfinished image and broken line. Again, the perceived pointlessness of the writing process is not only signaled by the description of an inadequate end-product, but also by the portrayal of initial failure. The poem concludes with the ultimate collapse of creative possibility and an acceptance of defeat:

> Rock pulled away from rock
> Till the sea went out of its mind;
> And my road in a sudden triangle
> Warned how the dreamer is in danger
> When his dream begins, like that,
> With the weather. (*OBB*, 11)

Poetic consciousness, depicted as male in its failure, remains the solitary subject of this poem. As "apple flesh," it is situated somewhere between its past image as a wholesome symbol of female-generated knowledge and its failure as a creative idea.[47] There is no space left for the reader to contribute, or initiate an act of composition by participation. The creative performance is buried within the insipid "weather" of the poem and its symbolic success in conveying the eventual collapse of meaning.

"Sea or Sky" (*OBB*, 15), following in the footsteps of "Apple Flesh," traces the journeying of ideas within the poetic consciousness. The creative construction of words is likened to inadvertent incidents that come about isolated from the governing authority of the mind:

> Small doses, effleurage will do,
> Because I never garden. Wednesday comes
> Out of the rim of bones with a port-wine
> Stain on its face, a day of possible
> Excitements, no sky, yet you know immediately
> The colour it should be. (*OBB*, 15)

The subtle inclusion of birth imagery[48] signals a negative economy of language, where word production is likened to the involuntary expulsion of the fetus ("comes / out of the rim of bones"). Creativity is implied as the unattainable, the idea that materializes as the conditional "should be." However, the source of the creative impulse, the "agitated sky of my choice" becomes visible as a mere "echo of light," "the sun / improperly burning" (*OBB*, 15), hinting at incompleteness and failure. In a complex set of images McGuckian attempts to convey the conceptual hiatus that exists between the inspirational desire and its embodiment as lines of poetry:

> . . . In a sea of like mood
> A wave is trying to break, to give a reason
> For water striking something else, and the grey

> Below the wave is a darker version
> Of the moisture-laden sky I should be working in.
> (Not the clear water of your sleep where you
> Seem lighter, and the garden's voice has gone inside.) (*OBB*, 15)

"Sea" and "sky," in their indefinable, yet overpowering, corporeal presence, signal the pressures exerted on the creative consciousness toward production. Set in opposition with the effortlessness of the "clear water" of dreams, literary construction takes on the "darker version" of the poetic mind. The outcome of this psychic struggle is a materialized corporeality which significantly exists in the context of human relations:

> . . . my new, especially
> Dense breasts can be touched, can be
> Uplifted from the island of burned skin
> Where my heart used to be, now I'm
> Seeing eyes that, sea or sky, have seen you. (*OBB*, 15)

The concluding lines seem to suggest that the creative effort produced a physical reality, which is accomplished in the "touch" conducted by the generic "you" of the poem. Interpreted as an address to the reader, the final line construes the poem as the "eyes" that, having been read, have "seen" the participating reader. The creative process, therefore, is involuntary for author and reader alike; it "happens" and remains as indistinct as the blurred moisture trapped between sea and sky.[49]

The space created by the productive effort and its realization as poem holds McGuckian's interest in "Blue Vase" (*OBB*, 28). Blue, a color associated with creativity all throughout her poetry, takes shape as a virtual space of inspiration. The first stanza positions the body and the garment covering it at opposite ends of the creative spectrum:

> My overblouse is a garment made
> For rest, work, movement. I permit
> On my body only that which glides,
> The roving ache of all shared things—
> Love, rest, and dreams. (*OBB*, 28)

The "overblouse," once removed from the physical reality of the body, is significantly the catalyst of creative production: "work." The body itself remains unfocused and the host of the imagination (the gliding "dreams"). However, what makes this stanza interesting is the occurrence of the word "rest" in both contexts. As the hiatus in the compositional (and reading) process, it is symbolic of what Wolfgang Iser termed the "virtual dimension" of the text. Iser argues that the creative act of reading produces this dimension, which is not the text itself, nor the imagination of the reader, but "the coming together of text and imagination."[50] The gaps left between the composition and the reading act in Iser's argument

> have a different effect on the process of anticipation and retrospection, and thus on the "gestalt" of the virtual dimension, for they may be filled in different ways. For this reason, one text is potentially capable of several different realisations, and no reading can ever exhaust the full potential, for each individual reader will fill in the gaps in his own way, thereby excluding the various other possibilities; as he reads, he will make his own decision as to how the gap is to be filled. In this very act the dynamics of reading are revealed. By making his decision he implicitly acknowledges the inexhaustibility of the text; at the same time it is this very inexhaustibility that forces him to make his decision.[51]

However, this poem *writes* the gap, rather than allowing for a space in the reader's efforts to be filled. In other words, the gap is not presented as the hiatus between the lines, or authorial omissions (which would require conscious and imaginative efforts to decode) but rather, the lines themselves embody the imaginative blockage between writer and reader. The second stanza reinforces this recognition, by presenting the creative produce as a present "difficult to give" (*OBB*, 28). The poetic consciousness does not let go of the compositional process ("being / Held too tightly by my own / Determined touch") and the reader's efforts are knowingly integrated in the course of writing, symbolized by the way in which a painting captures light:

> Determined to steady your heart,
> As a painting that gathers up
> The light of some astonishing hair,
> The rare dimming of a ship
> Early in the voyage. (*OBB*, 28)

Again, the reading process is prefigured within the writing, and the assumed reader is converted into a *created* one. Naturally, all writings create their own readers,[52] but it is rare to configure the process of the reader's response into the text. This response is not concerned with a critical reaction to the work (the poem is not asking the reader to like it, neither does it assume otherwise) instead it re-creates the creative process whereby the reader is created alongside the poem. The authorial presence, although strong, does not assume power over this process, and in fact the final line asserts the reader's words as the ultimate invention of the poem:

> . . . In the dream
> That preceded the poem, I was standing
> Outside a house that had your face;
> From opposite ends
>
> Re-chose you in my dream-speech,
> Without telling you or anyone what it meant:
> To be the insouciance of the room,
> Interrupted, re-created—to be the innocence
> You have just learned to say. (*OBB*, 28)

Internalized within the reader's consciousness (the "house"), the authorial presence creates a virtual space which symbolically accommodates the combined creative maneuvers of the creator and decoder of the poem. This "interrupted, re-created" artistic effort is indicative of McGuckian's conceptualization of the creative process in several of her poems and remains one of the uncharted territories within her work.

On Ballycastle Beach is a volume which pays particular attention to the poems' self-formation and reception. "Harem Trousers" explores the position of the speaking subject within the writing process and opens up with a commanding proposition:

> Asleep on the coast I dream of the city.
> A poem dreams of being written
> Without the pronoun 'I.' (*OBB*, 40)

The desire to eliminate the speaking subject from the poem results in the advantage shifting to the subject *of* the poem. As Danielle Sered argues:

> [the] fluidity results in the placement of the poem itself in the position of subject: it is the poem which dreams, not the poet. This mobile relation compounds the instability of meaning in McGuckian's verse and also exhibits what Docherty will term "an alienation in [her] own relation to her language."[53]

However, Sered seems to disregard the fact that the speaking subject is reinstated later on in the poem and that the elimination of the "I" is unrealized.[54] This detail is significant both for the compositional and reading processes: the poem is "dreamed" as subject only before it is written and read, but its eventual interpretation is dependent on the physical presence of author and reader alike.[55] As in the previous poem, McGuckian carefully charts, stages, and (re)creates the joint inspirational performance of the authorial parties. As the lines are written and the poem takes shape, the compositional space for the poetic consciousness is created, and the speaking subject reenters:

> It straightens, stands, it walks
> Timid and incongruous
> Through roadblocks and breadlines.
> It holds the hundred and first word
> In its fingers and tears it apart,
>
> So the openness within the sound
> Is forced to break, dislodging
> Its already dove-grey music.
> An extreme and simple feeling
> Of "What if I do enter?—
>
> As I run to fetch water
> In my mouse-coloured sweater,
> Unkempt, hysterical, from
> The river that lives outside me,
> The bed whose dishevelment
> Does not enchant me. (*OBB*, 40)

The "unkempt," "hysterical" figure of the speaking subject enters the gap (the "openness within the sound") created by the poem's compositional process. Significantly, the appearance is physical, not transcendental, and the actual presence of the subject accelerates the completion of the poem.[56] The now only missing subject—the reader—appears as the generic "you" in the last stanza, and is approached for interpretation. The "room," here representing the interpretative space of the reader's mind, is furnished with the analytical tools of decoding ("a stem, a verb, a rhyme") and is acknowledged as the unpredictable mechanism of interpretation:

> Your room speaks of morning,
> A stem, a verb, a rhyme,
> From whose involuntary window one
> May be expelled at any time,
> As trying to control a dream
> Puts the just-completed light to rest. (*OBB*, 40)

The final word of the poem, "rest," reiterates the ambiguity introduced at the opening. It is uncertain whether the rest indicates a success or a failure, and whether the apparent collapse of the "dream" ("to be written without the pronoun 'I'") is the ultimate triumph of the poem. In other words, the speaking subject collides with the dreaming subject, and the outcome of this encounter is seemingly unresolved. However, the poem is completed, ("crawled into words") signaling yet again McGuckian's awareness of the intricacies of the compositional performance.[57]

"The Dream-Language of Fergus," probably the best-known poem from this collection, brings together disparate critical strands in relation to interpreting McGuckian's work. However, all readings agree that this poem is a type of *ars poetica*, a poetic manifesto that describes McGuckian's writing process. Clair Wills pointed out first in 1993 that the poem "borrows" heavily from three essays by Osip Mandelstam, a claim that was further developed by Alcobia-Murphy in a later study.[58] The poem is a good example of the kind of self-reflexive poetry in which McGuckian demonstrates her creative process. The borrowed lines not only incorporate seamlessly into the intended content, but their presence gives meaning to McGuckian's conceptualization of writing. The first section describes a "pregnant silence"[59] that precedes creativity: silence here becomes a visual space full of potential, a "shape" and a "shadow" that forms in the unconscious:

> Your tongue has spent the night
> In its dim sack as the shape of your foot
> In its cave. Not the rudiment
> Of half a vanquished sound,
> The excommunicated shadow of a name,
> Has rumpled the sheets of your mouth. (*OBB*, 57)

"Cave" and "shadow" recall Plato's allegory of the cave, and his theory of forms, which argue for the supremacy of "forms," or ideas, over sensory reality. In Plato's allegory one reality merges into another, and it becomes the philosopher's task to distinguish between the two. McGuckian takes up this idea of merged realities in the second stanza. However, instead of arguing for the supremacy of one over the other, she describes her artistic truth as a "scattered alphabet" and a "sky" that is "stabbed by their exits / And the mistaken meaning of each" (*OBB*, 57):

> So Latin sleeps, they say, in Russian speech,
> So one river inserted into another
> Becomes a leaping, glistening, splashed
> And scattered alphabet
> Jutting out from the voice,
> Till what began as a dog's bark

Ends with bronze, what began
With honey ends with ice;
As if an aeroplane in full flight
Launched a second plane,
The sky is stabbed by their exits
And the mistaken meaning of each. (*OBB*, 57)

This section of course carries a rich source of referential material. The first line gains novel interpretative layers in the context of Mandelstam's essays and, as Leontia Flynn points out, Dante, Frost, and Seamus Heaney also reverberate throughout this work.[60] Some critics see these lines as a reflection on the duality of the Irish and English language within her work, yet others read them as a manifestation of McGuckian's maternal conceptualization of language.[61] While all these interpretations add rich layers of imaginative possibilities, lines 6–8 carry, in my opinion, the most significant message of the poem. "Till what began as a dog's bark / ends with bronze, what began / with honey ends with ice." (*OBB*, 57).These images not only describe the unconscious and uncontrollable progress of ideas to words, they also hint at the qualitative difference between the two. The original ideas, here described as "dog's bark" and "honey," are fluid, temporal, and formless concepts that escape containment, and which also carry dual qualities. A bark is unpleasant but can be useful; honey is pleasant but can be sticky. On the other hand what they become in the process, "bronze" and "ice," are cold, touchable, and contained substances, reinforcing McGuckian's earlier conceptualizations of writing as failure. While this might sound an overly particular reading, it offers, I believe, an insight into the way McGuckian views her poems and explains her aesthetic urge to return the reader's gaze toward the development of her creative process. The finalized words lose their ambivalence and become a reality that cheats their original intent, as described by the "second plane" that diverts the creative objective of the work, becoming a "mistaken meaning" in the process (*OBB*, 57). In other words, the imagery describes a derailed interpretative process that is unable to recover either the source, the process, or the result of the creative work. The final section of the poem offers a conceptualization of readerly attitude that can be more successful in retrieving authorial intent. It suggests, in my reading, an approach that is not one-directional, in other words an interpretation that surpasses the urge to recover tangible sources and ideas (be it textual references or biographical explanations), but rather, goes back and forth between text and origin, like a "pendulum."[62] The key is to read in the "now," with an overt acceptance of the "double-stranded words" that McGuckian offers (*OBB*, 58).

Although this attitude potentially unravels critical textual analysis, it allows for readings that involve the reader creatively. Arguably this can lead to a cavalcade of misreadings and misinterpretations from a critical point of view. However, the author expresses skepticism toward definitive readings ("no text can return the honey / in its path of light from a jar" (*OBB*, 58)) and instead seems to ask for a questioning readerly stance and creative involvement.

In conclusion, *On Ballycastle Beach* sees the tentative development of a more coherent writing self. Written into the poems as a creative idea, poetic consciousness is still portrayed more as a failure than an articulate authority. However, even as a negative entity it is given space in which to maneuver the creative process. The poet in this volume toys with the idea of "unwriting" her creative self, giving over authorial responsibility to the reader and the created artifact, nevertheless her artistic identity keeps "crawling" back onto the written page.

"Clouds within Hesitation Quotes": *Marconi's Cottage*

The created artifact as subject takes central stage in McGuckian's 1991 Gallery Press collection, *Marconi's Cottage*. "Words," "lines," and "the poem" are the focus, and the aesthetics of the volume consider the poetic mind's troubled liaison with its work. "The Sun-Moon Child," for instance, succumbs to the problematized "half-room" appearance of the composition and states: "I accepted the dream's / Standpoint and decision, like a false season."[63] The ensuing half-breed, the "sun-moon child," is the self-contained and autonomous subject, the poem itself, which accepts its double bind as both success and failure.[64]

"Turning the Moon into a Verb" (*MC*, 76) develops this theme even further and introduces the reader to the methodology of compositional performance: the surrealistic act of verbalizing something that is, literally, beyond our reach becomes emblematic of the impossibility inherent in the creative process. The image of the "Moon" evokes a complex symbolism. It is the feminine satellite charting the rhythm of the tides and the menstrual cycle. Although in itself dead and motionless, it encompasses time, change, and movement, thus symbolically turning *itself* into a verb. The first stanza of the poem exposes the infertile image of winter turning into the fertile beginning of creation:

> A timeless winter
> That wants to be now
> Will go on taking shape in me.
> Now everything can begin. (*MC*, 76)

The uncanny in the compositional process appears as the initiation of fertility by winter and the transformation of "timeless" into time in the word "now," that reverberates to the "now" of the earlier discussed poem "The Dream-Language of Fergus." In other words, the first stanza repeats the act of the title where the motionless becomes mobile and the infertile is transfigured as fertile, thus imagining a space where the creative birth is initiated. (The third line clearly refers to pregnancy.) With the voice of the yet unborn poem inside her, the second stanza investigates the delicate balance between creator and the created composition. The "new listening" prepares both poet and reader for the arrival of the poem. However, being pregnant with the poem "weakens" the desire for new creation, and this creative pregnancy develops a new sense of timelessness where the usual rhythm of life, the seasons, lose their significance:

> Everything can reach much
> Further up; with this new
> Listening, the longing at the window
> For the missing seasons weakens. (*MC*, 76)

This is the disjointed time of the birthing process, where time both begins and ends. The next stanza, however, reaches back to the time before the conception—conceptualization—of the poem and explores the role of the male subject:

> When springtime had need of him,
> He did not offer me the winter,
> He took away each of the seasons
> In its visual turn. (*MC*, 76)

In the season of symbolic spring, the time of conception and growth, the male fails to deliver his compositional contribution and instead robs the speaking subject of fertile time. In other words, the conventionally male performance of composition where details are gathered and then re-presented to an audience as a self-contained unity is denounced. The feminine subject's compositional process transforms "springtime," "winter," and all the seasons into creative acts, at the expense of the male within. However, the "need" of the masculine is significant and signals the cooperative performance necessary for completion. The last missing link, the reader, in this interpretation makes an appearance in the subsequent stanzas as the nonspecific "you" left in the dark. S/he is looking for particulars which would make sense in the darkness, "a green / A little darker than all other greens" (*MC*, 76). Seemingly all participants fail, and it is the figure of the mother who remains the sole performer of the composition. Transposing the process into the "secret year" and "secret time" of pregnancy—the carrying of the poem to full term—allows for the eventual release. When time is up, its "flight is a written image / Of its cry" (*MC*, 76)—the poem concludes in its surfacing through the birthing canal. This "capacity" of the poem to talk about its own delivery signals the real "timeless" time of creation:

> . . . The experience
>
> When the sky becomes a womb,
> And a vision of rivers slanting
> Across the doubly opened page
> Of the moon turns her into a verb. (*MC*, 76)

The appearance of the words "written" and "doubly opened page" directly introduce the subject of composition. The poem is eventually written on the moon, which in itself is an active participant in the creation:

> An image I have consciously
> Broken like a shoulder on your hearing,
> The inconstancy within constancy
> That is the price of a month. (*MC*, 76)

The consciously broken image, the moon turned into a verb, will represent the creative process, "the inconstancy within constancy" which operates in a time out of time. McGuckian's aesthetic builds on the recognition of a temporal and spatial dimension dedicated solely to the compositional process, which bends the rules of ordinary linguistic expectations. Unlike in the Wordsworthian model of inspiration, where past experiences are recollected in the tranquility of a focused and well-defined space and time, McGuckian discredits these boundaries and formulates an inspirational mechanism which creates its own dimensions. Thus both the writing and reading processes are performed within the intersubjective economy of McGuckian's poetry, where time and space are simultaneously created and destroyed by the joint efforts of writer and reader. Derek Attridge's notion of reader performance[65] therefore does not account for the writer's consciousness of the reader, and in McGuckian's case it disregards the poet's effort to instigate responsive cooperation.

Once the performance is over, and the poem is "born," the concept of inspiration ostensibly loses its significance. However, because McGuckian writes poetry with a more organic sense of creation, the finished composition enters the intersubjective nexus of her imaginary. Attridge argues that the lines of a written work "come to life" when read. McGuckian, on the other hand, writes poems as already *read* and reflective on their delivery. "Branches" (*MC* 78), a poem which exemplifies this mechanism, traces its own formation and culminates in its actual birth. It opens with floating images, disconnected from the poetic consciousness, as well as from their "original" character:

> This window, clumsily inserted,
> Was originally a door.
> So am I detached
> From the fabric which claims me. (*MC*, 78)

These discrepancies are consolidated under the "one rain" of the performance of composition. This performance subverts both the classical notion of mimesis (art imitating an imitation of the divine image) and the Romantic idea of summoning up images seen before, by denying the legitimacy of the concept of a primal and original "image":

> Under one rain, the same rain,
> I sleep two dreams in one,
> And am softened like a touch
> Blurred by a curtain. (*MC*, 78)

The softened vision of the subject authorizes its speech, which is no longer reliant on the conventional progress of creation going from image to page. Instead, the gaze turns inward, where the "two dreams in one" resides and reflects on its self-image. The eyes are looking at themselves, "diffused with blood," "veins . . . powerful as open arms" (*MC*, 78). This sight is evocative of a fetus's view of the interior of the maternal womb. Pregnancy, in McGuckian's own declaration, is the central theme of *Marconi's Cottage*,[66] and its association with creative production gains increased significance in this particular poem. Like the fetus, the speaking subject considers herself interned within the confines of a maternal space, which creates her, but also from which she is created. This duality symbolically appears as the "larch in the stairs" (*MC*, 78) in the next stanza, the substance which creates the stairs but which also gains existence through its materialization *as* stairs. The poetic voice eventually surfaces as the potential creation of the written page:

> I force the closely written page
> To bend me, as though it had created me.
>
> Slow-forming, the most changeable of all,
> Sky on sky in crescent-like sequence
> Overcomes the touch of another,
> Intertwines hedgelessly with the garden. (*MC*, 78)

The traumatic side effect of birth, the ultimate severance of mother and child, troubles the poetic voice on a literal, as well as a metaphorical, level. McGuckian was seriously distressed by the birth of her daughter Emer, and, in her mind, poetry and actual birth came together. She describes this in an interview:

> Well you see the birth itself was absolutely inhumane. Everything exploded and erupted: my relationship with my father and mother, my husband, and with the Church . . . my unresolved moral thing with sexuality. For six weeks I didn't sleep, and my whole body seemed to be weeping with liquid from every orifice. The whole body was just seared and opened and the mind as well. I was totally confused. . . . I was put into a mental home for three or four weeks, and I had the baby taken away from me. I went absolutely bananas. I was on all sorts of drugs and things. I was told not to write poetry and told I would never write poetry again.[67]

The anxiety of losing herself in the birthing process by simply "leaking" away is reflected in "Branches" (*MC* 78) as the relationship between creator and created forms. The "hedgeless intertwining" subverts the corporeal threat of loss and formulates instead a space where the performance of composition can be safely played out. The speaking subject responds to the danger of separation inherent in delivery and ultimately comes to inhabit this in-between space, which captures the moment of birth:

> . . . brings its shape to bear twice over
> On only one of our hours, unrelieved,
> Loaded down like a bookshelf,
> And content with bearing, nothing else. (*MC*, 78)

However, this space remains "unrelieved" and "loaded down" with the burden of its offspring, and its contentment with "bearing, nothing else" reflects the subversive resolution the speaking subject arrives at in this poem. The completion of the poem *is* its process of composition, and its writer and reader alike ultimately will share the labor pains of its delivery.

Marconi's Cottage is probably the volume in which McGuckian explores the concept of the performance of composition in most detail. The trauma of giving birth coincides with the also distressing (side-)effects of poetic creation. Questions of beginning and end surface in relation to the compositional process, and poems often conclude in negating a poetic or subjective essence at the center of creation. The "in-between" dimensions of space and time frame these explorations. In "The War Ending," for example, the poetic subject is likened to "a rainbow or a painting being torn / within" (*MC*, 82) and "Oval of a Girl" compares the process of composition to "a kind of forlorn frenzy leaking over into sound" (*MC*, 78). In this volume, "without the help of words, words take place,"[68] the reader inhabits "the spaces between words in the act of reading"[69] and "that irreducible / quality of createdness"[70] is expressed by "the awareness / of the silence, the form of the sentence yet to come."[71] The central concern of *Marconi's Cottage* gains momentum in explorations of the poetic self, which, as the embodiment of a voice of origin, questions inherited myths of inspirational source. Clair Wills argues that McGuckian's strategy of personalizing public narratives disables myth's claim to universality by "introducing discontinuity into their version of the myths by privatizing them, by taking them out of the public realm in which they are everybody's story and everybody knows their significance."[72] Wills's argument considers McGuckian's exploration of the female body as part of the public myth of nationhood, but it equally fits McGuckian's subversion of myths of origin. In this volume, significantly, there is no voice of God, angels, or other authorities. The only acknowledged voice of origin is that of doubt, duality, ambiguity, and labor. Childbirth, as a central metaphor, embodies the processual representations of these aspects of composition. Stuck in the birth canal, held captive in between the two dimensions of life and death, the poetic subject questions its own laboring deliverance. "From the First Underworld" (*MC*, 86–87) stands as a suitable representation of the problematization of poetic voice in *Marconi's Cottage*:

> And it is not the semi-soul
> Of a neo-nate in its uncontrolled dreaming,
> Or the listening behaviour
> Of 'mere foam, aura or melody',
>
> But such an ensouled thing
> As if you had died
> Fighting in a holy war

For some inert and unobtrusive God.
My wholly this-worldly question,

Without end though not without beginning,
Is whether, with the possibility of cruelty,
We are indeed such choice creatures
Or clouds within hesitation quotes
Felt, heard, finding the imageless air. (*MC*, 86–87)

The poem traces the development of the voice that originates in the underworld of the unconscious and prenatal realms. The lines contain quotations from philosophical works by Aristotle and Anthony Flew that ponder the meaning of life in the light of death, signaling the ambiguity of the poetic voice.

Marconi's Cottage also contains several male figures in her poems that can be read in the context of McGuckian's conceptualization of muses. If the female muse in the poet's work is interpreted as the projection of feminine poetic agency that threatens, as well as assists in, the performance of poetry writing, McGuckian's male muse certainly subverts readerly expectations of this creative partnership. The men that appear in her poems as possible aides rarely fit stereotypical descriptions of masculinity. Her male muse is an imaginary construct that cannot be separated from his feminine originator. He is not a man, but a woman-made man. If we appreciate the limitations of the traditional figure of the female muse as a male imaginary construct, then the same holds in the case of the woman-made male muse. This has crucial implications for reading McGuckian's poetry in a cultural and political context.[73] Creating a male muse is not only a subversion of the sexual determinants of a "muse tradition," but it is also a comment on the nature of gender as seen by McGuckian. The act of creating a poem becomes intertwined with creating sexualities: the performance of writing reflects on the performance of gender. McGuckian draws critical attention to the interconnectedness of performing her identity as a woman and as a poet, and her male muses provide the opportunity to demonstrate an increased awareness of discourses of gender in her poetry.

"Open Rose" (*MC*, 80) offers an accomplished exploration of this idea. The masculine pronoun that appears in the second stanza provides a startlingly clear image of the male muse:

His head is there when I work,
It signs my letters with a question-mark;
His hands reach for me like rationed air. (*MC*, 80)

The first line places the male muse in a somewhat conventional position. "His head" is "there," somewhere out of the reach of the poet, at a distance from which inspiration could arrive. However, instead of divine stimulus the muse provides the poet with a "question-mark" and then leaves his place, reaching out to the poet in existential hunger ("like rationed air"). In terms of creating a connection between the performances of poetry and gender, the male appears as a fundamental participant in the process of writing, profoundly influencing the identity of the poet-speaker. Now the relationship is seen from the speaker-subject's point of view:

> Day by day I let him go
>
> Till I become a woman, or even less,
> An incompletely furnished house[74]
> That came from a different century
> Where I am a guest at my own childhood. (*MC*, 80)

The construction of womanhood is seemingly inseparable from the process of discarding an interfering masculinity. However, the poem suggests that without the male muse the female poet is incomplete: she is a woman but not a poet. This line of thought has a strange resonance with what Toril Moi terms "social magic." She says: "Social magic is a socially sanctioned act which attributes an essence to individual agents, who then struggle to become what in fact they already are declared to be. In other words: to cast women as women is precisely to *produce* them as women."[75] The "letting go" of a possessive male muse produces a lack in the feminine, which reinforces the "essence" of a subdued second sex. The poetic subject appears as "less than woman"; she is a woman of past centuries who does not have control over her own life, being merely a "guest" at her own development.[76] It seems, however, that the most significant symbolic capital[77] of the speaking subject, the ability to write the poem, remains in the woman's control:

> I have grown inside words
> Into a state of unbornness,
> An open rose on all sides
> Has spoken as far as it can. (*MC*, 80)

The imagery of pregnancy serves as an ultimate exclusion of a masculine presence. However, the completion of the poem paradoxically remarks on its own incompletion ("unbornness"). It seems, then, that the conclusion of the poem acknowledges the assumed masculinity with which it opened. It is left open to interpretation whether the male is a necessary contributor in the creative reproductive process or whether he is a hindrance. McGuckian seems to circumvent a straightforward declaration of ideological positioning in terms of gender politics. Her male muse in this poem seems to be an extension of the self, whose existence, even if it creates an obstacle to fulfilling an ideal of "womanhood," suggests creative completeness. However, this is less a manifestation of androgynous creative powers than a demonstration of how the two genders perform one another. In "Dovecote" McGuckian says that "you cannot reproduce in your own shade" (*VR*, 40). In "Open Rose," however, she seems to be doing just that.

The relationship with the male muse becomes (in my reading) the central focus in "The Man with Two Women" (*MC*, 14). The poem takes its origin, as Alcobia-Murphy points out, "from a monograph detailing a ménage-à-trois, namely Ann and Samuel Charters' *I Love: The Story of Vladimir Mayakovsky and Lili Brik.*"[78] The three poetic subjects, apart from representing sexual innuendo, also stand as representative facets of a compound poetic self. The two women arguably signify a differentiation between "woman" and "poet." The first woman we see is on her way to the seashore in a "stylish sundress" reading other people's letters. The other is locked up somewhere with a monumental male figure "pulling off his shirt." The former is a woman "free" from poetic activity. The latter is the one entrapped with her man:

> My tired skin
> was letting the rain
> Get inside the halves
> of my collar when
> He entered as he
> would his own home. (*MC*, 14)

The masculine imagery of a penetrating rain, beyond being overtly erotic, also precipitates the strategic entrance of the male muse. He enters with an assumption of possession and dominance, occupying yet again the subconscious domestic space of the "house":

> Placing himself
>   There in the square
> Like a monument
>   and suddenly,
> In the doorway,
>   pulling off his shirt.
> Though I never promised

my long kiss
To anyone,
he turned his yard-wide
Shoulders as if
harnessed, like a
Grand piano,
suspended upside-
down, over
my head. (*MC*, 14)

The eroticized threat of the male muse's symbolic violence is imposed "over" the poet-speaker's "head," suggesting its influence on the cognitive faculties.[79] This has a profound effect on language, and the last stanza demonstrates this in the startling imagery of "sand" being poured into "his mouth":

I could have
edged the breeze,
Never within a house,
to pour sand
Into his mouth,
But getting dark
Is the world's fault:
Send me
My winter. (*MC*, 14)

The sand might signify a poem's process of development, which negates the source idea to become the written word: thus when a poem is born the muse becomes silenced.

The production of a poem strategically implies a process of constructing gender. Simone de Beauvoir famously declared that one is not born a woman but becomes one.[80] "Woman," theorized this way, is a social construct, always dependent on and formed by her social surroundings. "Man" is a fundamental part of that. "The Man with Two Women" is a particularly instructive poem on this point. The male muse, through his simultaneous enticement and threat, is the backdrop against which composite feminine subjectivity is eventually formed.[81]

The male muse emerges again in complex form in the poetry inspired by McGuckian's reading of the Russian poet, Marina Tsvetaeva. Meeting Rainer Maria Rilke, whom she considered her male muse, was of crucial importance to Tsvetaeva. Her long letters to him are all centered on their planned, but never realized, encounter.[82] Their relationship focused exclusively on poetry. They both considered each other an important source of inspiration. Rilke once wrote:

> We touch each other. How? With wings that beat,
> With very distance touch each other's ken.
> *One* poet only lives, and now and then
> Who bore him, and who bears him now, will meet.[83]

Nevertheless it was not only "circumstances" that prevented the two poets from ever seeing each other. Tsvetaeva's attitude to Rilke was complex and passionate. She desired the meeting but at the same time feared and maybe even resented it. In her letter of August 22, 1926, she wrote:

> What do I want from you? What I want from all poetry and from each line of a poem: the truth of this moment. That's as far as truth goes. Never turns to wood—always to ashes. The word, which for me already is the thing, is all I want. Actions? Consequences?
>
> I know you Rainer, as I know myself. The farther from me—the further *into* me. I live not in myself, but outside myself. I do not live in my lips, and he who kisses me misses *me*.[84]

This ambiguity becomes the subject of McGuckian's poem "Visiting Rainer Maria" (*MC*, 10). The influence of Tsvetaeva and Rilke is discernible throughout *Marconi's Cottage*. Therefore, one can assume that the complexities that defined the relationship between Tsvetaeva and Rilke are translated into this poem, and the presence of a male muse can be observed in these terms.[85] Tsvetaeva, particularly after his death, considered Rilke as a "higher power" inspiring her work. In a letter to Rilke's Russian secretary who stayed with him in his last days, she wrote:

> Rilke's role has changed only in that while he was alive he collaborated with a "higher power" and now he himself is that power. Please don't see this as Russian mysticism. We are talking about earthly things. The most divine inspiration isn't worth a fig if it isn't applied to earthly activity.[86]

Although the male muse of this poem is recognizable as Rilke, his actual presence is far removed from the poetic subject.[87] "Visiting Rainer Maria" describes Tsvetaeva's turmoil in handling that friendship, and through this it reflects, yet again, on the forming of a feminine poetic identity. At the start, the poem outlines the emotional charge experienced by the speaker-subject when contemplating the encounter with "Rilke":

> He said he was just leaving
> As I was just arriving, in my blue[88]
> Smock, yesterday, without meaning to. (*MC*, 10)

In this imaginary construct, the male muse and the writing subject fail to meet up. This is potentially a representation of the arbitrariness of the creative process. The muse's influence is unintentional and randomly applied. The second half of this stanza reflects on this when the writing subject reminds the readers of the uncertainty and fragility of the poetic construct:

> Though this first sentence would
> Have been equally suitable
> For the last, for a poem made
> From a kitchen conversation. (*MC*, 10)

Unlike in "The Man with Two Women," in this poem the male muse is suggestive and spectral. His influence is not directly applied through his physical dominance, but rather, through the medium of the subdued passion that permeates the poem. The writing subject, a container of poetic identity, is created and shaped by this continuous emotional tension:

> So was my shape dictated by
> The curved outer wall, the eccentricities
> Of the corridor, all sorts of untils.
> And I thought to myself, if he touches
> My sleeve even softly, whole streets
> Of shops near the sea will be extinguished
> In the most intentional darkness. (*MC*, 10)

The "intentional darkness" of this poem greatly differs from the darkness that comes about in "The Man with Two Women." While in the previous poem it was seen as a threat to creativity, here darkness is the very element where creation takes place. Interpreted as a representation of subconscious sexuality, it becomes apparent that, while the sexuality of the male muse in "The Man with Two Women" is threatening and suffocating, in "Visiting Rainer Maria" it is accepted and desired. However, what really triggers creativity is the unfulfilled nature of this desire. The male muse of this poem, instead of "pulling off his shirt," remains absent:

I said, I must find it,
Using the feminine form of must,
What *you* want, what *I* want, what can be done.

For four more virgin months I have been
Not his, *not* his, *his*,
A sea-kitten rolling up in his
English shirt like a tray of Persian
Tea, neutral as a cloud. Because
The *it* of his translation may mean silence,
But the *she* of mine means Aphrodite. (*MC*, 10)

Sarah Broom interprets "Aphrodite" as "an affirmation of McGuckian's femininity, and in a sense that of Rilke as well; it is the active, female necessity for and solution to creation."[89]

The result of his absence is a kind of "virgin" creativity where dreaming about fulfillment brings satisfaction to the poet. Whatever reality may be, the poetic process "translates" it into passion.[90] The poem starts and finishes by saying that an encounter never took place. In between, there is a passionate, sensual unification, but only in the conditional: "*If* he touches my sleeve"; "*if* he mentions a river" (*MC*, 10). The actual poem is born out of the tension between the poet and her muse, just as Tsvetaeva's beautiful and passionate letters were a result of her own paradoxical desires. McGuckian's male muse in this poem is not simply Rilke but Tsvetaeva's Rilke. He inspires through his absence and the passion of unfulfilled desire. The influence of the male muse is played out both in the construction of the poem and of the writing subject, "adding a feminine ending to / whatever parts are dream" (*MC*, 10).

Recognizing the inspiring male voice in herself and entering into a relationship with him empower Medbh McGuckian and her poetry. Her relationship with this man in herself is extremely passionate. In "Venus and the Sea" she says: "The incomplete opening of his mouth / Lives in my hand like a wound" (*MC*, 81). Throughout her poetry she tries to heal this wound by forcing the mouth of her male muse completely open and literally "waking" in it:

It begins in an hour like the door-mirror
Of a wardrobe cracking the memory
Of an over-remembered window-door

Wiping off the painted pinpoint pupils
And the ringlets of music with a smile
Waking in the separate mouth beside me. (*MC*, 81)

Marconi's Cottage is probably the most intertextual volume among McGuckian's works. Several poems take lines from the correspondence between Tsvetaeva, Rilke, and Mandelstam. References can be found to the Brontë sisters, Byron, Gilbert-Gubar, and the collection as a whole ponders upon the anxiety of influence.[91] On a personal level the volume also celebrates the poet's daughter's birth in 1989 and foreshadows McGuckian's father's death.

In conclusion, the poetic tension between communication and expression on the one hand, and a growing awareness of McGuckian's compositional processes on the other, characterize the four volumes discussed in this chapter. When considering these collections consecutively with the Blanchotian objective of allowing the experience of the work to surface, the degree to which McGuckian's creative performance is intricately connected to a conscious shaping of the creative self becomes strikingly evident. From the playful revealing/concealing of *The Flower Master,* through the dark chaos of *Venus and the Rain* and the uncertain emergence of a more coherent writing self in *On Ballycastle Beach,* to the investigation of the compositional process and the introduction of her male muses in *Marconi's Cottage,* the composite of these volumes combine to offer a dazzling exploration of the performance of creativity.

Notes

1. Medbh McGuckian, e-mail message to author, October 15, 2012
2. Following the sequence brought out by The Gallery Press.
3. Medbh McGuckian had published two pamphlets previously: *Single Ladies: Sixteen Poems* (Devon: Interim 1980); and *Portrait of Joanna* (Belfast: Ulsterman Publications, 1980).
4. McGuckian, *FM*, 25.
5. Elin Holmsten, "Signs of Encounters in Medbh McGuckian's Poetry," in *The Poetry of Medbh McGuckian: The Interior of Words*, ed. Shane Alcobia-Murphy and Richard Kirkland (Cork: Cork University Press, 2010), 93.
6. For alternative readings of this poem see Alexander G. Gonzalez, "Celebrating the Richness of Medbh McGuckian's Poetry: Close Analysis of Six Poems from *The Flower Master*," in *Contemporary Irish Women Poets: Some Male Perspectives*, ed. Alexander G. Gonzalez (Westport, CT: Greenwood, 1999), 51; Michaela Schrage-Früh, *Emerging Identities: Myth, Nation and Gender in the Poetry of Eavan Boland, Nuala Ni Dhomhnaill and Medbh McGuckian* (Trier: WVT, Wissenschaftlicher Verlag Trier, 2004), 156; Peter Sirr, "'How Things Begin to Happen': Notes on Eiléan Ní Chuilleanáin and Medbh McGuckian," *Southern Review* 31, no. 3 (Summer 1995): 464; and Peggy O'Brien,

"Reading Medbh McGuckian: Admiring What We Cannot Understand," *Colby Quarterly* 28, no.4 (December 1992): 243, 247.

7. Included in both the 1982 Oxford University Press and the 1993 Gallery Press editions of McGuckian's *FM.*

8. Shane Alcobia-Murphy points out similarities between Seamus Heaney's poem "Digging" and "The 'Singer,'" arguing that both works "contrast manual work with writing" and point toward "a break with family continuity." Shane Alcobia-Murphy, *Medbh McGuckian: The Poetics of Exemplarity*, Aberdeen Introductions to Irish and Scottish Culture (Aberdeen: AHRC Centre for Irish and Scottish Studies, 2012), 26.

9. Included in both the 1982 Oxford University Press and the 1993 Gallery Press editions of McGuckian's *FM.*

10. See Michaela Schrage-Früh, "Speaking as the North: Self and Place in the Early Poetry of Medbh McGuckian," in *The Poetry of Medbh McGuckian: The Interior of Words*, ed. Shane Alcobia-Murphy and Richard Kirkland (Cork: Cork University Press, 2010), 29.

11. Scott Brewster, "The Space that Cleaves: The House and Hospitality in Medbh McGuckian's Work," in *The Poetry of Medbh McGuckian: The Interior of Words*, ed. Shane Alcobia-Murphy and Richard Kirkland (Cork: Cork University Press, 2010), 108.

12. For more readings see Ann Beer, "Medbh McGuckian's Poetry: Maternal Thinking and a Politics of Peace," *Canadian Journal of Irish Studies* 18, no.1 (July 1992): 193–94; and Clair Wills, *Improprieties: Politics and Sexuality in Northern Irish Poetry* (Oxford: Clarendon Press, 1993), 72.

13. Tom Clyde argues that "McGuckian dissolves her being into that of the object, which thereby becomes subject." Tom Clyde, "An Ulster Twilight: Poetry in the North of Ireland," *Krino* 5 (Spring 1988): 102.

14. For an alternative reading of this poem see Borbála Faragó, "Artfully Placed Mirrors: The Poetry of Medbh McGuckian," *AnaChronisT* 3 (1997): 175–77.

15. Probably a reference to Tsvetaeva, who said, "All my doors are entrances, with no exits. Understand?" Marina Tsvetaeva, "Letter to Boris Pasternak," in *Letters Summer 1926: Correspondence between Pasternak, Tsvetaeva, Rilke*, quoted in Wills, *Improprieties*, 169.

16. Thanks are due to Shane Alcobia-Murphy for pointing out this intertextual comparison.

17. Timothy Clark, *The Theory of Inspiration: Composition as a Crisis of Subjectivity in Romantic and Post-Romantic Writing* (Manchester: Manchester University Press, 1997), 22.

18. Donna L. Potts argues that McGuckian in these lines "alludes to Buddhism. . . . The 'eight valleys' refer to Buddha's eight fold path to end suffering and attain Nirvana—the eradication of all desires." In Donna L. Potts. *Contemporary Irish Poetry and the Pastoral Tradition* (Columbia: University of Missouri Press, 2011), 128.

19. Shane Alcobia-Murphy, *Sympathetic Ink: Intertextual Relations in Northern Irish Poetry* (Liverpool: Liverpool University Press, 2006), 66.

20. Inspiration here is used in the literal sense of in-breathing.

21. For a comprehensive analysis of the imagery of the house in McGuckian's first five volumes see Charles L. O'Neill, "Medbh McGuckian's Poetry: Inhabiting the Image," in *Contemporary Irish Women Poets: Some Male Perspectives*, ed. Alexander G. Gonzalez, 65–78 (Westport, CT: Greenwood Press, 1999). Clodagh Rafferty also interprets the "truth room" as "a place of creativity, [where] dreams, fruit, poetry, and the color blue

are some of the products of this "secret place." Clodagh Rafferty, "'*Breaking the Blue*': A Study of Female Voices in Contemporary Irish Poetry," PhD diss., Vassar College, 2006.

22. Leontia Flynn, "Domestic Violences: Medbh McGuckian and Irish Women's Writing in the 1980s," in *The Oxford Handbook of Modern Irish Poetry*, ed. Fran Brearton and Allan Gillis (Oxford: Oxford University Press, 2012), 426.

23. It is worth noting, however, that some of McGuckian's critics at the time of publication saw this volume as "about male-female relationships that are on the verge of marriage" (Gonzalez, "Celebrating the Richness," 62). Douglas Sealy, on the other hand, noted that "Medbh McGuckian presents an exotic jungle of metaphor and image where tracks peter out or lead back in on themselves but never connect." Douglas Sealy, "Review of *The Flower Master*, by Medbh McGuckian," *Poetry Ireland Review* 5–6 (1982): 58.

24. Medbh McGuckian, *Venus and the Rain* (Oxford: Oxford University Press, 1984), repr. (Oldcastle, Ireland: Gallery Press, 1994). Citations are to the Gallery Press edition (hereafter cited as *VR*).

25. Michael Allen, "Barbaric Yawp, Gibbous Voice," review of *Venus and the Rain*, by Medbh McGuckian, *Honest Ulsterman* 77 (Winter 1984): 59.

26. Ibid., 64.

27. The volume received eleven reviews, ten of them written by men.

28. Moynagh Sullivan, "The Woman Poet and the Matter of Representation in Modern and Postmodern Poetics," PhD diss., University College Dublin, 2001, 292.

29. Derek Attridge, *The Singularity of Literature* (London: Routledge, 2004), 104.

30. Ibid., 98.

31. Sullivan, "The Woman Poet," 207.

32. Ibid., 207.

33. Attridge, *Singularity of Literature*, 19.

34. Mary O'Connor comments on McGuckian's "black" in this poem that it is "the work of the poet, the artist—not passively enduring the darkness, but actively resisting the light." Mary O'Connor, "'Rising Out': Medbh McGuckian's Destabilizing Poetics," *Éire-Ireland: Journal of Irish Studies* 30, no. 4 (Winter 1996): 163.

35. The concept of the "abject maternal body" was theorized by Julia Kristeva in her work *Powers of Horror: An Essay on Abjection* (New York: Columbia University Press, 1982).

36. Sullivan, "The Woman Poet," 174–75.

37. In this case, the bodily matter of the written poem.

38. Leaking meconium also signals the distress of an infant when still in utero, symbolically disallowing the waste of an infant to mix with the before-life environment of the amniotic fluid.

39. Robert Brazeau, "Troubling Language: Avant-Garde Strategies in the Poetry of Medbh McGuckian," *Mosaic: Journal for the Interdisciplinary Study of Literature* 37, no. 2 (June 2004): 135.

40. See Susan Stanford Friedman's notion of the "childbirth metaphor." Friedman argues that when used by women writers, this metaphor originates in conflict with themselves as Other. Quoted in ibid., 135.

41. For an analysis of McGuckian's relationship to painting see Wendy J. Eberle, "Painting a Pictographic Language, Beyond Sound Boundaries: Medbh McGuckian's Poetic Making," *Canadian Journal of Irish Studies* 22, no. 1 (July 1996): 61–70.

42. The use of water imagery underscores this point. The sister calls the painting a "failure of the tampering rain / To go right into the mountain" (*VR*, 18.)

43. Beer, "Medbh McGuckian's Poetry," 196.

44. Shane Alcobia-Murphy identifies the source as *Women Artists* by Karen Petersen and J. J. Wilson, where the authors discussing Cassatt's painting *The Loge* state that "the fan seems to separate one Alice from the other Alice in the looking glass." See *The Poetry of Medbh McGuckian: The Interior of Words,* eds. Shane Alcobia-Murphy and Richard Kirkland, (Cork: Cork University Press, 2010), 5–6.

45. Because of the volume's close association with McGuckian's postpartum depression, it might be worthwhile for future scholarship to revisit these poems in light of trauma theory and investigate to what extent these works are written out of (or against) that experience.

46. Medbh McGuckian, *On Ballycastle Beach* (Oxford: Oxford University Press, 1988), repr. (Oldcastle, Ireland: Gallery Press, 1995). Citations are to the Gallery Press edition (hereafter cited as *OBB*).

47. In metaphorical terms, this is the difference between the images of the biblical apple and a completed meal made out of "apple flesh."

48. "Effleurage" is a light massage that glides over the skin but does not use pressure or movement of deep muscle masses. Effleurage is performed by the laboring woman or by her partner/husband or her labor support (doula). Rhythmic slow circles are "drawn" with fingertips on the abdomen, thigh, or arms. The sensation of pain is reduced by varying amounts, depending on the individual, (Birthsource.com [accessed October 21, 2013]).

49. This indistinctiveness is exactly what irritates several of McGuckian's critics. Elizabeth Lowry, for example, calls this "the source of the problem" and vehemently argues, in connection with this poem, that

> words are not like paint, which is infinitely flexible in what it may represent, but have quantities already assigned to them. In our lazy way we say that a picture "speaks" to us, but of course it doesn't: the colour blue does not necessarily signify the Irish Sea, the summer sky or my new jumper, but the words "the Irish Sea", "the summer sky" and "my new jumper" do just that.

Elizabeth Lowry, "Dream On," review of *Selected Poems*, by Medbh McGuckian, *Metre* 4 (Spring–Summer 1998): 52.

50. Wolfgang Iser, "The Reading Process: A Phenomenological Approach," in *Modern Criticism and Theory: A Reader*, ed. David Lodge (London: Longman, 1994), 215.

51. Ibid., 216.

52. See Umberto Eco's theory of the "model reader," who, as opposed to the "empirical reader," is created by the text to the extent that his/her understanding of the text is dependent on "following the rules" and contexts of the text. To become a model reader, one has to accept (understand) the paradigms set out by the text. In Eco's view therefore

"a text is a device conceived in order to produce its Model Reader." Umberto Eco, *Interpretation and Overinterpretation* (Cambridge: Cambridge University Press, 1992), 64.

53. Danielle Sered, "'By Escaping and [Leaving] a Mark': Authority and the Writing Subject of the Poetry of Medbh McGuckian," *Irish University Review: Journal of Irish Studies* 32, no. 2 (Autumn–Winter 2002): 276.

54. Unrealized, but, significantly, desired. The loss of a determinate speaking subject is, in Maurice Blanchot's theory, the starting point of literature. He argues, that "to write is to break the bond that unites the word with myself" and, furthermore, that "the writer belongs to a language that no one speaks, which is addressed to no one, which has no center, and which reveals nothing." Maurice Blanchot, *The Space of Literature*, trans. by Ann Smock (Lincoln: University of Nebraska Press, 1982), 26.

55. Robert Brazeau recognizes this point when he argues that "this first stanza offers the very interesting suggestion that, just once, a poem would like to be written that does not subordinate itself to the exigencies of a private, speaking subject." Further on, however, Brazeau acknowledges the importance of the return of the speaking subject when he says that "the 'I' of the first line returns to serve as an ordering device for our reading." Brazeau, "Troubling Language," 132–33.

56. Blanchot terms the appearance of the speaking subject the "silent affirmation of the effaced 'I.'" This is the speaker who "is no longer himself, but neither is it the sheer slipping away of no one's word." Blanchot, *Space of Literature,* 27.

57. Shane Murphy successfully points out Marina Tsvetaeva's "influence" on this poem and argues that "Harem Trousers" is riddled with "intertextual borrowings" from the Russian poet. Painstakingly unveiling all the hidden sources, Murphy comes to the somewhat self-evident conclusion that "it is, in one sense, a pity to track down and isolate the sources, thereby demystifying the beguiling use of pronouns and imagery," and later concedes that "despite the absence of footnotes and clear acknowledgement of her source material, one should not describe her work as in any way 'plagiaristic'." Shane Murphy, "'You Took Away My Biography': The Poetry of Medbh McGuckian," *Irish University Review: Journal of Irish Studies* 28, no. 1 (Spring–Summer 1998): 121, 132. Although it is undoubtedly interesting to delve into the writings of Tsvetaeva and trace her influence on McGuckian, it adds little, in my opinion, to the overall interpretation of this poem as an expression of creative performance.

58. Wills, *Improprieties*, 172–82; Alcobia-Murphy, *Sympathetic Ink*, 238. Critics also discuss the referential significance of the name Fergus. The name is McGuckian's mother's maiden name, her son's name, and the name of an Irish mythological figure.

59. "Pregnant silence" is Elin Holmsten's expression. See Holmsten, "Signs of Encounters," 97.

60. Leontia Flynn, "Re-Assembling the Atom: Reading Medbh McGuckian's Intertextual Materials," in *The Poetry of Medbh McGuckian: The Interior of Words*, ed. Shane Alcobia-Murphy and Richard Kirkland (Cork: Cork University Press, 2010), 178–83.

61. See Schrage-Früh, *Emerging Identities*, 185; Catriona M. Clutterbuck, "A Gibbous Voice: The Poetics of Subjectivity in the Early Poetry of Medbh McGuckian" In *The Poetry of Medbh McGuckian: The Interior of Words* ed. Shane Alcobia-Murphy and Richard Kirkland (Cork: Cork University Press, 2010), 63.

62. Clutterbuck also points out "the dual movement towards origin and away from it," in "A Gibbous Voice," 64.

63. Medbh McGuckian, *Marconi's Cottage* (Oldcastle, Ireland: Gallery Press, 1991), 37 (hereafter cited as *MC*).

64. The poem, therefore, is successful in its completion, but fails to represent the autonomous creative consciousness.

65. Attridge, *Singularity of Literature*, 98

66. As she states in an interview: "Obviously the new book [*Marconi's Cottage*] will be about Emer's birth. The pregnancy will be the central event, that last pregnancy. Every time I do poetry readings I stand up and say, 'This is a poem about early pregnancy' and 'That is a poem about late pregnancy'. And all these men are sitting there and the women are bored and the men I think are not too excited either, you know. But I think it probably has been for me a very fecund period till now, though it's not easy to reconcile the two forms of creativity." Medbh McGuckian, in interview with Susan Shaw Sailer, *Michigan Quarterly Review* 32, no.1 (Winter 1993): 113.

67. Laura O'Connor, "*Comhrá*: Conversation between Medbh McGuckian and Nuala Ní Dhomhnaill," *Southern Review* 31, no. 3 (Summer 1995): 595.

68. "She Which Is Not, He Which Is," in *MC*, 93–94.

69. "Breaking the Blue," in *MC*, 84.

70. "Almond," in *MC*, 91.

71. "Vibratory Description," in *MC*, 95.

72. Wills, *Improprieties*, 75.

73. There have been several discussions as to whether McGuckian's poetry can be considered "political" in any sense, given its overwhelming focus on the private. My views on this point, as outlined in the next chapter, concur with those of Robert Brazeau, who says that "her [McGuckian's] sustained reflection on language as both integral to political systems and the facet of such systems that can be used to potentially reinscribe them represents the most enduring discussion of politics that we find in her work." Brazeau, "Troubling Language," 142.

74. "House" is a recurring metaphor in McGuckian for the inner spheres of poetic subjectivity. Examples from other poems are "Journal Intime," (*MC*, 26) where the poet leads us into a "child's first (and most satisfying) / House," her subconscious, which is "so light / To her, so dark to us," or "Marconi's Cottage," (*MC*, 103) where the "you" of the poem is described as "small and watchful as a lighthouse" and the speaker "lock(s) and unlock(s)" his door to gain access to his concealed self.

75. Toril Moi, *What Is a Woman?: And Other Essays* (Oxford: Oxford University Press, 1999), 290.

76. See Bourdieu's argument that the process of symbolic consecration is essential to the reproduction of "mythico-ritual" systems, quoted in ibid., 290n30.

77. See a discussion of Bourdieuian "capital" in ibid., 288–95.

78. Alcobia-Murphy, *Sympathetic Ink*, 63.

79. To give this a "lighter" reading, consider this description: "The archetype of the muse does not work very well when one attempts to reverse the traditional genders—just try to visualise, without snickering, a woman writer at her desk while some hunk of celestial beefcake floats nearby." See Katherine McAlpine and Gail White, *The Muse Strikes Back: A Poetic Response by Women to Men* (Brownsville, OR: Story Line Press 1997), xvii.

80. Simone de Beauvoir, quoted in Moi, *What Is a Woman?*, 290.

81. The layout of the poem, the broken lines, is also a sustained reflection on the overlapping gender codes present in this process.

82. Yevgeny Pasternak describes this connection: "The idea of their meeting and of the sacred joy it would bring them, mentioned by Rilke at the end of his letter and seized upon by Tsvetaeva, was to become the leitmotif of their relationship." Yevgeny Pasternak, et al, *Pasternak, Tsvetaeva, Rilke. Letters: Summer 1926*, trans. Margaret Wettlin and Walter Arndt (Oxford: Oxford University Press, 1988), 80.

83. Ibid., 81.

84. Ibid., 202. Tsvetaeva didn't know that Rilke was mortally ill at this stage and was never able to respond to her.

85. Sarah Broom gives a convincing reading of this poem in which she concentrates exclusively on the influence of Rilke. Sarah Broom, "McGuckian's Conversations with Rilke in *Marconi's Cottage*," *Irish University Review: Journal of Irish Studies* 28, no. 1 (Spring–Summer 1998): 145–50.

86. Pasternak, *Pasternak, Tsvetaeva, Rilke*, 214.

87. The fact that only his first names are used in the poem might also underline a distancing intention.

88. Peggy O'Brien suggests that in Medbh McGuckian's poetry blue "is the color of idealization, aspiration, memory." Peggy O'Brien, "Reading Medbh McGuckian: Admiring What We Cannot Understand," *Colby Quarterly* 28, no. 4 (December 1992): 245. I would also say it is the color of expectation and of creative activity, for example: "the blue of my / weather fights the cloud of your voice" in "Liontamer," (*MC*, 24).

89. Broom, "McGuckian's Conversations," 150.

90. An example of this can be found in the correspondence between Tsvetaeva and Rilke which took place for four months in 1926 before Rilke's death. Tsvetaeva's main concern was always Rilke's love for her and she constantly was worried that his emotions might turn "neutral" towards her. Regardless of the crude reality of Rilke's dying, her last postcard reads: "Dear Rainer, This is where I live.—I wonder if you still love me?" (Pasternak, *Pasternak, Tsvetaeva, Rilke*, 204).

91. For a detailed discussion of her sources see Alcobia-Murphy's chapter on Medbh McGuckian in his *Sympathetic Ink*, 44–91.

2

The Politicized Aesthetic in *Captain Lavender*, *Shelmalier*, and *Drawing Ballerinas*

This chapter explores Medbh McGuckian's collections *Captain Lavender* (1994), *Shelmalier* (1998), and *Drawing Ballerinas* (2001), in the order of their publication with The Gallery Press and traces the poet's complex engagement with her political and cultural environment. The 1990s were a period of significant political change in Northern Ireland. Although the earlier years of the decade were pockmarked by horrific incidents in the continuing conflict, such as the Teebane and Sean Graham betting shop massacres of 1992 and the Shankill Road bombings and Greysteel atrocity of the following year, the Hume-Adams talks of April 1993 marked a major breakthrough in the quest for peace. In December 1993 the British and Irish governments issued the Joint Declaration on Peace which was followed by the IRA and Loyalist ceasefires of 1994. Although the first ceasefire did not last, it was renewed in 1997, and the decade came to an astonishing conclusion with the coming into force of the Belfast Agreement.[1] It was also an era of rapid economic development as the Northern Irish economy benefitted from the onset of the Celtic Tiger in the South and grew more rapidly than any other sector of the United Kingdom. The changing and less threatening societal environment was reflected in McGuckian's work during this period, allowing for a more overt political voice to emerge. But personal factors were also of critical relevance. The last of McGuckian's children, Emer, was born on August 23, 1989, so she no longer had to deal with very young infants, and the postpartum depression from which she had suffered after the birth of her first child Liam in 1980 was now firmly in the past. However, her father passed away on October 7, 1992, which had a major effect on the poet. Indeed, the first of the volumes under consideration in this chapter was in part a reflection on McGuckian's relationship with her father and on his death, which is echoed by the collection's unusually dark tone.

CHAPTER 2

"Born in Little Pieces": The Speaking Subject in *Captain Lavender*

Published in 1994, *Captain Lavender* opens with a motto from Picasso: "I have not painted the war . . . but I have no doubt that the war was in . . . these paintings I have done."[2] The political changes of the early 1990s provoked a public response from Medbh McGuckian. Introducing a poem from this collection, she said:

> I was sort of accused by my own side really of not taking issue, or of not supporting them or of escaping. Then I began to feel a bit conscious-stricken as an artist. I think I'm basically, if I'd been born in a different time, I'm just a love-poet you know. So I'm not a war-poet. So this is a love-poem to the war if you like. . . . But I'm not sure whether Picasso improved his art by looking at the war directly.[3]

Images of war and death permeate these poems as the speaking subject embarks on a quest of conscience. The ethics of voice is the central enquiry, and the process of composition takes on the extra burden of morality.[4] "The Silkwinder" examines the site of composition as the dark center of the poetic consciousness:

> The heart stays blooded
> with summer seeds, as the trees
> which I always think of as bare
> bubble up to a pool in my mind
> in which the forging leaves
> slowly exchange their line-pattern
> and relics of flowers wind a wristlet
> around the impression of a perfect rose. (*CL*, 26)

The compositional process as a creation of something out of nothing is fundamentally subverted here as the images "forge" and "exchange patterns" to form an "impression" of perfection. The idea of origin is denied (the heart *stays* and does not become "blooded"). However, unlike in her previous volume, in this poem the culmination of creative effort is pain, injury, and collapse, rather than metaphorical delivery. The creative performance becomes associated with negation and death, and the futile "addings up of days" result in "several graves" and "images . . . of the depths / of the sea" (*CL*, 26). Poetic expression hurts, and the "raw spot between wrist / and elbow I touched / each time I came into it" (*CL*, 26). It develops into the compositional wound into which the speaking subject returns. This metaphorical "inner arm" of creation symbolically writes the poem, which, on its completion, revisits its initial negation:

> I began to conceive of the room as a whole
> in relation to the picture
> of the silver vase and long flower
> from the dining-room:
> how the flower was folded up
> inside its lip, then came loose,
> like waking wider, leaving the inner arm
> as dark as it was before. (*CL*, 26)

The collapse of composition into darkness signals the futility of poetic expression as perhaps a meditation on current politics. However, the voice is compelled into speaking, and the pain and dark of the notion of war become intricately entangled in the lines of the poem.[5]

The formation of a narrative voice becomes the central subject of the poem "Dante's Own Day" (*CL*, 34). Starting off as a (masculine) "sub-sea, birth-green river / of eggs in a private nest of smell," the speaking subject eludes the public eye and is internalized in the female body. Its formation is conceptualized as a fundamentally physical process,

> The struggles of a series of intertwisted minds,
> arranged by no mind, one on top of another,
> in a growing ribbon of warmth. (*CL*, 34)

As a fetus within the maternal womb, the narrative voice formulates itself in a process similar to cells growing. However, the symbolic womb which hosts the voice is inhospitable, signaling the intersubjective anxiety inherent in the relationship between the poetic consciousness and the poetic body. The body, interpreted here as the ultimate source of the poetic performance,[6] hinders the compositional process, while at the same time initiating it. Like "the unwritten / part of an angel, that unhealthy tissue / around the moment" (*CL*, 34), the maternal womb becomes the beginning and end of the writing performance. Similarly to the previous poem, the end product of the composition is a symbolic collapse. However, here it happens at the source and even the possibility of progress is denied. On the other hand, the formation of the poetic voice takes center stage. There is no subject written, but there is a subject who writes. Starting from the vantage point of this negation, the voice surfaces as "an acorn of a blind, denuded, unbegun, / unsheltered and unfinished" (*CL*, 34) negation, which "draws across a floor / on the mortal side of language" (*CL*, 34). Emphasizing yet again its physicality and embodiedness, the speaking voice denies a modernist vision of an essential subject inhabiting the depths of the poetic ego. Instead, this voice emerges as

> a leaf detaching itself
> from the narrative 'tree'
> attempts to seal its meaning. (*CL*, 34)

Separated from a "grand narrative" most "meanings" become "sealed" and internalized.[7] McGuckian's concern to partake in political discourse finds some resolution in the attitude of her "leaf." As part of the tree a leaf is an organic component, however, as a detached entity, its interpretation remains concealed. In plainer terms, if one takes the leaf as a symbolic representation of poetry, its function as social commentator is inherent in its origin, yet obscured in its expression. Thus the poetic voice remains entangled with the sociopolitical narrative and yet it remains fundamentally "outside" it:

> Then the voice that supplied the story
> will be a character rounded-off outside it,
> writing itself into those fumbling breaks
> through which desire is completely trained:
> bound in the bed like an account book. (*CL*, 34)

The ultimate locus of the poetic subject is the hiatus, the "fumbling breaks," which is created within the poetic performance. The circular collapse is represented by the voice's restraint within the metaphorical "bed," from which it originates. The stress of speech and anxiety of expression is signaled by the unlikely positioning of the "account book" within the bed, and, as the ultimate image of the poem, it becomes the ironic representation of the poetic self.[8] Thus "Dante's Own Day" traces the process of creation towards its collapse and sees the emergence of the poetic self as a hesitantly politicized speaking subject.

In *Captain Lavender* the speaking voice embarks on a quest of conscience and the formation of a creative self becomes entangled in sociopolitical commentary. "The Over Mother" (*CL*, 64), a poem[9] that was written at a time when McGuckian was running a creative writing workshop at the Maze Prison,[10] looks at the symbolic "birthing" of the reader. The emotional frustration that precedes the appearance of the "audience" is portrayed in the first stanza:

> [. . .] Play kisses
> stir the circuits of the underloved body
> to an ever-resurrection, a never-had tenderness
> that dies inside me. (*CL*, 64)

The "underloved body" is a composite image simultaneously referencing the abstinent prisoners ("passion exhausts itself at the mouth" [*CL*, 64]) and the poet-mother who is pregnant with her work. The "play kisses" and the "never-had tenderness" come from an audience which has limited access to a freedom of understanding. Thus, the audience is invoked as the cause of the emotional turbulence that triggers the poem:

> My cleverly dead and vertical audience,
> words fly out from your climate of unexpectation
> in leaky, shallowised night letters—
> what you has spoken? (*CL*, 64)

The imprisoned readers are conceptualized in a somewhat shocking image of the "dead and vertical" fetuses of the "over mother." They themselves are not burdened, (having a "climate of unexpectation") but still produce the "words." Put in a different way, the reader is carried by the author and is therefore incapable of consciously sharing in the experience of the creative process. However, this inability becomes a potential to create. The imprisoned reader "leaks" the words of this poem to the page and speaks. ("What you has spoken?") The severance of the two subjectivities, that of the author and the reader, is denied by disallowing a symbolic birth. Thus the moment of reading never follows the work, but accompanies it:

> I keep seeing birds
> that could be you when you stretch out
> like a syllable and look to me
> as if I could give you wings. (*CL*, 64)

This "as if" is a recurring phrase throughout McGuckian's work. It provokes the reader actively to reflect on the performance of a readerly identity through which the poetry is generated. Maurice Blanchot's argument on the relationship between the reader and the work provides a relevant theoretical demonstration of how the poem "gives birth" to the reader:

> The reading of the poem is the poem itself, affirming itself in the reading as a work. It is the poem giving birth, in the space held open by the reader, to the reading that welcomes it; it is the

> poem becoming power to read, becoming communication opened between *power* and *impossibility*, between the power linked to the moment of reading and the impossibility linked to the moment of writing.[11]

However, several poems in *Captain Lavender* step outside of self-reflection and become more overtly political. The best example for this is probably "The War Degree" (*CL*, 74), which in 1995, in a radio interview, McGuckian introduced as a "love poem to the war," that "masculinises" the war and "plays on the word 'degree'. Like extent and also qualification."[12] The absurdity of writing a love poem to the war is explained by the poet's expressed inability to relate to, and simultaneously to ignore, the war around her. In an emotional twist the unbearable political (social, cultural) situation haunts her imagination as a lover would do. Addressing the war as a lover also suggests a defense mechanism: by "masculinizing" it, it becomes human, more predictable and less fearsome. The first three lines evoke and describe the war. "You smell of time as a Bible smells of thumbs" hints at the eternal presence of war in the history of humanity. However, the time conception of war is different: it is "not time elaborately thrown away / . . . but time outside of time." This "time outside of time" describes the inhuman nature of war where time loses its meaning.[13] The fourth line of the poem, "you wound yourself so thoroughly into life," emphasizes further the impossibility of ignoring war (the past tense verb "wound" forms a telling homograph with the noun "wound" here). The second line, "a bank of earth alive with mahogany-coloured / flowers," can be read as the description of human blood that "vitalizes" war. The first verse thus describes the inescapability of war. That the poet approaches the war by "re-falling in love" with it does not however mean that she celebrates violence. On the contrary, the poem brings to the fore the impossibility of relating to violence in any "normal" way. When war is constantly "drumming at the back of my skull," a reaction is provoked and "re-falling in love" indeed becomes a "must."

The second stanza explicitly mentions a political event of the "treaty," which is the ceasefire that was declared in September 1994. (*Captain Lavender* was published in November 1994.) Thus the first line places the poem at a particular time when war and violence were, supposedly, "killed" by peace. The treaty moves "all tongues," not only English and Irish, but also the language of violence that had permeated Northern Irish political life. The "sweet Irish tongue in which / death spoke and happiness wrote" hints again at the complexities of relating to national identity and the impossibility of reconciling violence with love. Speech and writing are also contrasted in an interesting way here. Is death "audible" because of its immediacy, and is happiness "written" because it communicates through the medium of the signed treaty? The third stanza evokes the horrors of the war and the blocked interaction of love:

> a wartime, heart-stained autumn drove
> fierce half-bricks into the hedges; tree-muffled
> streets vanished in the lack of news.
> Like a transfusion made direct from arm
> to arm, birds call uselessly to each other
> in the sub-acid, wintry present. The pursed-up
> fragrances of self-fertile herbs
> hug defeat like a very future lover. (*CL*, 74)

The only realized love in this poem is that of violence and death and defeat. This is an inverse love poem that subverts the very meaning and function of love as a life-affirming force. Instead, love is frozen and destructive, devoid of communicative faculties. The poem concludes with describing this infertile, "demolished," and desolate emotional landscape in which the poetic self dissolves into a "nobody":

> Now it is my name and not my number
> that is nobody now, walking on a demolished
> floor, where dreams have no moral,
> and the door-kiss is night meeting night. (*CL*, 74)

This "kiss" does not carry the promise of happiness. As a reference to the peace process it foreshadows pessimism and probably refers back to the sarcasm of the title that describes the treaty as a "degree" in (and of) war.

Captain Lavender is a book that addresses the contemporary political situation in a circuitous way, allowing her social commentary to emerge from hidden allusions and metaphorical twists. In addition, as demonstrated, the reader in McGuckian's poems is prefigured as a constructive subjectivity "writing" the work. McGuckian's portrayal of the authorial voice as a hesitantly politicized subject that conveys morality through her containment of pain and violence makes space for reading this volume not only as a personal memento for the poet's father's death but also as a subtle introduction to McGuckian's commitment toward sociopolitical commentary.

CHAPTER 2

"It Was Not My Hand Writing": The Power of Words in *Shelmalier*

Shelmalier was published in 1998 on the bicentenary of the 1798 Irish Rebellion.[14] In the "Author's Note" McGuckian remarks:

> I found that what I had written in the form of epitaph and commemoration or address for the present-day disturbances in the North fitted like an egg into its shell that previous whirlwind moment when, unbelievably, hope and history did in fact rhyme. (*SHEL*, "Author's Note," 13)

The encounter with this critical era in Irish political ideology inspires McGuckian to challenge the contemporary straitjacket of inherited political affiliation. However, there is something odd about McGuckian's reference to the "rhyme" of hope and history.[15] If anything, what 1798 proved was the utopian nature of the aspirations of the United Irishmen: a rebellion in which so many, Wolfe Tone among them, died and which eventually fuelled further sectarian violence could be considered a problematic model for contemporary political thinking.[16] McGuckian herself states that the theme of her book is

> less the experienced despair of a noble struggle brutally quenched than the dawn of my own enlightenment after a medieval ignorance, my being suddenly able to welcome into consciousness figures of an integrity I had never learned to be proud of. (*SHEL*, "Author's Note," 13)

What, in fact, the poet sees as giving integrity to these political figures is what Declan Kiberd terms their "freed consciousness,"[17] their capacity to surpass rigid notions of identity, in other words, the poetical aspect of their political engagement. This poeticity of politics is then translated into, or made visible as, lines of poetry. This volume, therefore, offers a series of poems in which McGuckian meditates on the United Irishmen of 1798, imaginatively "welcoming" them into her consciousness and yet avoiding the articulation of rigid political ideology. Her approach is fundamentally emotional—these "figures of integrity" are viewed and dramatized in an often eroticized setting, and any political agenda takes second place to romanticized notions of personal dialogue.

The title poem of part 1, "Script for an Unchanging Voice" (*SHEL*, 16), considers the role of language in passing on a poeticized political awareness. The "unchanging voice," silence, is represented by the metaphor of the stone:

> Here is a stone with a stone's mouth inside,
> a shell in which a lighter shell has died,
>
> one with a honey bullet in its heart,
> one that has lain full-length from the start. (*SHEL*, 16)

The serial and cumulative metaphor of "bullet" within "heart" within "stone's mouth" within "stone" depicts the incarceration of language which, significantly, is violently dead. Dead language, silence, is inherited from the past. The language of new expression, however, must stem from this silence. A new "script" is written for the old, "unchanging" voice:

> The leaves are tongues whose years of blood are locked
> in the wrong house, time feels unclocked
>
> or has been dead too long by now to cast
> its freshly slaughtered shadow from the past. (*SHEL*, 16)

This new language, however, exists not as a commemoration of historical actions and events, but rather as an unstable text, in McGuckian's words a "welcoming into consciousness" of metaphorical connections between past and present, politics and poetry, language and silence.[18] Access to the past, therefore, is not possible by conscious recollection, only by creative reimagining. The focus of "Script for an Unchanging Voice," as a result, is this peculiar oscillation between historical and poetical realities,[19] which creates a palimpsest effect and sets the tone for the entire volume of *Shelmalier*.

"Dream in a Train" (*SHEL*, 17) elaborates on the theme of an incorporative and multilayered poetic consciousness. The writing of the past, history, appears again as silence, out of which comes poetry:

> The world shovels snow
> into a pond without an echo.
> This image of water made visible
> is a cry as warm as life. (*SHEL*, 17)

The juxtaposing of cold and warm, the solid snow and fluid water, the echoless, silent shoveling and a cry of life emphasizes McGuckian's method of creating politicized poetry. The events of the past are freed from their rigid historical, and, necessarily, verbal settings, becoming silent and thus allowing them to seep into consciousness, which in turn shapes them and "makes them visible" as lines of poetry.[20] In the next stanza, the metaphor of the "house" epitomizes this new poetic consciousness and its method of "rewriting" the silent past:

> The house is a perfect body
> surpassing, unwriting me,
> as the density of black repairs
> light, even grows it. (*SHEL*, 17)

Blackness grows light, silence writes language; anomalies create consistencies. McGuckian, like many of her contemporaries, recognizes poetry's ethical stance concerning politics.[21] However, she believes that only by identifying with, and then surpassing ("unwriting"), the past can her poetry develop a credible political awareness. Significantly, her poems display a more markedly politicized authorial presence, rather than any overtly political or ideological stance. This process, however, is not without pain.[22] In the second part of "Dream in a Train," McGuckian describes her consciousness before this new "awakening" as "sleeping or dead," a "tightened up light / I was sheltering for years" which, in her words, "destroy something other / than flowers" (*SHEL*, 17).[23] The awakening is by no means a conscious effort, as the closing metaphor of the swimmer describes:

> . . . eluding
> by means of their own surface
> the unchanging sea
>
> around a swimmer
> whose sigh is a fold
> imposed upon the waves,
> suggestive of an awakening. (*SHEL*, 17)

The "swimmer," who in this reading is identifiable with the emerging authorial presence, upsets the equilibrium of the "unchanging sea," the poetic consciousness.[24] And just as her strokes make it impossible for the swimmer to appreciate the unchanging, even surface of the sea, so is it impossible for the poet to grasp consciously the process of creating a new language. However, by allowing a free flow of influences to go both ways, the "awakening" can take place. The quoted lines are also indicative of the nature of this process. The sea surrounds the swimmer as history and society surround the poet. The poet, in return "imposes" her "sigh," that is, her words on the waves, which is suggestive of the process of history becoming incorporated into poetry.

"Circle with Full Stop" (*SHEL*, 31) further demonstrates the poet's fragmented, nongender-specific exploration of creativity in the context of a politicized aesthetic. The title encapsulates the concept of transformation: the reader is left to speculate about the visual approximation of "circle" to "full stop." The tautological closure inherent in the title warns the reader about self-reflexive rhetoric. The opening lines of the poem develop the idea of duplicity further:

> Birds are the only creatures who can feel
> two things at once. I see and hear nothing
> but the cheesemonger and chandler,
> I've lain in the shallow dents where
> sleep breaks all day with a pistol
> by me, when I could have been swimming
> under fire across the Danube. (*SHEL*, 31)

The metaphor of the birds suggests a strategy of understanding which is based on becoming capable of feeling "two things at once." In a politicized context it could be argued that McGuckian is expressing an ameliorative viewpoint about Northern Irish politics, where through creative application divisions are potentially overcome. It is interesting to note, however, that the speaker of the poem places a great distance between the metaphorical "birds" of the sky and herself, who lies "in the shallow dents" (*SHEL*, 31).[25] In addition, while the birds can "feel," the speaker can "see and hear nothing." Interpreted in an aesthetic context, what seems to emerge, then, is that by identifying her readers with the distant birds McGuckian actually draws them closer to the meaning of the text, rather than pushing them away. The reader is situated at a vantage point from which the text becomes more transparent. The paradoxical nature of coming nearer to something through distance is aptly expressed in the metaphor of birds being able to "feel / two things at once," and is also indicative of McGuckian's politicizing aesthetic. It is distance and approximation, and not ideological rhetoric, which most successfully convey the poet's political awareness. Meanwhile, in the first stanza the site of creation remains out of reach for the conscious mind: the dream of "swimming under fire" is juxtaposed with the brutal awakening in the lines of "sleep breaks all day with a pistol / by me."[26] The opening verse thus puts all the basic actors of the compositional process on stage. The source becomes identified with the process; the inspired poet appears, and so does the interpreter, the reader. The second stanza plays with the concept of creativity in a temporal dimension:

> But to bring out the taste of the month
> I've had my dive into your head
> where it was summer till three-thirty
> and always afternoon.

> In the dance of the months I was August,
> now I've gone back into winter clothes,
> a March sea, the glacial white of the reading-room. (*SHEL*, 31)

The phrase "bring out the taste" relates both to the process of creation (bringing the words out of the mouth) and, simultaneously, to the process of interpretation (bringing meaning out of a text). The reader in this interpretation is directly addressed in the second person singular of "your" head in the next line. In an aesthetic context, McGuckian enters the mind of her reader. However, in a different reading the interpretative function represented by the birds is fulfilled by the politicized authorial presence. "Diving into" the head therefore reproduces the self-reflexive tautology of the title and suggests a reading in which political ideology is played out within the confines of the writing self. This unification blurs the boundaries between reader and author, writing and interpreting. This is also underscored by the intertextuality of this poem. Quoting liberally from the diary of Virginia Woolf, as well as from Byron's family papers, the poet presents a rich nexus of interpretative possibilities.[27] Interestingly, while the previously mentioned distance between author and reader proved fruitful, the total amalgamation in the second stanza brings forth images of void: the "three-thirty summer afternoon" is in stark contrast to the benevolent and creative night-time of the previous stanza. In summary, the middle stanza contains images of creative inactivity, where the "dance of the months" results in the "glacial white" sterility of "the reading room." Interpretation fails, signaling the need for a more unambiguous intersubjective dialogue, which the last stanza appears to deliver:

> I am pinning together a chair-cover
> from the flaring fragments of your shirt,
> drawing my hands to and from my lips
> like dusk adding truth to the chain
> of pictures lining the house.
> When sleep flings its inkstand, everything
> is a few degrees clearer. (*SHEL*, 31)

The "flaring fragments" aptly describe the chaos of the previous stanza. This chaos, created by the blurring of boundaries between different constructs of self, the reader and the author, or the political and the aesthetic writing self, provokes a desire for structure and order. Thus, "pinning together a chair-cover / from the flaring fragments of your shirt" becomes symbolic of comprehensible expression, where words follow a discernible pattern of intelligibility. The process of interpreting thus becomes synonymous again with the process of creating: what is clarification for the reader is creation for the writer. Alongside the concept of creativity, images of darkness and sleep emerge. "Dusk is adding truth to the chain / of pictures lining the house" (*SHEL*, 31). [28] Darkness not only assists the process of creation, but also the process of interpretation. The poem is written and read, and for author and reader alike "everything / is a few degrees clearer." In this reading then the title of the poem, "Circle with Full Stop," describes the circular, interdependent process of creation and interpretation. The textual symbol of the "full stop," which represents a fixed point of reference, is either the reader who, in the process of reading, is surrounded by the text, or vice versa, the text itself, which attracts the reader's mind to circle around it (as a symbol of closure, the full stop also represents the final point, the terminus of the interpretative—and creative—process).[29] Through this title, McGuckian captures an image of the relativity of text, reader, and author. In political terms, the poem is a reflection on the instability of ideology, on the single-minded point of view of political rhetoric, and it arguably formulates a need for creative reimaginings within political discourse. McGuckian thus constructs a metaphorical language, which is aware of its own instability, and in its making reflects its own deconstruction.

This interactive aesthetics also appears in McGuckian's representations of female subjectivities in this volume. "From the Weather-Woman" (*SHEL*, 33) describes the presence of an unidentified, suffering other, whose silence makes direct interaction impossible. Elin Holmsten sees this figure as the other "who gains primacy over the egocentric needs of the speaker," leading her into an open-ended encounter that allows for both subjectivities to retain their alterity.[30] Read in the context of McGuckian's interest in the figure of the muse, the poem arrives at a similar conclusion, where the muse and poet enter into an interactive relationship that facilitates their creative alterity. The first few lines of the poem deconstruct the stereotypical figure of the muse:

> Not even a dead letter
> a pseudohope from your pseudohome.
>
> You are dissolved in me
> like the death of the century. (*SHEL*, 33)

Read in this context, the muse is displaced and distanced from the male ego, which is portrayed as a fake and pretentious dwelling, a "pseudohome," where communication is nonexistent.[31] Taken out of her conventional role she is "dissolved" in the poet's mind. This act symbolizes a rearrangement of power relations between muse and poet. While in her "pseudohome" the muse is a subordinate extension of the male ego, here the two parties are equal: by dissolving her, the muse becomes interchangeable with the poet. This evokes the demise of a tradition and therefore is aptly compared to the "death of the century." The next two-stanza sentence takes a closer look at the interdependence of muse and poet:

> I need your summer movements
> as the spirit needs the world,
>
> my non-world the inner
> gospel of your letters. (*SHEL*, 33)

The words "spirit" and "gospel" have an obvious biblical resonance, but, characteristically, McGuckian subverts their associations. The concept of divine inspiration is an integral aspect of Old Testament biblical prophecy. The prophets received their words from God in a fundamentally physical experience.[32] The divine source was a giver of language, and language represented the living, spoken truth.[33] That is also true of the New Testament, most famously in John 1:1, "In the beginning was the Word, and the Word was with God, and the Word was God." This process is fundamentally revolutionized in "From the Weather-Woman," insofar as inspiration, the "spirit" itself, is displayed as the one in need of "the world." Again, the term "gospel" refers to the inner world of the poet and not the muse. Thus, the poet becomes muse and the muse becomes the poet, but, significantly, their intertwining and complicated relationship does not drown out creativity, rather, it is compared to a "road of openness":

> From the unhardened nature
> of the memories, your prison
>
> look, that mood, that number,
> leads a road where nothing
> can unhappen, to the meeting
> of two opennesses: the one
>
> I write before the visit,
> the one you will write after it. (*SHEL*, 33)

"Memories" remind the reader again of a past that represented a "prison" for both the poet and the muse. The "road where nothing / can unhappen" may be seen as the road of rewriting history and, simultaneously, of writing the poem. The poem closes with a final interpretation of the relationship between poet and muse: both figures represent openness, an ingenuity which allows them to influence and be influenced, to give and receive inspiration, and to be the reader, as well as the writer, of the poem. The meeting of muse and poet results in "inspired" poetry, but the source of inspiration is not one or the other, but rather, their encounter itself. The "visit" of the poem, therefore, represents the moment, or rather performance, of creation, which is the focal point of writing. Anything, which has been written "before the visit" or will be written "after" it, is an "openness" which represents nothing more than the possibility of creativity. The title of the poem, "From the Weather-Woman," therefore carries a twist in its meaning: the poem derives from the muse, the "weather-woman," in the sense only that she is part of the circular process of creation, from muse to poet and back to the muse. As Simon Critchley argues: "Inspiration, far from completing the artwork, and bringing it to formal perfection, destroys the possibility of the artwork by transgressing its law in an act of impatience."[34]

"Self-Portrait in the Act of Painting a Self-Portrait" (*SHEL*, 65) explores a more conventional representation of the creative process. Like in the earlier poem "The Sitting" (*VR*, 18), the poem introduces a model who is being painted and a painter: muse and artist are both present.[35] However, the reader should note that positions are switched, and, in the act of painting a self-portrait, muse becomes artist and artist becomes muse. This, we read, is the "outer position of a double / circle of positions, / where her musehood has withdrawn / into a single drop" (*SHEL*, 65). In other words, the classic metaphor of inspiration is questioned from the inside—the painting in the poem looks at its model with "her ears closed" and "her lifetime's gaze . . . on her own reflection, undigested" (*SHEL*, 65). The ultimate self-portrait of the poem is, of course, a self-portrait in the act of writing a poem about a "Self-Portrait in the Act of Painting a Self-Portrait." This circular image thus offers a metaphor for inspiration where the unilateral relationship of female muse to male creator is replaced by a mutual interdependence of muse and artist, process and product, writing and interpreting.

"The Potter" (*SHEL*, 32) is especially instructive in reinscribing the role of the male muse from a feminine point of view. Called "the word spouse," the male muse is reinvented as a writing subject who has lost the iconic woman as his inspirer:

> To my word spouse
> I was not Eve nor Helen,
> Not Mary nor Sophia,
> But the fool of the house. (*SHEL*, 32)

Stripped of her traditional attributes the feminine poetic subject is formed in tandem with the masculine. The inspiring "breath" does not originate from the muse or travel into the writing subject. On the contrary, it comes from the "I" and is extinguished by the "he" ("He followed my breath / and left it in the face / of one who was pronounced dead / by the history of faith" [*SHEL*, 32]). His effect on the woman poet is simultaneously damaging and constructive. The poem is an explicit commentary on the type of lyrical discourses that assign the female muse her conventional roles, and it is meant to highlight the unsustainable poetic reality when these roles are reversed. The male muse is domesticated and familiar; he communicates with the "fool of the house," and it is merely his imaginary (constructed) presence that influences the creative process in this poem. The speaking subject positions herself in "the lotus of courtly love," the traditional space reserved for the muse, and from there strategically denies a masculine influence:

> and deny that he is
> all spices commingled,
> with my entire body sown,
> deny that he is light. (*SHEL*, 32)

However, as the subject of "The Potter," the male remains a significant reality that assists in the formation of a feminine identity. The title of the poem is strategic and directs our attention to Plato's potter, who strives for perfect roundness in making his plate in imitation of the divine. Similarly, the feminine subjectivity in this poem is the imperfect imitation ("not Eve nor Helen, / not Mary nor Sophia") whose actuality contains the masculine.

In *Shelmalier* McGuckian's politicized poetry carries with it several layers of meaning, identity, and consciousness. It is constantly on the move and in the making. The poems demonstrate the dense and intricate nature of her language, the complex visualization of every aspect of her creative process. This is especially obvious in her dealings with the political. Diverging from the commentary on actual and historical situations of conventional political poetry, McGuckian's peculiar conceptualization of history as textual idiom—where past events surface via the poet's unconscious as lines of poetry—succeeds in creating a new poetic language of politics. Obviously, in some ways all utterances have political and social significance. Nevertheless, detection of this phenomenon in McGuckian's poetical texts is rendered more difficult because the main body of her vocabulary remains within the realm of what could more easily be considered private.[36] In her poems, McGuckian recreates the process of reading and interpreting and presents her own readers with the challenge of rereading and reinterpreting. Thus, tracing her unique creative process becomes essential for the interpretation of her politicized poetic texts. Within such a context, Medbh McGuckian's words in her preface to *Shelmalier* become easier to comprehend. When she says this book is "the dawn of my own enlightenment," she is in fact explaining her role as the *reader* of history before her role as the writer of poetry. Emphasizing the power of words, the collection witnesses the emergence of a politically conscious author, one who nevertheless shies away from political rhetoric. By presenting the reader with an imaginative interaction between past and present, as Leontia Flynn argues,[37] *Shelmalier* invites readings that take cognizance of politics and history in the context of aesthetic composition.

"Word against Word": Aesthetic Violence in *Drawing Ballerinas*

Drawing Ballerinas, Medbh McGuckian's seventh volume of poetry, was published in 2001, at a moment in time when the Northern Irish peace process was still on shaky grounds. Decommissioning and policing remained contentious issues which increasingly challenged the terms of the 1998 Good Friday Agreement and the functioning of the Northern Irish Assembly.[38] Sectarian violence was a simmering force in the background which resurfaced in the summer of 2001 when a group of Catholic schoolgirls were stoned on their way to school. Medbh McGuckian at this point in her life had already published six volumes of poetry as well as a *Selected Poems* which were more often than not reviewed positively, although with covert criticism for her lack of engagement with the Northern Irish political situation. This was her first, and arguably, up to now at least, her only collection, which aimed to address this perceived lacuna in her work. The title of the book, *Drawing Ballerinas*, is taken from Henri Matisse who, when asked how he managed to survive the war artistically, replied that he spent the worst years "drawing ballerinas."[39] Matisse will be discussed in more detail below, but first it is necessary to consider what this artistic approach to violence means. Is it escapism into a subjective universe which is divorced from political actuality, or does it represent a philosophical engagement with the reality of violent acts?

Slavoj Žižek in his work *Violence: Six Sideways Reflections* distinguishes three kinds of violence. The first of these is the most obvious type, the visible or "subjective" violence which is performed by a clearly identifiable agent.[40] The second and third both come under the category of what he terms "objective" violence: these are "symbolic" violence, which is embodied in language and its forms, and "systemic" violence, which is invisible because it is inherent in the economic and political structures in which we live. Žižek thus explores three layers of the same thing: the visible and tangible acts of violence, the endemic structures that support and create it, and the language which encapsulates and expresses it. He also argues cogently that it is impossible to give account of violence with any kind of clarity: dispassionate narratives undermine the true horrors of experiencing violence, while more passionate or subjective reports become unreliable and "contaminated" by their very subjectivity. What he proposes is a "sideways" glance which interestingly enough evokes poetry as its most natural linguistic medium. He suggests that

> Adorno's famous saying . . . needs correction: it is not poetry that is impossible after Auschwitz, but rather *prose*. Realistic prose fails, where the poetic evocation of the unbearable atmosphere of a camp succeeds. That is to say, when Adorno declares poetry impossible (or rather, barbaric) after Auschwitz, this impossibility is an enabling impossibility: poetry is always, by definition, "about" something that cannot be addressed directly, only alluded to.[41]

This "enabling impossibility" seems to be the driving force behind much of what McGuckian is trying to express in *Drawing Ballerinas*. The volume's central desire to "draw ballerinas," that is, to evoke subjectivities that cannot easily be associated with violence, enables the poet to express through circumnavigation that which, because of its impossible violence, resists direct disclosure. This can be demonstrated by a closer examination of three poems from the volume which can be rewardingly read through the prism of Žižek's sideways glances at violence.

The first of these, the title poem from *Drawing Ballerinas,* is set in the realm of symbolic violence. It basically poses the question of how one can talk about the violent events that underpin and accompany the Northern Irish conflict. There is a footnote accompanying the poem which explains that it "was written to commemorate Ann Frances Owens, a schoolfellow and neighbour, who lost her life in the Abercorn Café explosion in 1972" (*DB*, 15). The opening sentence immediately combines the imagery of dance with violence: the innocent sounding ballet term "scissor-steps" becomes aesthetically charged with violence through the preceding expression "we are the focus of storms," which also serves to draw the reader into communion with anticipated victimhood. The young girl, the model of the painting, is given an ambivalent position in the first stanza: she is between adulthood and childhood, between innocence and moral ambiguity, and also between being the object or subject of the painting and poem. Most importantly, however, her identity is irrevocably tied to our interpretation: we make sense of her by association, "as we would tie / the leaves to the trees and the trees to the forest" (*DB*, 14).

The second stanza describes the model's hair, again aesthetically jolting it into the dimension of violence by the conspicuous placing of the word "machine-gun" at the end of the second line. Nothing violent "happens" here, and yet the innocence presumed in the title is comprehensively shattered. This is followed by the visual shock of the third stanza, where a blown-up body's scattered lines attempt to redraw themselves into a coherent whole:

> And the lines' desire is to warp to accommodate
> A body, a lost and emptied memory of a lost
> Body, the virgin mind emptied from or of it,
> To discover the architecture of pressed-together
> Thighs, or lips that half-belong to a face. (*DB*, 14)

Suddenly the meaning of drawing completely changes: it is not an innocent pastime that reproduces what is seen, but a desperate attempt to make whole again what is irrevocably shattered. And just as it is impossible to "tie leaves to trees and the trees to the forest," it is also impossible to reconstruct a broken life and, in turn, to make sense of violence. Drawing in this poem is not about visual representation, but rather, about aesthetic and moral reconstruction of the consequences of violence. This aestheticized violence appears as the "enabling impossibility" mentioned by Žižek. The following stanza describes the hopelessness implied in representing the broken body which restlessly turns and "reveals opposing versions of itself." Although the point of view of the painter-poet is not challenged in these lines (we are still looking at the body from the outside), the act of drawing or representing no longer belongs to a master-narrator. Instead the body narrates its own impossibility, finally settling into its own disaster in stanza five, "let loose by one last feeling" and "obligingly joining those imprisoning arms" (*DB*, 14). It is as if the act of drawing was tracing the actual event of violence. This symbolic, aesthetic violence gains another interpretative context in stanzas six and seven, which direct our gaze toward the head and "the astonishingly open, misaligned eyes / that suffer like a camera" (*DB*, 15). The ruined body is not only looking back at us, but it also offers itself as the site of creation as the "paper [which] possesses the entirety of sheets they occupy" (*DB*, 15). Shane Alcobia-Murphy has pointed out how these lines were borrowed from a book by John Elderfield on the drawings of Henri Matisse, where Elderfield describes how the drawings "share an absolute sureness, a sense of having been drawn with ease, at ease. The entirety of the sheets is addressed."[42] McGuckian takes the idea of filling the page with lines from Matisse. However, in this poem the contours of the broken body take possession of their own narrative, severing themselves from the model, or the original idea of the unviolated body:

> The contours become brittle and start
> to fracture, as if the body-burden
> with its stripped-down beauty, having rested,
> removed her necklace, had put her gown
> back on, tied back her hair, resettled her hat. (*DB*, 15)

The idea of the body as beauty, which is evoked in the title of the poem as the model posing as ballerina, seems to have "rested" while the violence played out on the "other" body destroyed by the bomb. In some sense representation failed: neither the ballerina, nor the blown-up woman were "accurately" described, and it would probably be futile to say the poem was "about" either of them. The dead body is dissociated from gory details and transformed into the image of a dancer, which merely alludes to violent possibilities. However, this alienation process is deeply shocking and brings the victim even closer.[43]

The last stanza unites the two images within the idea of a "breathing white," which symbolically becomes the space of creativity, the enabling whiteness of the page. In some sense this is also an erasure: the page of the poet and the sheet of the painter are emptied of representation. However, this emptiness is filled with the reverberation of violence that the poet and painter witnessed: it is in fact the enabling impossibility of the symbolic language of violence. Matisse is of crucial relevance in this respect. The painter noted that "the essential thing [in art] is to . . . express the bolt of lightning one senses upon contact with a thing. The function of the artist is not to translate an observation but to express the shock of the object on his nature; the shock, with the original reaction."[44] This suggests that the figure of a ballerina is capable of exerting shock just as much as a destroyed, blown-up body. The shock comes from the inherent language of violence which emanates from the artistic encounter. Matisse also described his creative association with the white page. He said:

> Once my emotive line has modelled the light of my white paper without destroying its precious whiteness, I can neither add nor take anything away. The page is written: no correction is possible. If it is not adequate, there is no alternative than to begin again, as if it were an acrobatic feat.[45]

"Whiteness" here is also seen as an enabling possibility, what McGuckian terms in her poem "that simplest of solution" (*DB*, 15). Completion is associated with origin: the "precious whiteness" must remain intact. Thus on the one hand there is the fragility of the creative idea, symbolized by the whiteness of the page, and on the other hand there is the violence of representation. When the complexity and difficulty implied in this process is taken into account, drawing ballerinas in times of strife no longer looks like an escapist pastime which ignores political violence. The examination of one of Matisse's most famous ballerina paintings reinforces this point.[46] This particular ballerina seems displaced, uncomfortable, unsupported, and in limbo. Her unfinished, undefined right foot rests in a blood-red streak. Feet are probably the strongest, most important descriptors of a dancer, which on this picture are dissolved into the redness. The strong bands of color completely displace and misplace her; it is not even clear what she is sitting on. When compared to Degas's mobile, graceful dancers who are accompanied by a stage and props helping the dancers' pictorial representation of their "dancerness," this painting suggests that Matisse did not so much escape describing violence as merely avoided being drawn into its symbolic dialectic.[47] The fundamental question in relation to both Matisse and McGuckian is whether theirs is a refusal to witness (as some of their critics claim) or, rather, a refusal to witness on violence's terms. In their art the language of creation removes the immediate reality of things. The subject of violence is encountered through symbolic representation of the act of violence which is inherent in the very act of representation. Violence thus becomes the driving force of creation, as the last line of the poem expresses: "the same whiteness everywhere" (*DB*, 15).

Medbh McGuckian states in an interview that her collection *Drawing Ballerinas* "tries to face up to . . . some of the easiest kind of horror."[48] Such a horror is represented in this volume as a violent, destructive act of self-realization where the words are structured around the ever-present idea of death. McGuckian says:

> Death is always a crux around which I write. It's the only thing you can be sure about, but it also brings you up so short against everything. Death is what poets are supposed to define, not deal with

> death or even understand or to cope with it, and not give answers but just meditate, not on death but on life as curtailed by death, or broken by death and whether it is just broken or whether it is broken completely. To try and find, I suppose, the answers to all those huge questions. When I say death, what I really mean is life, because I don't believe that death is the end of things because of my faith.[49]

That death is of central significance to McGuckian in *Drawing Ballerinas* is aptly illustrated by the next poem under discussion, "The Dead Are More Alive" (*DB*, 12–13), which traces the speaking subject's journey of destruction and creation. The poem, according to McGuckian, is a direct reference to her son, who was "caught" watching live coverage of the group of mourners at a nationalist funeral attacking and killing two off-duty British soldiers in 1988.[50] It is not about an individual's death but about institutional death, about the death of the "British Soldier," and the violence which is implicated in the Northern Irish norm. In Žižek's terminology we could suggest that "The Dead Are More Alive" (*DB*, 12–13) is about mapping systemic violence. But the starting point of violence in this poem, death, is also the starting point of creativity. Figures of the dead dominate the poem. However, as the title suggests, the dead do not pose a threat to life but, rather, redefine it. McGuckian once remarked that "talking to the dead for me is the most natural . . . really there's lots of other things wrong for me to do. I can't see anything wrong and I would never feel guilty."[51] The poem opens with a powerful image of dead faces, strangely filled with life:

> As if their eyes could still open,
> were resting from their beauty, still
> burning very quietly, like candles,
> there is something in them that goes beyond
> murder, something denied to the eyes,
> the eyes being used for movements
> denied to the limbs. (*DB*, 12)

The eyes, as the metaphorical representations of words on the page, embody McGuckian's conceptualization of the creative process, where meaning does not precede writing but follows it. She explains this through the example of the previous poem, "Drawing Ballerinas" (*DB*, 14–15). She says:

> I pinned that meaning onto it afterwards. At the same time, by pinning it onto something like that I do give the poem a dimension, even though she died at one time, the poem was written at another time, and the meaning was tacked on at another time, and it's been published at another time. But all of those times are irrelevant because we are in another world, we are in a world where time isn't.[52]

The eyes of the dead are burdened with the potential of expression, but the performance of meaning, as in most of McGuckian's poems, is contingent on the joint participation of the reading and writing subject. The next stanza duly brings in the reader through the observing son's eyes (we read the violence through his watching eyes). This is not an invitation, but an assertion: the reader, "you," cannot remain intact: "Even if you did not see it, nevertheless / it grazed the skin of your mind . . . slicing everything in two" (*DB*, 12).[53] Violence is introduced as the driving force of the concurrent acts of destruction and creation. Constructing the poem does not follow the patterns of creativity of the earlier poems of McGuckian. The question is no longer where "meaning" comes from or whether there is a starting point and a finishing point. However troubled these concepts have already become in her work. The issue in this poem, and indeed in the whole volume of *Drawing Ballerinas*, is whether the creative process exists at all. By opening the poem with the void faces of the dead, but also their inherent life and energy, the idea of progress is made redundant. The performance of creation starts where it ends and ends where it starts. This is the world "where time isn't"[54] and creation is "denied to the eyes" (*DB*, 12). McGuckian explains: "It's sort of like a kind of despair, I cannot be understood, and I cannot even understand myself. If I upset the whole normal process enough then maybe I will reorganise everything and start all over again, go back to square one."[55] The middle section of "The Dead Are More Alive" attempts to recreate a recognizable "starting point." The reader ("you") is distanced from the speaking subject and observed in her/his attempt to make sense of the violence experienced. On one level, this violence refers to the killing of British soldiers at a nationalist funeral in 1988 but, on another, it is a direct allusion to the violent delivery of this poem:

> You were shielded against what you saw
> only by never looking away,
> you broke down what you saw
> by not turning your head,
> as one stares at a map so as never
> to be outside the world. (*DB*, 12)

Not only do the resistance and negative participation of the reader not halt the poem, they also adversely create it. McGuckian consciously draws a parallel with public resignation toward political violence:

> Your seeing did not change you,
> your eyes grew accustomed
> to remaining open, and gathering
> the senselessly scattered things. (*DB*, 12)

However, this resignation is the necessary driving force behind the provoked reader participation, as it is contrasted and simultaneously paired up with the writing subject's avoidance of violence ("I avoided reading any items / about them, but listened to the sounds / of the day stretching across the city" [*DB*, 12–13]). The resulting tension drives the poetic self toward encountering the dead ("I looked for a head as though / to follow its directions" [*DB*, 13]). However, in contrast to the opening scene of the poem, the dead are not subjected to the authorial gaze but are physically met: "I passed four heads in the living-room" (*DB*, 13). This encounter however, now affects the writing subject just as the reader was "grazed" by their presence earlier. As an "ultimate breath" the dead are internalized, bringing with them the violence of their subverted "existence":

> The day clashed inside me, till
> I felt its blood-filled collapse,
> and wanted to tear out from my soil
> everything it had planted, then invite
> people into my emptiness. (*DB*, 13)

Yet again, surpassing, but drawing on, the political urgency of these lines, the poem writes about its own creative violence. The "soil," as the mind of the poet, accommodates the arranged words on the page, which are then violently disrupted to create the "empty" space of potential. McGuckian uses the same metaphor to describe her technique of writing in an interview: "It's like they [the words] are growing in a garden and I pull them out of the garden and put them into my garden, and yet hope they take with them some of their original soil, wherever I got them."[56] However, this process is reversed in this poem as, inversely, it is the "tearing out" of the living to make space for the dead which initiates production. Like "a fire laid in readiness" (*DB*, 13), the dead submerge in the poetic consciousness, transforming into the communal "we" of the last stanza. This uncanny union, which also incorporates the reader, fuses together the impossible performance of the "more alive" dead:

> But mute as peacocks released
> from their vividness, we would not
> have been speaking so gladly
> about the same thing. (*DB*, 13)

Creation is denied to the last: the poem is deprived of a unified performance of the writer-reader-subject, unable to speak about "the same thing." However, in a creative twist, the destruction of the poem simultaneously signals its completion. In political terms, therefore, the poem could be seen as an invitation to view an internalized perspective on the Northern Irish conflict and the violence which assists in the creation of language that is capable of expressing it. The specific political event of the murder of the British soldiers does not appear as straightforward thematic content, yet it informs the personal response to violence that permeates the poet's environment. There is a well-known saying, as Žižek recounts, that "an enemy is someone whose story you haven't heard."[57] McGuckian in this poem seems to go a step further and offers the story of the dead as a representation of systemic violence, which is as much part of her society as the dead that occupy social consciousness.

The third poem under scrutiny, "Gaeltacht na Fuiseoige" (*DB*, 43), is about subjective violence, about the agents who took part in the visible violence of the Troubles: the IRA prisoners. It queries and maps their agency to speak outside violence. The title signals that it, unlike other poems, is thoroughly political. The name refers to a segregated area (block six) in the H blocks in Long Kesh Prison, where republican prisoners spoke Irish and gained access to Irish language books and newspapers and where McGuckian ran poetry workshops in the early nineties. The prisoners are politically and linguistically defined and demarcated as Irish speakers who find linguistic "freedom" in their created environment.[58] However, the poem also traces McGuckian's conceptualization of her creative process, which, in this poem as in the previous one, is fraught with ambivalence. The first stanza gathers the performing participants: the "light" of the source of inspiration—which controversially turns out to be "silence"—and the reader, "you," who is the crucial facilitator of the poetic performance:

> Cubes of sky-wielded silence
> yellow the light: the light
> that would be glad
> to bathe itself in you. (*DB*, 43)

The silence simultaneously marks the solitude of the prisoners and the writer. The poetic consciousness thrives on this identification. Solitude, as Maurice Blanchot remarked, is an essential element of the creative process. He argues that "the work is solitary: this does not mean that it remains uncommunicable, that it has no reader. But whoever reads it enters into the affirmation of the work's solitude, just as he who writes it belongs to the risk of this solitude."[59] The prison block, where there is a "different" language spoken, signifies this imaginary space, where writer and reader unite in solitude. However, McGuckian not only anticipates this metaphysical union of reader and poet but also writes it into the very beginning of the poem. In other words, interpretation and reception precede writing, and the act of reading the rest of the poem becomes a fundamental partaking in the process of creating it. The remainder of the poem is one sentence in three stanzas, which denote the violent possibility, but not the affirmation, of creation:

> When for years I have months
> and my soul chimes
> like an inhabited word,
> a thinking which sucks
>
> its substance, barer now,
> enticing meaning, laying
> word against word
> like pairs of people,
>
> broods in the wound,
> an admitted infection,
> the highroad's central
> greatest ought. (*DB*, 43)

The performance of creativity is likened to an infectious wound, where the battling words create a compulsion toward the fulfillment of creation. This "greatest ought," however, is where the poet leaves the poem, to reflect on the solitude of creation. As Blanchot argues:

> The writer writes a book, but the book is not yet the work. There is a work only when, through it, and with the *violence of a beginning* which is proper to it, the word *being* is pronounced. This event occurs when the work becomes the intimacy between someone who writes it and someone who reads it. One might, then, wonder: if solitude is the writer's risk, does it not express the fact that he is turned, oriented toward the open violence of the work, of which he never grasps anything but the substitute—the approach and the illusion in the form of the book? The writer belongs to the work, but what belongs to him is only a book, a mute collection of sterile words, the most insignificant thing in the world [my italics].[60]

However, McGuckian circumnavigates this process by opening the poem with the intimate encounter between reader and writer and then proceeding to depict the "violent beginning" of the creative process. The emphasis is on the contained violence of the written, but not yet understood, words. This in-between state of violence, the pressure of the unaccomplished work, is reminiscent of the anxiety experienced by many prisoners, who are trapped in an existence alien to life. "Gaeltacht na Fuiseoige," the designated linguistic territory of prisoners, is then also the designated linguistic center of poetic creation. In Blanchot's words, "The central point of the work is the work as origin, the point which cannot be reached, yet the only one which is worth reaching."[61] Thus the symbolic violence of the prisoners becomes also the symbolic violence of the poet and the reader.

Drawing Ballerinas is permeated with violent images, which act as dual referents to Northern Irish politics and the creative process. Although the volume directs the readers toward politicized interpretations, significantly, the poems themselves repudiate political paraphrase. Because McGuckian's technique is driven both by political and aesthetic concerns,[62] the poetic outcome is always ambivalent. The narrative of violence—be it subjective, systemic, or symbolic—is constantly infused with the aesthetics of violence. Furthermore, introducing the concept of death to her aesthetic, McGuckian refocuses the reader's attention onto negation that creates meaning and energized content.

In conclusion, these three volumes trace a growing awareness of a politicized aesthetic absent from her earlier work.[63] One of these collections, *Shelmalier*, contains direct dedications to the Irish rebellion of 1798, its aftermath, and its political "heroes." However, what emerges from the poems is more a sense of a politically conscious author than actual political content. The poems' main focus remains an aesthetic investigation of the performance of creativity and the author's personal engagement with her cultural heritage. Significantly, therefore, the increased politicization is represented in a circuitous and often confusing way, where the signaled content is frequently different from the words written on the page. In many of her poems, McGuckian gestures toward a distinct political referent, only to venture into a seemingly disjointed vocabulary. Her declaration of Irish historical and ideological themes does not provide straightforward political meaning, and the poems continually break loose from political decoding. McGuckian's codes of representation arguably serve a different purpose altogether, one which places an imaginative interaction with past and present in their focus. This means that McGuckian *poeticizes* political content and suggests an attitude of almost spiritual engagement with it. She lucidly describes this in an interview:

> And gradually I became more and more interested in Irish history, which I hadn't been before. I thought Irish history, ah . . . it's too sad, and too miserable, and there is no poetry in it, its source is misery, and let's forget. And now I think no, and not to forget but that there is a source of poetry in it which I think about some times.[64]

Notes

1. Paul Bew and Gordon Gillespie, *Northern Ireland: A Chronology of the Troubles 1968–1999*, 2nd ed. (Dublin: Gill and MacMillan, 1999), 256–404.

2. Medbh McGuckian, *Captain Lavender* (Oldcastle, Ireland: Gallery Press, 1994) (hereafter cited as *CL*).

3. Medbh McGuckian, "Interview with Michael Longley, Edna Longley, Medbh McGuckian, and Ciaran Carson," by Simon Armitage, BBC STANZA, radio interview, recorded at John Hewitt International School, July 28, 1995, broadcast August 19, 1995, on BBC 4.

4. Not that McGuckian's critics have uniformly appreciated this "change" in her interests. Des O'Rawe, for example, argues that the success of her political poems "is limited by post-ceasefire pessimism and the fact that McGuckian's very private public voice is (thankfully) ill-suited 'to set a statesman right.'" Des O'Rawe, review of *Captain Lavender*, by Medbh McGuckian, *Irish Review* 19 (Spring–Summer 1996): 123.

5. McGuckian acknowledges the Northern Irish conflict as one of the main sources of her poetry in several interviews. In "An Attitude of Compassions" she says: "No one here can be an observer. Everyone has lost someone or been scarred over twenty years. More than half of my life—all my adult life—has taken place in this war. It's impossible not to see the poetry as a flower or defence mechanism, so the relationship is a complex one." "An Attitude of Compassions: Q and A with Medbh McGuckian," by Kathleen McCracken, *Irish Literary Supplement: Review of Irish Books* 9, no. 2 (Fall 1990): 21.

6. This is consistent with McGuckian's metaphorizing of the pregnant body.

7. See Lyotard's argument about the crisis of narratives in *The Postmodern Condition: A Report on Knowledge*. There he states that "the narrative function is losing its functors, its great hero, its great dangers, its great voyages, its great goal. It is being dispersed in clouds of narrative language elements—narrative, but also denotative, prescriptive, descriptive, and so on. Conveyed within each cloud are pragmatic valences specific to its kind. Each of us lives at the intersection of many of these. However, we do not necessarily establish stable language combinations, and the properties of the ones we do establish are not necessarily communicable." Quoted in Lawrence E. Cahoone, ed., *From Modernism to Postmodernism: An Anthology* (Oxford: Blackwell Publishing, 2003), 260.

8. The title "Dante's Own Day" is probably also a joke at the expense of the idea of a male grand-narrator.

9. For an intertextual analysis of this poem see Shane Alcobia-Murphy's "Introduction," in *The Poetry of Medbh McGuckian: The Interior of Words*, ed. Shane Alcobia-Murphy and Richard Kirkland (Cork: Cork University Press, 2010), 15–16.

10. Her Majesty's Prison Maze, also known as Maze Prison, The Maze, The H Blocks, or Long Kesh, was a prison in Northern Ireland that was used to house paramilitary prisoners during the Troubles from mid-1971 to mid-2000. At least ten thousand men were held there over the course of thirty years. It was situated in the former Royal Air Force base of Long Kesh, on the outskirts of Lisburn. This was in the townland of Maze, about nine miles (fourteen kilometers) southwest of Belfast. The prison and its inmates played a prominent role in recent Irish history, notably in the 1981 hunger strike. The last prisoners were moved out of the H Blocks in September 2000, and demolition began on October 30, 2006. See Louise Purbrick, "The Last Murals of Long

Kesh: Fragments of Political Imprisonment at the Maze Prison, Northern Ireland," in *Archaeologies of Internment*, ed. Adrian Myers and Gabriel Moshenska (New York: Springer, 2011), 263–83.

11. Maurice Blanchot, *The Space of Literature*, trans. Ann Smock (Lincoln: University of Nebraska Press, 1982), 198.

12. McGuckian, "Interview," by Simon Armitage, July 28, 1995.

13. Ellen S. Fine argues that "The concept of time that governs life in normal conditions . . . changes radically in the concentrationary universe." Ellen S. Fine, "Witness of the Night" in Harold Bloom ed., *Bloom's Modern Critical Interpretations: Night* (New York: Chelsea House, 2001) 52. In his autobiographical account of the holocaust, *Night*, Elie Wiesel describes this phenomenon the following way: "So many events had taken place in just a few hours that I had completely lost all notion of time. When had we left our homes? And the ghetto? And the train? Only a week ago? One night? One single night? How long had we been standing in the freezing wind? One hour? A single hour? Sixty minutes? Surely it was a dream." Elie Wiesel, *Night*, transl. Marion Wiesel (New York: Hill and Wang, 2006) 37.

14. Medbh McGuckian, *Shelmalier* (Oldcastle, Ireland: Gallery Press, 1998) (hereafter cited as *SHEL*). In the summer of that year a sporadic series of insurrections, loosely organized by the Society of the United Irishmen who hoped to instigate an Irish republic on the French revolutionary model, broke out in different parts of the island, particularly in Wexford and in East Ulster. They were ultimately suppressed with savage violence. See Dáire Keogh and Nicholas Furlong, eds., *The Mighty Wave: The 1798 Rebellion in Wexford* (Dublin: Four Courts Press, 1996); and also A. T. Q. Stewart, *The Summer Soldiers: The 1798 Rebellion in Antrim and Down* (Belfast: Blackstaff Press, 1995).

15. The expression "when hope and history rhyme" is drawn from Seamus Heaney, *The Cure at Troy, A Version of Sophocles' Philoctetes* (London: Faber and Faber, 1990), 77. It has become one of the most frequently quoted lines of contemporary poetry in Ireland, mostly in political contexts.

16. See Marianne Elliott, *Wolfe Tone: Prophet of Irish Independence* (New Haven, CT: Yale University Press, 1990).

17. Declan Kiberd, *Irish Classics* (London: Granta Books, 2000), 242.

18. In a 1995 interview McGuckian, when asked about the poem "On Ballycastle Beach," declared, "The real language is dead, and the new one is anathema—for emotional reasons." "'My Words Are Traps': An Interview with Medbh McGuckian," by John Hobbs, *New Hibernia Review/Iris Éireannach Nua: A Quarterly Record of Irish Studies* 2, no. 1 (Spring 1998): 113.

19. Wolfgang Iser discusses the importance of an "as if world" in bringing about an interplay between the "bracketed world" of the text and empirical reality. See Wolfgang Iser, "Towards a Literary Anthropology," in *The Future of Literary Theory*, ed. Ralph Cohen (London: Routledge, 1989), 216–17.

20. This is very much in contrast to Seamus Heaney's aspiration to create a pristine, aesthetic language in opposition to political brutalities, as discussed in Michael Bernard-Donals, "Governing the Tongue: Seamus Heaney's (A)Political Aesthetic," *Canadian Journal of Irish Studies* 20, no. 2 (December 1994): 75–88.

21. She says: "I think poetry is part of the society's developing consciousness of itself in a way that the individual cannot control and may not be aware of." "A Dialogue

with Medbh McGuckian, Winter 1996–1997," by Rand Brandes, *Studies in the Literary Imagination* 30, no. 2 (Fall 1997): 46.

22. In her 1995 interview McGuckian describes art and poetry as "a metrical controlling of pain and experience." Hobbs, "My Words Are Traps," 112.

23. It can be speculated that these "flowers" refer to her own earlier poetic work such as her 1993 collection, *The Flower Master*.

24. Note the reference to the "unchanging voice" of the previous poem, which was interpreted as silence, history's unchanging consciousness.

25. This strongly echoes Paul Ricoeur's idea of "distanciation." In "Phenomenology and Hermeneutics" Ricoeur says: "To interpret is to render near what is far (temporally, geographically, culturally, spiritually). In this respect, mediation by the text is the model of distanciation which would not be simply alienating . . . but which would be genuinely creative. The text is, *par excellence*, the basis for communication in and through distance." Paul Ricoeur, *Hermeneutics and the Social Sciences*, trans. John B. Thompson (Paris: Éditions de la Maison des Sciences de l'homme; Cambridge: Cambridge University Press, 1998), 111.

26. "Swimming" contrasts with "awakening" in the earlier poem "Dream in a Train" as well, where it was taken to represent creativity (*SHEL*, 17).

27. See Virginia Woolf, *The Diary of Virginia Woolf 1920–1924*, ed. Anne Olivier Bell (New York: Harcourt, Brace, Jovanovich, 1980), vol. 2, 45; Byron Guiccioli and Teresa Guiccioli, *The Last Attachment: The Story of Byron and Teresa Guiccioli as Told in Their Unpublished Letters and Other Family Papers*, ed. Iris Origo (New York: C. Schribner's Sons, 1949), 33.

28. The house is also a recurring metaphor in McGuckian's poetry, often denoting poetic consciousness.

29. As Steven Matthews has noted, Ciaran Carson, a contemporary Belfast poet, frequently uses textual symbols to reflect upon the violence in Northern Ireland. Steven Matthews, *Irish Poetry: Politics, History, Negotiation* (London: Macmillan Press, 1997), 197.

30. Elin Holmsten, "Signs of Encounter in Medbh McGuckian's Poetry," in *The Poetry of Medbh McGuckian: The Interior of Words*, ed. Shane Alcobia-Murphy and Richard Kirkland (Cork: Cork University Press, 2010), 101.

31. This aptly describes the passive role of a romanticized muse. It is interesting to note that at the beginning of her career Medbh McGuckian saw the role of the poet as a male one: "I wanted to do something that would make me into a man, or give me the status of a man." "Interview with Medbh McGuckian," by Rebecca Wilson, in *Sleeping with Monsters: Conversations with Scottish and Irish Women Poets*, ed. Rebecca Wilson and Gillean Somerville-Arjat (Dublin: Wolfhound Press, 1990), 4.

32. "Then the Lord put forth his hand, and touched my mouth. And the Lord said unto me, Behold, I have put my words in thy mouth" (Jeremiah 1:9). All biblical references are from the King James Version.

33. Indeed, the prophets had no choice but to accept this divine gift, even though it was often painful to receive, as for example for Jonah, who attempted to escape. Malachi mentions the "burden of the word of the Lord" (Malachi 1:1), and Isaiah describes the physical effects of this divine inspiration: "Therefore are my loins filled with pain: pangs have taken hold upon me, as the pangs of a woman who travaileth: I was bowed down by the hearing of it" (Isaiah 21:3).

34. Simon Critchley, *Very Little . . . Almost Nothing: Death, Philosophy, Literature* (London: Routledge, 1997), 43.

35. And so are we, spectators of the painting and readers of the poem. One is reminded of Lacan's *voyeur*, visible to someone else, while still seeing. As Rosalind Krauss observes, "The price, then, for being in the picture is that I am there as function, not as subject." Rosalind Krauss, "The Future of an Illusion," in *The Future of Literary Theory*, ed. Ralph Cohen (London: Routledge, 1989), 286.

36. Words from the two previously discussed poems like "stone," "leaves," "house" or "sea" were interpreted as signifiers of history and politics, although the immediate associations which they evoke carry resonances of the quotidian and private. As Clair Wills argues, "[Northern Irish] poets construct an alternative relation between public and private registers, in which a work's political responsibility no longer derives from its public or communal reference." Clair Wills, *Improprieties: Politics and Sexuality in Northern Irish Poetry* (Oxford: Clarendon Press, 1993), 191.

37. Leontia Flynn, "Reading Medbh McGuckian," PhD diss., Queen's University Belfast, 2004, 227.

38. See Jennifer Todd, "The Changing Structure of Conflict in Northern Ireland and the Good Friday Agreement," Working Papers in British-Irish Studies, no. 26 (Dublin: Institute for British-Irish Studies, University College of Dublin, 2003), http://www.ucd.ie/ibis/filestore/wp2003/26_todd.pdf (accessed January 20, 2012).

39. Medbh McGuckian, *Drawing Ballerinas* (Oldcastle, Ireland: Gallery Press, 2001), 15 (hereafter cited as *DB*).

40. Slavoj Žižek, *Violence: Six Sideways Reflections* (London: Profile Books, 2008), 1.

41. Ibid., 4.

42. Shane Murphy, "Sonnets, Centos and Long Lines: Muldoon, Paulin, McGuckian and Carson," in *The Cambridge Companion to Contemporary Irish Poetry*, ed. Matthew Campbell (Cambridge: Cambridge University Press, 2003), 201.

43. Žižek also claims that alienation is often not the problem but the solution. Žižek, *Violence*, 51.

44. Jack Flam, *Matisse: The Man and His Art 1869–1918* (Ithaca, NY: Cornell University Press, 1986), 85.

45. Jack Flam, *Matisse on Art* (Berkeley: University of California Press, 1995), 131.

46. Henri Matisse, *Ballerina*, 1927, oil on canvas, 65 x 50 cm, held in the State Hermitage Museum, Saint Petersburg, Russia. Online see http://www.arthermitage.org/Henri-Matisse/Ballerina.html (accessed October 21, 2013).

47. On a sidenote relevant to this point, Žižek recounts that "according to a well-known anecdote, a German officer visited Picasso in his Paris studio during the Second World War. There he saw *Guernica* and shocked at the modernist 'chaos' of the painting, asked Picasso: 'Did you do this? Picasso calmly replied: 'No, *you* did this!'" Žižek, *Violence*, 9.

48. Medbh McGuckian, "'I Am Listening in Black and White to What Speaks to Me in Blue': Medbh McGuckian," interview by Helen Blakeman, *Irish Studies Review* 11, no. 1 (April 2003): 62.

49. Ibid., 62.

50. Flynn, "Reading Medbh McGuckian," 229.

51. Medbh McGuckian, "In the Country of Comparative Peace: Interview with Medbh McGuckian," by Philip Harvey, *Encounter*, ABC Radio National, December 12, 2004.

Transcript available at: http://www.abc.net.au/radionational/programs/encounter/in-the-country-of-comparative-peace/3427894 (accessed October 18, 2013).

52. Blakeman, "I Am Listening," 67.

53. Leontia Flynn notes that these lines are a direct reference to the previously mentioned incident with McGuckian's son, who was "caught" watching live coverage of the group of mourners at a nationalist funeral attacking and killing two off-duty British soldiers in 1988. Flynn, "Reading Medbh McGuckian," 229.

54. Blakeman, "I Am Listening," 67.

55. Ibid., 68.

56. Ibid., 67.

57. Žižek, *Violence,* 39.

58. The English translation of the title is "the gaeltacht (Irish-speaking territory) of the lark." "Lark-wing" was also the code-name for Bobby Sands, the most famous inmate of the prison.

59. Blanchot, *Space of Literature*, 22.

60. Ibid., 23.

61. Ibid., 54.

62. The blurb for the volume reads: "Constantly affirming the validity and necessity of aesthetics, the muse of this book is not so much Peace as what Edward Said calls "peace with justice" (*DB*, back cover).

63. The American publication of her later poems, which incorporates some of *Drawing Ballerinas* and *The Face of the Earth*, does not completely fit the description of progress outlined here. In *The Soldiers of Year II* the focus, on the one hand, is more overtly political, on the other, the national iconography noted in her Irish publications is less markedly present. Thus when Guinn Batten describes the collection in her afterword she says: "In *The Soldiers of Year II* Ireland's past remains present: the Famine and its epidemics, 1916 and its aftermath, all appear alongside happenings in Hollywood and in Ulster during the last half of the twentieth-century. Throughout the volume the poet is concerned with the difficult necessity of representing fairly contemporary events whose consequences offer multiple trajectories not only into the future but also into the past." Medbh McGuckian, *The Soldiers of Year II,* with afterword by Guinn Batten (Winston-Salem, NC: Wake Forest University Press, 2002), 125. For a more detailed discussion of this volume, see Flynn, "Reading Medbh McGuckian," 242–46.

64. Medbh McGuckian, "An Interview with Medbh McGuckian," by María Jesús Lorenzo-Modia, *European English Messenger* 13, no. 2 (Autumn 2004): 40.

3

Death and Spirituality in *The Face of the Earth*, *Had I a Thousand Lives*, and *The Book of the Angel*

THE VOLUMES UNDER CONSIDERATION IN THIS CHAPTER were published in the course of three short years between 2002 and 2004, concluding a four-year period when the poet produced a new collection annually. While the violence of the previous decade was largely absent, during these years the fragility of the peace process was all too apparent. The issue of decommissioning bedeviled all attempts at normalizing democratic politics, and the issue of the relationship between the IRA and criminal activity was brought sharply into relief by the Northern Bank robbery of December 2004. In the same month the Democratic Unionist party turned its back on a comprehensive agreement because of its opposition to power-sharing with the nationalist community and the Good Friday Agreement.[1] Thus Northern Ireland seemed still to teeter over the abyss, and genuine confidence about the durability of peace was frequently difficult to sustain. *Drawing Ballerinas* had signaled the arrival of a new thematic voice and interest in Medbh McGuckian's work, which reflected on the Troubles from a more internalized, almost philosophical perspective. The following three collections continue with this theme, allowing the experienced violence and darkness to surface in an increasingly spiritual tone. Religion and faith appear as comfort and creative impetus, suffusing McGuckian's language with otherworldly and sacred imagery. The political violence experienced through the Troubles had surfaced in thematic, allegorical forms in McGuckian's more overtly political volumes, *Shelmalier* and *Captain Lavender*. This resulted in a darker tone that considered death as a creative origin and also as the ultimate expression of futility. A tentative spirituality had risen out of this voice in *Drawing Ballerinas*, which continues and strengthens in the consecutive three volumes under discussion in this chapter. Religion as a thematic focus follows these spiritual reflections and leads the poet back to meditations on the creative-writing self. The performance of creativity is arguably still at the center of her focus; however, the wider thematic range infuses and inflects some of McGuckian's earlier compositional techniques. In these volumes death, spirituality, and religion become the source of creative performance, where divinity enters and reconfigures her poetic language.

Colliding with Absence in *The Face of the Earth*

The Face of the Earth[2] is centered on the evocation of spiritual renewal through corporeal and natural images. The motto of the book, taken from the Psalms, is: "Thou sendest forth thy spirit, they are created: and thou renewest the face of the earth." The focus is on renewal, creating something fresh out of something old. The face of the earth becomes the surface which bears all the marks of the past but which is still in need of rejuvenation. The question this volume poses, both in political and poetical terms, is whether rejuvenation is indeed possible or whether, due to the scars of the past, it remains an illusion. In terms of McGuckian's creative process, the focus shifts to nature and its innate ability to revivify death and decay. In political terms, the collection muses on ideas of progress and their relevance to the individual.

The opening poem, "The Brood-bird" (*FOE*, 11), introduces the poetic language that characterizes this collection. The "bird" here becomes a signifier both of authorial intent and spiritual content:

> My encircler, I am placing a lock
> upon my lips, though nine deaths
> were in my unhemmed mouth
> or thy mouth breast-white to my breast. (*FOE*, 11)

The "white" of the Holy Ghost encounters the "unhemmed mouth" of the speaker. Death is the source of language and expression. The innate tautology of this statement is the theme of the next stanza, where the speaker explicitly articulates that death as creative source can only be viewed as language that recognizes its own futility:

> The tongue and knot and pulsing oil
> of death without death goes round
> in a thread, so I see neither the black
> nor the white, tonight, in the upper chamber:
>
> only the knee-woman, the world-woman,
> the woman of songs. (*FOE*, 11)

When death becomes the source, rather than the object of poetic expression, language becomes disabled and paralyzed for cognitive expression: the black and white of the world become blurred, and the only thing that remains visible is humanity, in this case represented in the corporeality of the woman. The three figures represent facets of femininity: the "knee-woman" is a midwife assisting in birthing, the "world-woman" is the corporeal, living human being,[3] and the "woman of songs" *is* the poet and the poem, containing all the paradoxical, tautological or simply nonsensical language of poetry. In this *ars poetica* McGuckian signals her intent for this collection, where dichotomies complement, rather than contrast with each other, and meaning emerges from the healing grace of understanding.

"The Worship of the Plough" (*FOE*, 16–17) turns attention to the language of nature, depicting tangible images of soil, water, and vegetation. The poem retraces and reinterprets a universal, indeed somewhat hackneyed, image of creation, the sprouting of a seed from moist earth. However, the first stanza commences with the iconography of death:

> Only old women like the colour
> of deep water, when the body is thrown
> into a running stream and becomes
> the ghost of a childless person. (*FOE*, 16–17)

Death, in a manner reminiscent of the Beckettian "I can't go on, I will go on," becomes the starting point of creation rather than a finitude which renders life irrelevant. Simon Critchley, following Adorno, argues that the only possible expression left to artists is the "concrete reconstruction of the meaning of meaninglessness."[4] This meaninglessness is represented here by images of death. However, incorporated within the poem the picture of void, the "colour of deep water," is filled with meaning, as it becomes the "nocturnal source"[5] of writing. At this stage, meaning appears as a "body," or, more precisely, as a "ghost of a childless person": not fully dead and not yet alive. This is the moment of desire, an Orphic yearning for life, an idyllic image of the meaning of meaninglessness. It is important to distinguish this approach from nihilism. McGuckian's imagery, here, does not recoil into itself creating a futile void. In this underwater death a genuine renewal takes place, although admittedly not in a manner the reader might expect. No resurrection of bodies occurs; no fresh vegetation grows out of the wet banks of the river. What actually happens represents, arguably, a more precise description of the creative process: the water, with all its decaying contents is poured straight into the epicenter of the poetic persona:

A coil of twigs brushing out
the sowing basket, like fluid opium
into a catch-basin, as soon as possible
before noon, before the rice flower forms,

drives the water full into
that absolutely level field,
a field left vacant in me,
well-white and smooth. (*FOE*, 16–17)

The creation happens at speed ("as soon as possible"), and the "vacant field," an agent as void as the "deep water" of the first stanza, represents a renewed receptive medium. The site of creation is, therefore, transferred from death to the living interior of the poet, from the darkness of the water to the "well-white" smoothness of a yet-unwritten page. However, this is still the fragile phase of the creative process. Inspiration has been described here as the experience of death, which, because of its very existence *as* experience, gives way to life. This is not, however, a completed work of art. It is merely its desire to materialize, the "moistening of the earth" as the following lines describe:

I go to the field by night,
to the place where the earth begins
to become moist, to a piece
of moist earth stamped and injured

by rain. . . . (*FOE*, 16–17)

The creative process is still located in darkness, in the realm of sexuality but also pain and suffering. "Rain," a frequently recurring image representing creativity in McGuckian's poetry, is seen "stamping" and "injuring" the "earth," the icon of the fertilized poetic mind. In the frail first steps of creation, what is carried away is a mere "helpless seed," the essence of conception. This fragility of beginning is emphasized by the "and if" of the sixth stanza. Significantly, the first words to emerge from this creative process are those of religious prayer. "Credos" and "Pater Nosters" are the only possible utterances as if, without embracing the supernatural, the birth of the Word would be impeded.[6] The appearance of the "plough" in the seventh stanza conjures up the imagery of writing. "Passed over the field," the plough produces scars but also leaves marks as if writing on the page of the earth. The new "shoots" that finally emerge incorporate in themselves the torment of their own creation; their growth is inseparable from their weakening. The last section takes the reader into a subversion of the Wordsworthian inspiration model. The poet's personality is entirely absent from the creative process. Nature is present but rather than recollecting its beauty in tranquility McGuckian allows its constituents to flow into each other, fuse, and emerge as their own production:

> . . . In the marriage
> of a grove to a well,
> or a well to an image,
>
> trees look their best,
> half-wearing the produce
> of one field less desired
> if you weed your fields in me. (*FOE*, 16–17)

The conclusion, as so often in McGuckian's poetry, is enigmatic. When read in a politicized context, the poem could be seen as a commentary on the stalled progress in political dialogue. However, in this case, an aesthetic interpretation yields more possibilities. Toward the end of the poem, certain dissatisfaction with this creation is detectable, as it is epitomized as "one field less desired," leaving all the others for the poet to "plough." The absurdity of "weed your fields in me" recalls the opening lines of the poem. Weeding implies killing what is unneeded, pulling up the undesired. However, this particular weeding seems to be the significant "if" of creation, the feat which completes the poem. It is as if the reader were to accompany the poet, or as if the act of interpretation (pulling the words or weeds out) had to take place simultaneously with the act of creation (putting the words or seeds in). The emphasis remains on this "as if," the ultimate fragility of the creative process which generates the distinctive emotional charge of all Medbh McGuckian's poetry. The physical landscape employed in "The Worship of the Plough" conjures up a suitable locus for the imagination, projecting the inherent ambiguity of the poetic self into the natural landscape it describes.

The poem "The Gas Curtain" (*FOE*, 74), by contrast, leaves nature behind and invokes war and a sense of danger. Although the exact reference is difficult to pin down, gas curtains were used in World War I to shield soldiers in their dugouts from a gas attack. Occasionally, however, soldiers would inadvertently bring enemy gas into the shelter in their boots, which was then prevented from escaping by the curtain. Thus, it was not uncommon for the men to be gassed in their sleep.[7] The ambiguous nature of the gas curtain (protective but also potentially dangerous) is what McGuckian comments on in this poem, which invokes the image of the fragmented female body as a metaphor of the self in the process of construction:[8] "I am showing one of me to each eye / believing she is seeing all there is to see" (*FOE*, 74). The positioning of the eyes is indicative of the destabilizing of a presupposed poetic perspective. The boundary between seer and seen is blurred, the presence of an unbroken vantage point denied. Maurice Merleau-Ponty, demonstrating a reciprocal intertwining of the seer and the visible argues that

> the seer is caught up in what he sees . . . the vision he exercises . . . so that the seer and the visible reciprocate one another and we no longer know which sees and which is seen. It is this Visibility, this anonymity innate to Myself that we have called flesh.[9]

Thus, the body, the corporeal matter, becomes a metaphor for vision as well as visibility; in other words the active participant in the creative constitution of self:

> If her eyes are asked, they act
> as if her body as a whole were moving
> in some brilliant boat action
> at the end of the sea. (*FOE*, 74)

A reciprocal motion is initiated whereby the act of seeing each other becomes the medium of self-interpretation. The locus of an identity is situated in between the seer and the seen, precisely in the axis of a peripatetic relationship. The "I" of the poem is seen carrying away "her head and shoulders, / her existing eyes, yellowed but whole, / the crushed brick of her lipless mouth" (*FOE*, 74). "Capturing" the self as an unbroken whole is an attempt doomed to failure, and cognitive approaches to self-definition result in a fragmented sense of identity. The only coherent entity emerging from this search is the text itself. The female body, "reduced to a mere / thread clothed with words," becomes the locus of identity as textual idiom. In other words, the poetic definition of self remains contained within the context of creativity. The act of definition becomes the definition itself ("a shadow often acts as the announcer"). Because the formation of self is thus eternally self-reflexive, it is also continually unstable and impossible to pin down in a temporal or visual dimension: "time may be dropped / like a corner cut / out of the face she has lost" (*FOE,* 74). The concluding stanza of the poem summarizes in a striking image the instability of the act of defining:

> Her bed half-opened and its clouds
> exhausting anyone who walks there,
> when her body closes does it close to all,
> its curtain slanting boldly as you look? (*FOE*, 74)

"Her bed" becomes the theatrical site of the dramatic quest for identity. The onlookers, exhausted by the clouds precipitated by a "half-opened" identity, are left with the only thing that remains constant, a boldly slanting curtain. The curtain, which symbolically signifies finality, its closing initiating the moment of return to "reality," receives a further twist in the title of the poem. As a gas curtain, it is robbed of its physicality, turning transparent and immaterial. Endowed with an innate sense of danger, the image of the curtain remains the ultimate question mark of the poem.

Among the several poems that consider faith and religion in this collection, "Navicella" (*FOE*, 38–39) stands out with its relatively more direct references to religious iconography.[10] Navicella is originally the name of a fresco by Giotto which can be found in St. Peter's Basilica in the Vatican City. The fresco was commissioned in 1298 and, as the guide to the Basilica describes "after four unfortunate transfers and various dismantling, recomposition and restoration activities, it was placed in its current location on the occasion of the Holy Year of 1675."[11] It is easy to see how the processes of de- and recompositions that the fresco underwent attracts a poet like McGuckian, whose writing technique similarly atrophies "original" sources, in order to create something new. The fresco depicts Christ standing on water, extending his right hand toward St. Peter, who seems to be sinking in a stormier section of the same stretch of water. The biblical reference in the context of McGuckian's poem is crucial: when Christ walked on water and his apostles saw him they were terrified and thought he was a ghost. Peter then asked Jesus to prove he was not a ghost by asking him to walk on water. Jesus did so and in turn asked Peter to walk toward him, but Peter became afraid and began to sink. Jesus stretched out his arm to save him and said, "O thou of little faith, wherefore didst thou doubt?" (Matthew 14:31). This was one of Jesus's most outrageous requests for a demonstration of faith from his disciples: walking on water does not make sense, unless in the context of faith. Putting cognitive faculties aside is also something that McGuckian seems to ask of her readers. Thus the title "Navicella" can be interpreted as both an apology to her compositional technique and an invitation to readerly faith.[12]

The first three stanzas of the poem open with a description of a damaged angel, who is covered within a tarnished fresco:

> Only your wings have survived,
> a few dark openings,
> your face in semi-shadow,

the pure gold azure of the window
partially filled in
with dusted red ochre. (*FOE*, 38)

The above lines can be read in several interpretative layers. Spiritually the image of the half-hidden angel hints at the fragility of faith. Read in the context of her compositional technique the lines describe the birth of a poem where the source text or idea is replanted in a new context. The overriding sense of frailty continues in the next lines, where the figure is described as a "flower between two abysses" (a phrase taken from Franz Liszt describing a Beethoven sonata[13]) and "a prisoner of your own image" (*FOE*, 38). These images also evoke the figure of the Virgin Mary who, at the moment of the Annunciation, is caught between the two worlds of divinity and profanity. Both of these worlds hold death for her, either in the form of her own personal demise or that of her yet to be born son. Between these "two abysses" she chooses divinity, becoming a flesh-and-bone woman whose life nevertheless symbolizes for women the unattainable and yet desirable acceptance of faith and fate:

your head is difficult to read;

age-old, unconsummated
emblem of charity, only ever young,
which of these worlds is ours? (*FOE*, 38)

"Navicella" is a meditation on faith, looking for a doorway that "truly leads into an interior" (*FOE*, 38). In its seventeen stanzas, the poet contemplates whether cognition ("there is /no other way than studying / the wax and honey of your face") or institutionalized religion ("your billowy mauve cloak, // the absence of punchwork in your halo, / your gestures set ominously to 'dead'") can lead to a Virgin Mary–like acceptance of faith. This question culminates in the description of "the snowfall of August 358," which is another religious incident describing miraculous belief. On the fifth of August that year Pope Liberius was visited by the Virgin Mary, who asked him to build a church where snow has fallen. The pope found the summit of the Esquiline Hill covered in snow that hot summer morning, and he sketched the outline of the future Santa Maria Maggiore Church there.[14] Whether it is walking on water, saying yes to a virgin pregnancy, or acknowledging snowfall in the height of summer, these examples point toward an invitation of faith that is not based on reason but acceptance:

> all of these people were healed
> by his shadow, that is no longer
> a blue or golden void,
>
> a rood screen, of Eucharistic grapes,
> but snowgrace,
> healing with its shadow. (*FOE*, 38)

The "shadow" refers back to the half-hidden angel of the first three stanzas and also to the healing sense of faith that evokes the biblical seeing "through a glass, darkly" (1 Corinthians 13). McGuckian invites her reader to be open to such faith when entering the world of her poetry, following the example of the Virgin Mary, Peter or Pope Liberius. As Lucy Collins explains:

> The Virgin Mary's words "My soul magnifies the Lord, and my spirit rejoices in God my savior" emphasise the power of acceptance within the act of praise. This receptiveness to the difficult or the unexpected is a particular requirement of McGuckian's readers.[15]

As well as introducing a stronger sense of religiosity, *The Face of the Earth*, in many ways, also marks a return to the themes of McGuckian's earlier volumes. The use of nature imagery and the female body as sites of identity constructs evoke poems like "Isba Song" (*VR*, 26) or "Lime Trees in Winter, Retouched" (*VR*, 49). However, the creative performance here is centered on absence: "I kept colliding with the absence" ("High Altitude Lavender," *FOE*, 47), questioning, and a deep-seated unease that permeates the volume. Words seem to arrange themselves arbitrarily and the contribution of the author appears involuntary: "my hand made a shining journey of its own" ("Christmas Eve Sky," *FOE*, 62). The writing self does not own the creative process: "let me arrange that pillow in your own words" ("Valentine Not to Be Opened," *FOE*, 55), and words seem to take on a life of their own: "the word wearing thin and hymnic" ("Image of Migratory Cranes," *FOE*, 40). In terms of her politicized aesthetics, this volume signals a temporary departure from the usage of more overt political vocabulary and bears witness to a sense of spiritualized reflection, foreshadowing the language of *The Book of the Angel*.

CHAPTER 3

Forcing Death to Speak in *Had I a Thousand Lives*

McGuckian's following collection, *Had I a Thousand Lives*, returns to some of her earlier historical and political interests.[16] The volume was written in 2003 for the bicentenary of the execution of Robert Emmet and Thomas Russell in 1803.[17] These "saintly" figures of Irish nationalist iconography are imaginatively appropriated for the purpose of pondering death and political sacrifice. The centrality of the dead in the Irish nationalist tradition, in which Emmet himself was a canonical figure, was powerfully reemphasized in the early twentieth century by Pádraig Pearse, whose metaphor of the disturbing impact of the unquiet "Fenian dead" became a defining image of Irish Republican ideology.[18] The loaded freight of the political Irish funeral, essentially originating with Daniel O'Connell, and reaching a contemporary peak in the lifetime of Medbh McGuckian with the hunger strikers of the 1980s, has also served to foreground the idea of communion between the living and the dead in a relationship doused equally in political and religious significance.[19]

The focus of the volume is, however, not purely ideological, as it avoids direct commentary and political analysis. Rather, these poems shadow questions of (national) identity and belonging through romanticized communion with Ireland's dead. It is in their death that Emmet and Russell "come alive," and in this volume death, in fact, becomes the driving force of the creative performance.

Representing death as a formative idiom poses several challenges to a reader. Death can never surpass its symbolic significance as the ultimate collapse of meaning: there can be life after death and before death, but the moment of death, as a black hole, carries with it a finite negation of existence. To overcome this negative economy, death is often represented as a threshold of meaning, a transitional phase between different modes of existence. The classical story of Orpheus, which has had a major influence on the shaping of elegiac poetry,[20] offers a suitable allegorical representation of this point. When Orpheus's wife, Eurydice, dies from a snakebite, he mourns her and in his grief descends to the underworld. There, with his speech and sweet music, he persuades Hades to release Eurydice from the dead. Hades agrees on one condition: Orpheus must not look back at her before they reach their own house. Orpheus, however, finds it impossible not to steal a glimpse and with his backward glance casts Eurydice back to the black hole of the underworld.

Eurydice, thus, dies twice, and Orpheus mourns twice. The acts of dying and mourning are duplicated, creating a heightened sense of everlasting grief, failure, and lack. Orpheus's eventual death symbolizes his entrapment in disjointed sentiment: he is torn apart, limb by limb, by a group of females known as the maenads. His head is thrown into the sea and washed up at the island of Lesbos, where it continues to sing until the Lesbians bury him.[21] Death, both his own and that of his wife, is thus represented as the threshold which connects the anxiety of life to the grief and mourning of after-death life.

The central question of the story, however, is why Orpheus turns back to look at his wife. As a powerful and successful poet, such weakness seems out of character.[22] Simon Critchley, following Blanchot, interprets this as the crucial moment of identity formation. He says: "The paradox of Orpheus's situation is that if he did not turn his gaze on Eurydice he would be betraying his desire and thus would cease to be an artist. Thus, the desire which destroys his art is also its source."[23] The close association between death and desire, lack and fulfillment, characterizes that crucial moment of identity formation, when one becomes fascinated by the vanishing face of Eurydice, entrapped in the double bind of origin and oblivion.

In the context of contemporary Irish poetry, death is often represented as a reservoir of identity formation, as for example in Seamus Heaney's bog sequences, and also as an ultimate collapse of meaning, as in some of Ciaran Carson's Belfast poems. McGuckian, in her poem "Forcing Music to Speak" (*HTL*, 102), revisits the death of Robert Emmet and the story of Orpheus (or rather, his severed head) to muse on identity. Although the title of this poem could be interpreted as a reference to Orpheus's speech to Hades in the Underworld, the poem opens with a quotation from the Bible, depicting Christ's funeral gear: "*And the napkin, which was about his head, not lying with the linen cloths, but rolled up in a place by itself*" (*HTL*, 102). The imagery of absence, lack, negation, and displacement sets the tone for the poem. Jesus has left, and the napkin is without its "content" and context, not with the other clothes, but all by itself. As a fragmented signifier, its purpose is to highlight the absence of Christ. At this crucial moment, the disciples only know that Christ is gone from their reality, but "as yet they knew not the scripture, that he must rise again from the dead" (John 20:9). The napkin induces grief in Mary and joyous belief in one of the disciples. The poem opens on this precarious threshold between death and life, grief and belief. The first three stanzas describe a church as "the shell of the bride of Christ," emphasizing again the discrepancy between the signifier and the substance it is supposed to signify.

The empty shell of the church, just like the head napkin of Christ, is deprived of its meaning, it collapses and "joins up with itself."[24] The void this creates evokes "illness spirits," voices of the underworld. At this point, life and meaning prevail, the narrative "I" has "no ear for their whispering" and is unaffected by their proximity. Stanzas 7 through 9 see the appearance of a "young man" who turns out to be Venantius Fortunatus, the sixth-century poet who recorded and celebrated the life of St. Radegund and her spiritually adopted daughter Agnes. Throughout his poetry, he rejoices in life's little pleasures. The chestnut and butter he receives from the two women symbolize the contrasting existences inside and outside the convent (the food having been sent from inside the convent, where it cannot be enjoyed, to the outside, where it is consumed). The print of Agnes's finger in the butter reinforces the discrepancy which exists between actual and signified presence. Up to this point, the poem is structured around ambiguities: Christ, the church, and Fortunatus's poetry represent ambivalence between life and death. As an embodiment of this hesitancy, stanza 11 describes the indistinct face of a man: "We cannot see his eyes, and can discern / only a hint of his mouth." The "harp" in stanza 13 suggests that he is, in fact, Orpheus, "delivering his body, his whirling, // musical body, musical glove, to the music / he knew in the sky." In the underworld, pleading for his wife, he invokes his music, which "answers to every touch." Stanza 15, however, evokes the figure of Robert Emmet, to whom the volume, *Had I a Thousand Lives*, is dedicated. Emmet, just like Orpheus, creates his identity in and through death. His famous proclamation, "When my country takes her place among the nations of the earth, then, and not till then, let my epitaph be written," contextualises his significance in terms of the politics of death. In following his dream and desire, he has taken the first steps toward his destruction: "his head / is cast in shadow and his lower body melts," and in stanzas 17 and 18 he becomes "post-human," "without a body, / broken in two by his fall." (This is a reference no doubt to his hanging and later beheading.) Significantly, however, the black hole of death is circumnavigated. Eurydice falls behind, but Orpheus emerges from the underworld. And even after being pulled apart he is "free of all body, his breath / giving out before his song" (*HTL*, 102). The encounter with the abyss of annihilation creates an identity for Orpheus and of course for Emmet as a national "saint," which is carried back to life. This identity is no longer congruent or harmonious. Anxiety, loss, and mourning are inseparable parts of his personality, and his voice, "with something dark and thirsty about it, / . . . / . . . states this lack clearly" (*HTL*, 102). The ambivalence of the first part of the poem is taken a step further. Not only are life and death divided, but their essential interpretation also founders. Death, as a giver of meaning and identity, ceases to fulfill its singularly destructive function, and life, because it is filled with the grief of encountering death, is no longer the blissful harmony represented by chestnuts and butter. Orpheus (Emmet) comes to life as an artist in this harrowing ambivalence when, in stanzas 22–23, "A shock wounds his windpipe, / one is too dark, the other splits his throat, / liable to rend from within" (*HTL*, 102). He is alive as an artist, but his human body is torn apart:

> His severed head continues to sing
> as it floats down the Heber
> and is immersed in stagnant winter water. (*HTL*, 102)

In a political context, Emmet's Irish identity and significance are created by his refusal to accept life or death in singular terms. The only epitaph that duly captures his significance is this ambiguous poem, which successfully depicts the universal impenetrability of the concept of identity. The identity of the poet Orpheus-Emmet is precariously balanced between origin and oblivion and its true realization does not come about until he is no more (or less) than a floating head landing on the island of Lesbos. Here he is "winnowed and purged and stellified— / true forge embroidered in gold and writing" (*HTL*, 102). The last two stanzas situate the speaker back at the moment of initiation in the underworld, where, glancing at death, the poet says to Orpheus and Orpheus to Eurydice:

> I don't want,
> I don't want you
> to rest in the leisure times of the cosmos:
>
> for we do not sing "Requiem"
> for such a soul,
> but the "Gaudeamus" Mass. (*HTL*, 102)

Euridyce, the face of death, the ultimate threshold between origin and oblivion, gives meaning to the concept of identity, which can only be seen, claimed, and articulated at that vulnerable moment when her face is still visible but already swallowed by darkness. In this text, standing on the docks, awaiting his death, Robert Emmet writes his own epitaph. McGuckian's self-confessed purpose in writing this poem was to commemorate Emmet's death in a way that would serve as a memorial to and apotheosis of his life.[25] However, the poem itself is less ideological cant for a political resurrection of a nationalist icon than a thoughtful meditation on death itself as a force inherent in identity formation.

"The Deadest Deaths Are the Best" (*HTL*, 47) has a somewhat more direct approach to mortality. The title is a quotation from Montaigne's essay "That to Study Philosophy Is to Learn to Die."[26] The central thesis of the essay is that facing death takes away death's greatest power over humans: fear. Montaigne argues that incorporating the thought of death into his life allows him to use his time wisely and without fear. Encountering death is the fulfillment of life. The deadest deaths are the best, he argues, because they portray mortality as total and immediate oblivion and with that gesture liberate the mind. He says, "The premeditation of death is the premeditation of liberty; he who has learned to die has forgot what it is to be a slave."[27] McGuckian opens the poem with the image of a corpse: "You lay, quiet, / herded into a ring / by the exploded tree" (*HTL*, 47). The dead body, maybe that of Judas, is "comely as a church." "But it was I who was / nailed there firmly" (*HTL*, 47), says the voice of Jesus perhaps. The juxtaposition of savior-betrayer sets the tone of the poem. Duality, which also dominates the previous poem, shapes the conceptualization of identity. The next stanza sees Narcissus, or, more precisely, his reflection:

> His arms mark
> the beginning of an embrace,
> the embrace that is
> only a splash. (*HTL*, 47)

The goddess, Nemesis, cursed Narcissus and condemned him to fall in love with his own reflection because he had ignored all the girls and nymphs who loved him. He sees himself in a spring and dies. Again, death happens through a fatal glance. Orpheus looks back to Eurydice, and Narcissus looks at himself. Both men see death at "the beginning of an embrace," and the identity of both men is formed by that encounter. "Deadest Deaths Are the Best" reads like a love poem to Robert Emmet,[28] whose epitaph provides the central energy of this volume. Created at the instant of departure, Emmet personifies and frames the Christian and classical references McGuckian lists in these poems. He is created when he is destroyed, and his art and memory come to life with his demolition. "Image and spectre . . . / snake within each other" (*HTL*, 47), and Emmet's undoing becomes the foundation for a national identity narrative. His name is saved from Lethe, the ancient river of forgetting, where the shades of the dead have to drink to forget about their past lives on earth.

Emmet therefore is rescued from oblivion and is portrayed as "the aisleless horizon" of remembering.[29] A sense of national identity for Medbh McGuckian is therefore constructed through the iconic image of a national hero. However, the threshold existence of Robert Emmet epitomizes the intricacies of identity formation. Achieving his goal in an unwritten epitaph, Emmet symbolizes the diverse pressures in claiming a singular and fundamental sense of identity. In other words, sometimes stating "the lack clearly" ("Forcing Music to Speak," *HTL*, 104) is all it takes to be heard.

The imagery of death in *Had I a Thousand Lives* characterizes the dynamics of identity formation. Identity, interpreted here as a construct of continual change and development, incorporates its own undoing. The political pressures of identity formation evoke a poetical response through reshuffling conventional metaphors of self. Death, in this context, is no longer interpreted only as the ultimate obliteration of life. Seen as a threshold, death gains center stage as the ultimate space and time which defines human, and poetic, expression. Written in memory of the execution of two nationalist heroes, the volume surpasses political veneration and rhetoric and concentrates again on the imaginative (and personal) interaction of past and present. *The Face of the Earth* explores the themes of death and violence as sites of identity formation, and addresses their influence on McGuckian's poetical consciousness. As she describes: "Death is not something that should be used as an excuse for not saying things. Life is short."[30]

Poetry and Prayer in *The Book of the Angel*

The Book of the Angel[31] offers a genuinely new departure within McGuckian's oeuvre. In this collection dedicated to angels,[32] McGuckian reconsiders issues of religion, spirituality, identity, and, perhaps most significantly, the linguistic erosion of prayer and death. The central theme of the volume, prayer, becomes an alternative language of poetic and political expression. The performance of composition is placed in the context of divine creation, and the figure of the angel is employed to represent transience and an alternative medium of communication. The process of writing is contextualized as prayer, and the unstable speaking (praying) self becomes the recipient of communication, who is simultaneously distanced as divine and pulled close as human. This peculiar language has no communicational purpose, and the reader is displaced as recipient and becomes positioned within the process of prayer (reading thus also becomes praying). However, this kind of poetic prayer is secularized and humanized, and the central idea remains to disrupt patterns of communication. In terms of politics, the volume is a metaphysical and spiritual meditation which seeks to explore alternative avenues of expression.

In the Old Irish text, *Liber Angeli*, or *Book of the Angel*, Saint Patrick discusses his ecclesiastical position in Armagh with an angel. Appropriating the title of this eighth-century work for her collection, McGuckian meditates on religion, national identity, and, most importantly, the unique, metaphysical composition as dialogue between the divine and the secular. Her volume is centered around the figure of the angel, who becomes the embodiment of transition. He is Christ, and she is the muse—the angel's gender, as well as its language, occupies the in-between spaces of the poetic imagination, connecting a powerful divine presence to a stubbornly real sense of self. The volume is divided into five distinctive parts, each focusing on a particular perspective of this metaphysical dialogue.

The opening sequence centers on the exploration of self. The angel is represented as a secular, corporeal being who is trapped and enclosed within the boundaries of the real. "The Publisher of Inwardness" (*BTA*, 11), the introductory poem of part 1, charts the inner workings of the poetic self: "I photograph asleep / like the detachable soul of a child." Words imitate divine creation to form a world in communion with the figure of the angel: ". . . taking his lifetime / into my mouth as a word / to make a world." The resulting language, however, remains "a word that ends up under / sea-ice, or a parable / by the seashore embroidering dawn." This claustrophobic setting introduces the voice of frustration that ripples throughout the first part of the volume. There is a tangible tension between the voices of the secular and the divine. "Four Voices without an Instrument" (*BTA*, 19) intricately traces the frustration of finding adequate channels of communications. The opening of the poem describes Easter as a perpetual, self-repeating process:

> Another March month has come
> to raise the temperature of the world,
> a self-opening, clear, in mourning,
> becoming light. (*BTA*, 19)

However, the "light" of resurrection is swallowed up by the eternal and irreversible cycle of the planets "where the moon falls awake / into its own mouth / till day and night are equal" (*BTA*, 19). Religion, and Catholicism in particular, frame the poem's main focus on language and communication. The next stanza introduces the imagery of the "blue city" which "has swollen / or returned to itself / in its dark ship / the reverberating sea." As an animate existence, the city is associated with the movements of the previous stanzas: the perpetual cycle of Easter, night and day, and the city's life expose an ultimate lack of communication with anything or anyone beyond themselves. Just as the moon speaks only to its own mouth, so does the city, most probably Belfast, return to its own darkness night and day. The political divides of the city are, therefore, portrayed as a self-perpetuating process, which is trapped in its own vicious cycle of silence.

It is not surprising, therefore, that the religious "light" of the resurrection is assumed "like a bell in the air / already out of tune" and without relevance (*BTA*, 19).[33] However, the next stanza introduces the most significant focus of the poem, communication:

> Yet since we have been a conversation,
> the three-in-one sign
> of your stained-glass voice
> has become my chosen one. (*BTA*, 19)

The "three-in-one sign," representing the Holy Trinity and the poetic self add up to the four voices of the title, still without their instrument. Thus the very existence of religion provides a framework of communication, "a garden surrounded by other gardens, / housing the seasons" (*BTA*, 19). It seems that reaching out is not possible without realizing that both sections of the religious and political divide are inherently involved with, and implicated in, each other. Religion here is not understood in an ecclesiastical sense as the church but rather as a spiritual foreboding of death:

> Though our lives may have overlapped
> the musicians that blew out their candles
> and left the stage, one by one,
> now blow for me
> a sunburst of winds
> on their lowest strings; (*BTA*, 19)

The "musicians" carry the only instrument heard equally by everyone: death. However, the poem does not end on a gloomy note. Rather, out of a mutual understanding ("we have been a conversation") appears the figure of an angel, who, with its transience and ambivalence, embodies the joy and frustration of finding an instrument for one's voice:

so that not without wings,
when the mist vanishes,
the brightening, endangered earth
is the year's first angel. (*BTA*, 19)

It is almost as if McGuckian has found in the image of an angel a way to express her "longing for wordlessness," a poem without its words.[34]

The tension of communication is also portrayed in "The Dream Theatre" (*BTA*, 12), an earlier poem in the volume. It displays the stage where the struggle between (secular) memories and (divine) dreams is played out, creating a schizophrenic backdrop to the formation of a coherent identity:

In the outline of your dream
you turn your head to the right,
but look to the left,

your mouth a little open as if
to bite, but never attacking thin air. (*BTA*, 12)

The poem concludes with the spheres of the otherworld taking center stage, where the realm of the unconscious dreams permeates the "empty, high-quality waking" of the poetic mind:

Until, note against note,
a dream comes on, and becomes
a place to live,

a dream-play in the open loop
of our dreams, now and equal,
white and coloured,

writing out the sleep debt,
a hundred minutes of dreaming,
underneath that late, inner star. (*BTA*, 12)

"Armed Dance" (*BTA*, 25) confers divine powers of creation on the poetic self. However, this does not involve the hubris of a human assumption of godly powers. Rather, the poem depicts the vulnerability and frustration of creativity:

I held in the same hand
male and female stones:
one blue variety giving
sweet light
like the sea close to shore;

and my increasing
certainty of touch
feared the virtue
of this weathered world
might be lost—(*BTA*, 25)

The creation of the world in Genesis takes place through the act of naming, by separating forms from the void. This biblical act of division, which produced the recognizable shape of the universe, functions as a source of anxiety in this poem. What if the waters would rather have stayed one with the earth and this brutal dissection is the origin of all human disquiet? The earth, "the original ark," holds the sky as its body "in its distant embrace" as "his limping heart." Yet, there is another dimension, another world, which interprets this anxiety. It is what McGuckian calls the "seed of language . . . the dark brown / re-enchantment of his voice" (*BTA*, 25). Poetic creation emulates divine language, but rather than forming a new universe, it remains, as the first poem indicated, the publishing of inward tension and frustration.[35]

Part 2 of the book is a powerful sequence of nine poems written in honor of the nine muses. The muses are differently portrayed as angels, Christ, the Virgin Mary, or a saint; their only constant is their characterization as mediators between the secular and the divine. The Gospel narrative, which frames this part of the book, takes center stage in "A Chrisom Child" (*BTA*, 30). The title refers to a child who dies before a month old, but the poem depicts the Annunciation, the moment when Gabriel offers his good news. Or, to be more precise, we see the moment when "it is impossible to tell . . . whether he has already spoken" (*BTA*, 30). Gabriel, as an angel, carries in him the ambiguity of divine happiness and human sadness, the joy of eternal life and the despair of death:

The cushion plays such a very ambiguous
role, and the fall of his hair
may be compared to a crucifix

that previously disfigured the sky.
The wood, cherry, that within so short
a radius, carried death at its heart. (*BTA*, 30)

The Annunciation thus also becomes the news of death. Christ, the chrisom child, carries his death at the moment of his conception. The relevance of this to poetic creativity is complex. Gabriel is the messenger of both life and death, and a poem about his image becomes a standpoint from which to contemplate the origin and purpose of writing.[36] From a religious perspective the Annunciation is the most significant proclamation of faith that makes God into man, but, as Lucy Collins argues, it is also a text that most deeply questions meaning within language:

> That the voice should exist prior to, yet also come after, wordless meaning is significant when exploring the trope of the Annunciation itself. If the words of the Angel Gabriel are productive of meaning, then they must be spoken in order for God to become Man. If, however, language is an expression of what is already understood, then it becomes inseparable from the divine will.[37]

The Virgin Mary's response to the Annunciation, the Magnificat, gains a very different interpretation in this context. As Collins argues, it can be viewed "as the text from which the Virgin Mary cannot escape, or the one in which she finds her most meaningful articulation."[38] "A Chrisom Child" in a sense is also a prayer of "magnificat" where the poet simultaneously accepts the creation of, and creates, the poetic language of life and death.

The fourth poem in this sequence, "A More" (*BTA*, 32), follows the theme of "A Chrisom Child" and looks at stained-glass representations of Christ, Gabriel, and the Virgin Mary. The stanzas trace the journey of contemplating eyes, from one figure to another. The images, though stationary, are full of subdued activity ("They sit in each other's presence / in a room neither can stand up in"; "she is caught with a breath half-taken" [*BTA*, 32]). The duality and tension between animate and inanimate existence are further enhanced, and toward the end of the poem it is the scrutinizing eyes that are rendered passive and submissive:

> What the simplified eyes experience deepest
> . . .
> is the candle-burned pearl on her head
> like a triple head within solar rays,
> her badly rubbed star-halo's
> long association of vases,
>
> the unfinished, leave-taking wings. (*BTA*, 32)

McGuckian defies the assumed perspectives of onlooker and object and transposes the reader into an interactive limbo of the in-between. "Saint Faith" (*BTA*, 38), the last poem of this sequence, positions the poetic self back in the lines, exploring its position vis-à-vis the divine agents who have dominated the previous pages:

> All in all, there were too many spires
> and waves, more than my own footsteps. (*BTA*, 38)

The method of portraying the angels as works of art (paintings, sculptures), freezing them in a moment, paradoxically results in capturing their transience: what we see is a *lack* of a smile or a movement. This absence of animation highlights the angels' inherent desire for life and reflects upon humanity's entrapment in the still finality of existence. The angel, portrayed here as "summer," eventually breaks out from its statuesque immobility. However, significantly, this takes place within the poetic consciousness:

> Summer stood nude, as alone as the rain,
> her family smile absent, as many sleepless
> eyes on her body as she has feathers.
>
> I heard a roar of wings, a darker flesh,
> and started walking, lest the mountain
> should soar right out of the book,
>
> then kneel down inwardly
> over a holy organ such as a feather. (*BTA*, 38)

The "book" gives birth to the monumental image of the angel, who "inwardly" encounters him/herself. However, this spiritual union happens only in the conditional. The poetic self walks away, hearing, but never actually comes face to face with the angel. This is because the only possible encounter is in "saint faith," where both parties communicate.[39] The immobility of the angel is in stark contrast to the walking image of the person, and it is the "book," or poetic imagination, which eventually propels an imaginary meeting between the divine and the secular faiths of this poem. Thus, as a fitting conclusion to the nine poems of this sequence, "Saint Faith" captures a frozen moment in the "life" of a divine identity, creating an atmosphere of unease about the finality and fragility of human existence.

The angels, who occupy these poems and accompany the reader on a spiritualized journey, remain ungraspable, shapeless, and in most poems genderless, yet lovingly humanized transient creatures: "Words remain on the shore, but when the angel / falls in love, with his different prayer movements, / he is the perfect human"("Poem Rhyming in 'J,'" *BTA*, 85). "Kaddish," although published in McGuckian's next volume, *The Currach Requires No Harbours*,[40] first appeared around the time of *The Book of the Angel* and thematically offers another instructive portrayal of the figure of the angel. A Jewish prayer of mourning, Kaddish is a form of thanksgiving for the life of the deceased. This poem is the closest the reader gets to McGuckian's angel: her hand, face, spine, eyebrows, and hair are poetically described in the first four stanzas. However, the description fits a corpse more than a living being: "her face at the lips of the sky / the colour of moonlight, without form, / without looking" (*CRNH*, 26). Is this the angel of death? Simon Critchley argues that

> the paradox at the heart of the representation of death is best conveyed by the figure of *prosopopeia*, the trope by which an absent or imaginary person is presented as speaking or acting, a form which indicates the failure of presence, a face which withdraws behind the form which presents it. The representation of death is always a mask—a *memento mori*—behind which nothing stands.[41]

In fact, the angel of this poem is significantly distanced from the speaking subject, set "away from my door." Her ethereal beauty is contrasted with the claustrophobic and depressing setting of the human heart in the stark shadow of the concentration camps:

> My heart that burns like an oven
> where the dead are locked
> and cold or warm memory
>
> lengthens out their shadow
> or buys them prayer. (*CRNH*, 26)

Prayer becomes the space which allows the interaction to take place between the angel and poetic self. However, whereas in the poems of *The Book of the Angel* the language of prayer is portrayed as the desire of humans, here it is the angel who internalizes desire, "coveting" the speaker's "indigo skirt." This transformation confuses the direction of communication: "And her desiring left its mark / on the child like glass in her womb" (*CRNH*, 26). The glass reflects a perplexing human incapability for interaction, and the poem concludes with the denial of faith:

> Now I do not see any colourableness
> in empty winds that could be
>
> spirit-laced, the turning over
> of the world by ankle-bells
> and sheer fabric-lack. (*CRNH*, 26)

The poem mourns the angel of death and also mourns a failure of encounter between the sacred and the secular. However, it celebrates its own lack and says Kaddish for a dead angel, symbolizing the ultimate deconstruction of the poetic language of prayer.[42]

The angels' dichotomy as divine and secular imaginaries embodies the ambiguity of poetry as experienced by McGuckian. The figure of the angel, her "winged muse," radically alters our preconceptions of human interaction. Alternating their position between sender and recipient, the angels fundamentally disturb routes of language transmission. The dislocated reader has no choice but to accept this dialogic relation to McGuckian's works, otherwise the poems simply get lost in the labyrinth of logical decoding. Part 3 of *The Book of the Angel* turns our attention from the heavens to the depths of the earth, and in the "small gaps of awkwardness between overlapping leaves . . . a rope vase / of flowers returns the angels / to the ground" ("Garden Homage," *BTA*, 39). In fact, most of these poems investigate how living things can turn eternally inanimate in their association with death. The angels of this section are saints whose death, rather than life, is celebrated ("her womb a transparent crystal / turning into a brown relic," ["Hand Reliquary, Ave Maria Lane," *BTA*, 40]). and Christ on the cross, whose "kind of everyday death" instigates the language of prayer, "something prior / to the sentences we speak," ("Fallen God of Bone," *BTA*, 53). The poem "The Gold That Is Worn by God,"[43] also considers the relationship of prayer to poetic creation. The poem opens by emphasizing the absence of tangible faith:

> The star or crown that an angel
> Once drew in the snow
> Is either not shown or trimmed away[44]

The fragile belief in the divine is inherent in human existence and is portrayed here as a "lack of desire," a "skin-tight coat of mail." The body has a central role to play in these lines: spiritual faith, which is portrayed as the fundamental frustration of lacking and desiring, seems to be physically attached to the self. The title of the poem, "The Gold That Is Worn by God," also reflects on physicality. The language of prayer, disguised in the multiplicity of "voices" in "differing fields, / pressed against the back / of a god-coloured valley," creates the space for the interaction between the divine and the human. However, McGuckian portrays this interaction in its absurdity, "like a bed of white bronze / looking out through the rent / in a strawberry," to emphasize the ambiguity inherent in the language of any kind of religious prayer (a transmission of information without a physical recipient). The gold that is worn by God, thus, represents the jewels of human frustration, the language of lack so skillfully mastered by McGuckian.

Part 4 of *The Book of the Angel* abandons the human perspective and turns toward the heavens again. However, the few poems of this section introduce a celestial perception, rather than a representation of the divine. In "Angel's Eye View of the Bridge of Sighs" (*BTA*, 60) the image of the window is made visible, becoming the central metaphor of the divine eye. "Recipe for Red" (*BTA*, 63) reflects on ruins and a "strangely molten landscape" where windows

> loom pale, particularly across water,
> their fire-polish rupturing the surface
> like rinse-waters in a mesh of darkness. (*BTA*, 63)

Possibly to reflect on the horrors of 9/11,[45] the colors of explosion and fog dominate the poem and create an otherworldly landscape where, from a human perspective, nothing makes sense:

> Sudden mists poise on the false edge
> in swathes and pockets whose colour is lowly,
> the humblest colour, the balance to green,
>
> or milled white—a spirit colour
> holding the world together, interlaced,
> however dreamy. (*BTA*, 63)

However, as in some of the poems discussed above, interaction with the divine creates space for interpretation and thus the poem concludes with the color of life, red:

> . . . And one visible arc
> that seems to share our incarnation
> then and now traces the earthy rose. (*BTA*, 63)

The scattering of colors throughout the poem is symbolic of the sense of loss and mourning experienced by the speaking subject. Grief, as Judith Butler argues,

> displays the thrall in which our relations with others hold us, in ways that we cannot always recount or explain, in ways that often interrupt the self-conscious account of ourselves we might try to provide, in ways that challenge the very notion of ourselves as autonomous and in control. I might try to tell a story here about what I am feeling, but it would have to be a story in which the very "I"

> who seeks to tell the story is stopped in the midst of the telling; the very "I" is called into question by its relation to the Other, a relation that does not precisely reduce me to speechlessness, but does nevertheless clutter my speech with signs of its undoing.[46]

The "earthy rose," therefore, is the color of the shared experiences of loss, but it is also a color which becomes the "one visible arc" of the expression of life.

Most of the fifteen poems of part 5 take death as their central theme. However, this somber subject is brightened by the preceding four sections, and the act of dying is more like a "delicate bridge" or a "sacrament" ("The Tenth Muse," *BTA*, 71), which completes the prayer-like language of the volume. In *The Book of the Angel* Medbh McGuckian has touched on a sensitive and highly politicized subject without succumbing to either religious romanticism or overt activism. Catholicism and its iconography in particular play a significantly stronger role in this volume than in any earlier collection,[47] signaling on the one hand a more relaxed identification with her upbringing, and on the other a subversive political and aesthetic interpretation of their role in contemporary life. The angels in these poems serve her well in formulating a subtle sense of spiritual and political awareness, one which nevertheless eschews straightforward ideological commentary. Her repeated assertion that the best poems would be written without words signifies a desire for formulating a specific language of poetry which would overwrite patterns of communication and political decoding. In this volume, McGuckian's poems, like her angels, delicately balance secular concerns with the language of unheard prayer, suggesting a newfound sensitivity to cultural embeddedness and spiritual understanding. *The Book of the Angel* signals a departure from the earlier volumes in its daring, yet subversive, engagement with overt Catholic iconography. Focusing on prayer, it suggests an alternative mode of expression that offers a different, and genuinely innovative, kind of poetical and political meaning.

Notes

1. Paul Arthur, "Republicanism and the Implementation of the Agreement—An Academic Perspective," Working Paper in British-Irish Studies, no. 44 (Dublin: Institute for British-Irish Studies, University College of Dublin, 2005), http://www.ucd.ie/ibis/filestore/wp2005/44/44_mmpa.pdf (accessed October 23, 2013).

2. Medbh McGuckian, *The Face of the Earth* (Oldcastle, Ireland: Gallery Press, 2002) (hereafter cited as *FOE*). There has been relatively little critical attention paid to this

particular volume. For a review see Moynagh Sullivan, review of *The Face of the Earth*, by Medbh McGuckian, *Irish University Review: Journal of Irish Studies* 33, no. 1 (Spring–Summer 2003): 237–40.

3. Explanations for the terms "knee-woman" and "world-woman" can be found in Noragh Jones, *Power of Raven, Wisdom of Serpent: Celtic Women's Spirituality* (Edinburgh: Floris Books, 1994), 79 and 179, respectively.

4. Simon Critchley, *Very Little . . . Almost Nothing: Death, Philosophy, Literature* (London: Routledge, 1997), 27.

5. Ibid., 32.

6. John's Gospel opens: "In the beginning was the Word . . . and the Word was God" (King James Version, John 1:1). McGuckian turns this process around and suggests that for the birth of the human word first there has to be God.

7. Michael Duff, ed., "Dug-Out," *First World War: The War to End All Wars*, May 25, 2006, http://www.firstworldwar.com/atoz/dugout.htm (accessed October 22, 2013).

8. Politically, the fragmented female body is also a signifier of Ireland, as McGuckian indicates through the image of her mother: "She's gradually losing her sight, her hearing, one leg is gone. It's a bit like if she symbolises Ireland, that it's been more and more destroyed, but it won't die, it's been chopped to pieces." In "An Interview with Medbh McGuckian," by María Jesús Lorenzo-Modia, *European English Messenger* 13, no. 2 (Autumn 2004): 40.

9. Maurice Merleau-Ponty, quoted in Richard Kearney ed., *Modern Movements in European Philosophy* (Manchester: Manchester University Press, 1994), 88.

10. Most of these refer to architecture and art that can be found in Rome today.

11. "The Navicella," in "The Companion Guide to Rome," by Georgina Masson, saintpetersbasilica.org, http://saintpetersbasilica.org/Interior/Navicella/Navicella.htm (accessed January 17, 2012).

12. One of the source texts of the poem is John T. Spike, *Masaccio* (New York: Abbeville Press, 1995), 42, which also describes a fresco attributed to Masaccio called *Navicella.*

13. James Holden, *In Search of Vinteuil: Music, Literature and a Self Regained* (Eastbourne: Sussex Academic Press, 2010), 30.

14. Linda Biesele Hall, *Mary, Mother and Warrior: The Virgin in Spain and the Americas* (Austin: University of Texas Press, 2004), 54. The original event is commemorated every August with a "snowfall" of white rose petals within the Santa Maria Maggiore Church in Rome.

15. Lucy Collins, "Joyful Mysteries: Language and Spirituality in Medbh McGuckian's Recent Poetry," in *Irish Women Writers: New Critical Perspectives*, ed. Elke D'hoker, Raphaël Ingelbien, and Hedwig Schwall (Oxford: Peter Lang, 2011), 44.

16. Medbh McGuckian, *Had I a Thousand Lives* (Oldcastle, Ireland: Gallery Press, 2003) (hereafter cited as *HTL*).

17. Thomas Russell (1767–1803) was a deeply religious Protestant of the established church, although his mother was probably a Catholic. He was an extremely close friend of Wolfe Tone and a founding member of the Society of United Irishmen, where he proved exceptional both for his interest in Gaelic culture and his respect for the common people. He was a determined campaigner for Catholic emancipation. It was his influence which helped convince Tone that a revolution was possible in Ireland. Russell was imprisoned

between1796 and 1802 for political activities. In 1803 he was captured in Dublin, where he had travelled in an attempt to rescue Robert Emmet. He was executed at Downpatrick Prison. Robert Emmet (1778–1803) was born in Dublin and educated at Trinity College. Although a brilliant student, he was expelled in 1798 for republican sympathies. He became active in reorganizing the United Irish Society after the failed rebellion of that year. Following the fiasco of his attempted rising in 1803, he was captured, tried, and hurriedly executed. See Marianne Elliott, "Thomas Russell (1767–1803)" and "Robert Emmet (1778–1803)," *Oxford Dictionary of National Biography*, ed. H. C. G. Matthew and Brian Harrison, (Oxford: Oxford University Press, 2004), online edition at http://www.oxforddnb.com/view/article/24339 and http://www.oxforddnb.com/view/article/8796

18. For a recent and comprehensive treatment of the 1916 Rising and its chief characters see Charles Townshend, *Easter 1916: The Irish Rebellion* (London: Penguin Books, 2006).

19. This subject has been addressed by Michael Laffan in a paper entitled, "Illustrious Corpses: Nationalist Funerals in Independent Ireland," unpublished paper presented at the "Politics of Dead Bodies" conference, School of History and Archives, University College of Dublin, March 10, 2006.

20. See Melissa F. Zeiger, *Beyond Consolation: Death, Sexuality, and the Changing Shapes of Elegy* (Ithaca, NY: Cornell University Press, 1997), 2.

21. The blatant gender politics is also an intriguing part of the story.

22. See Aurelia Ghezzi, "Quis Tantus Furor? Modern Versions of Orpheus Looking Back," *Southern Comparative Literature* 7 (May 1983): 9–10, quoted in Zeiger, *Beyond Consolation*, 12.

23. Critchley, *Very Little . . . Almost Nothing*, 42.

24. The church described is St. Catherine's on Thomas Street, Dublin, where Emmet's execution was carried out. Medbh McGuckian, e-mail to the author, March 9, 2004.

25. McGuckian, e-mail to the author, March 9, 2004.

26. Michel de Montaigne, "That to Study Philosophy Is to Learn to Die," in *The Complete Works of Michel de Montaigne*, ed. William Hazlitt, (London: J. Templeman, 1842), digitized by Google Books, May 2008, http://books.google.ie/books?id=YvcZAAAAYAAJ (accessed October 22, 2013).

27. Ibid., 29.

28. McGuckian calls this "more of a love poem [to Emmet], more personal, not an apotheosis." Medbh McGuckian, e-mail message to the author, March 9, 2004.

29. It is interesting to note that for McGuckian writing about Emmet is a highly "personal" experience, akin to "meeting" someone in person. She describes this in an interview with Leontia Flynn: "Well this is it, you see, this is poetry. And I've also met Robert Emmet, which is why I wrote the poem for Robert Emmet—because how could you write anything if you hadn't actually got some sort of experience or epiphany?" Leontia Mary Flynn, "Reading Medbh McGuckian," PhD diss., Queens University Belfast, 2004, 250.

30. Lorenzo-Modia, "An Interview with Medbh McGuckian," 40.

31. Medbh McGuckian, *The Book of the Angel* (Oldcastle, Ireland: Gallery Press, 2004) (hereafter cited as *BTA*).

32. McGuckian said: "The next book the only thread I've got through it is the word 'angel'. It's going to be for Gregory [Peck] and it's going to be called *The Book of the*

Angel. . . . But this is just corroborating, because I have this thing about angels." Leontia Mary Flynn, "Interview with Medbh McGuckian," in Flynn, "Reading Medbh McGuckian," 253.

33. Note the association of "bell" with Belfast mentioned by McGuckian in an interview. Lorenzo-Modia, "An Interview with Medbh McGuckian," 42.

34. "I find, in me, a longing for wordlessness almost or for something poetry can achieve through words but leaving them behind." "Interview with Medbh McGuckian," by John Brown, in his *In the Chair: Interviews with Poets from the North of Ireland* (Cliffs of Moher, Ireland: Salmon, 2002), 172.

35. Many of the titles in this section of *BTA* indicate a sense of imprisonment: "Closed Bells" (*BTA*, 16); "Poem Without Words" (*BTA*, 18); "Four Voices without an Instrument" (*BTA*, 19); "Addressed to Fanny on Her Confirmation" (*BTA*, 21); or "Armed Dance" (*BTA*, 25).

36. James Joyce also makes this connection when Stephen ponders on inspiration in *A Portrait of the Artist as a Young Man*. He says: "In the virgin womb of the imagination the word was made flesh. Gabriel the seraph had come to the virgin's chamber." James Joyce, *The Portrait of the Artist as a Young Man*, ed. Richard Ellmann, rev. ed. (London: Jonathan Cape, 1956), 221.

37. Collins, "Joyful Mysteries," 43.

38. Ibid., 43.

39. McGuckian is probably also hinting here at a receptiveness which she requires of her readers, a kind of communicative space of "saint faith."

40. The original publication of the poem "Kaddish" appeared in the *European English Messenger* 13, no. 2 (Autumn 2004): 45. Medbh McGuckian, *The Currach Requires No Harbours* (Oldcastle, Ireland: Gallery Press, 2006), 26 (hereafter cited as *CRNH*).

41. Critchley, *Very Little . . . Almost Nothing*, 26.

42. For an alternative and convincing reading of this poem see Collins, "Joyful Mysteries," 51–2.

43. Although not included in *BTA*, its publication coincides with it. *European English Messenger* 13, no. 2 (Autumn 2004): 46.

44. *European English Messenger*, 13, no. 2 (Autumn 2004): 46.

45. The back cover of the book jacket for *BTA* suggests that some of the poems "are responses to the apocalyptic wars engendered by September 11."

46. Judith Butler, *Precarious Life: The Powers of Mourning and Violence* (London: Verso, 2004), 23.

47. McGuckian claims in an interview that "recently the books would be more into Catholicism itself, you know, trying to look at Catholicism and speak for Catholicism." Lorenzo-Modia, "An Interview with Medbh McGuckian," 42.

4

Inward Journeys: *The Currach Requires No Harbours*, *My Love Has Fared Inland*, and *The High Caul Cap*

In her last three volumes published to date Medbh McGuckian returns to some of her earlier themes but also, simultaneously, conducts a retrospective journey through her creative oeuvre. *The Currach Requires No Harbours* and *My Love Has Fared Inland* are both collections about journeying, while *The High Caul Cap* reverses this theme and looks at loss and disintegration. The *Currach Requires No Harbours*, considers, in a manner familiar from the two preceding volumes, the effects and meanings of political violence. The poetic psyche is positioned as the observing and also as the suffering subject, and the reader is invited to partake in this introspection, rather than to evaluate. Similarly, *My Love Has Fared Inland* opens up a window into the depths of the creative self. Here the journey is purely contemplative and considers the significance of poetry writing and its implications. Published in 2006 and in 2008 respectively these volumes trace the author's increasingly rich and diverse language, and they bear witness to her unique manner of poetry writing. McGuckian's latest volume, published in 2012, returns to loss as its central metaphor, accompanying the poet's mother's journey toward death. This chapter offers a close reading of a variety of poems from all three collections which outline the poet's retrospection as well as developing new interests.

Violet-Lidded Eye: Suffering and Introspection in *The Currach Requires No Harbours*

This volume was born out of the violence McGuckian's daughter Emer experienced in Belfast one day coming home from school, which, understandably, had a profound effect on the poet. McGuckian recounted the details of the event in an interview as follows:

> This bus [the school-bus] would take all the children to begin with, but would then drop off the Protestant children in the Protestant area, and then ferry the Catholics up to the more Catholic districts. It's very clear where that border is. The bus was attacked there. All the Protestants got off and attacked the bus because they knew there were only Catholics left. Emer got a brick thrown at her head. She took an epileptic fit. It had hit her eye.[1]

The traumatic effect of this sectarian violence makes *The Currach Requires No Harbours* a heavily politicized volume, albeit in a lyrical sense. The first sixteen poems of the collection reflect on the injury her daughter suffered and on the poet's struggle to come to terms with the seemingly unchanged violent landscape she lives in, which is exacerbated by the helplessness she experienced as the victim's mother. These poems are scattered with the image of the "eye" with abundant explorations of this sensory organ's metaphorical meanings. "Seeing" and "blindness" are central concepts that shape the poet's understanding of politics, religion, and family responsibilities.

"A Book of Rains" (*CRNH*, 24) offers a good example of the poet's technique in fusing together the traumatic experience of violence with self-expression. The poem's title invokes meteorological imagery.[2] By manipulating nature and art together in the title McGuckian draws attention to the issue of control, where "book" and "rains" are at opposing ends of human controllability. The poem opens with the exploration of whether "knowledge" and "weather" (or nature and humanity) can ever be reconciled:

> Sheer weather, weather that can be felt
> with the eyes, as snow cover,
> selling spring, the first climax
> of the year.
>
> Bending, turning, standing,
> walking with closed eyes,
> the pendent half-moon
> pupil in her eye
>
> composes a path
> that does not stop unless
> forever, patches of her
> knowledge blasted away. (*CRNH*, 24)

The "eyes" function as representative agents of "humanness": the weather's function is to bring it to the dimension of "feeling" beyond seeing. The disabled, injured eyes remain closed, but, significantly, *sensing* throughout the destabilizing event. These stanzas evoke the epileptic fit where "patches" of "knowledge" are "blasted away." The "rains" of the title overpower the "book," and the powers of nature take control of human agency. These lines reflect on the abject helplessness experienced by the speaker on a very personal level. The injury to the eye is viewed as an inevitable and fateful weather event that overrides precaution and the illusion of control. The second half of the poem elevates the narrative of this personal reflection to a philosophical level. Shane Alcobia-Murphy has pointed out that much of the rest of the poem is "borrowed" from Emmanuel Levinas's writing on the Other. As Alcobia-Murphy states, for Levinas "to be is to be for the other."[3] McGuckian attempts to piece together a poetic response to the moment of encountering the face of the wounded other:

> Where one would expect
> added red, or a hat
> of darkness, the line is traced
> in the trajectory of the blow
>
> that was dealt. (*CRNH*, 24)

These lines reflect on the viewer, not the sufferer. The focus switches to the perpetrator, trying to gain understanding through the "tracing" of the violent act. However, the encounter results in coming face to face with violence itself:

> . . . Having nothing
> at its disposal
> to not yield
> to the provocation,
>
> the time of dying
> cannot give itself
> the other shore,
> the future that death gives
>
> is not yet time,
> when his forsakenness
> draws near, under the force
> of the lips of the blow received. (*CRNH*, 24)

The only change McGuckian inserted into the Levinasian text is the words "of the lips" in the last line, thus personifying death and death's kiss of violence. Levinas, near the place where these lines are taken from, argues that "beyond the visibility of whatever is unveiled, and prior to any knowledge about death, mortality lies in the other."[4] Seeing the wounded face in its vulnerability and nakedness creates an extreme exposure of self-expression. The "force" of the kiss of death refers back to the unpredictable violence of the weather experienced by the shut eyes of the first stanza. The personification of violence brings into focus not only the poet's empathy but also the poetic psyche's encounter with her own mortality through creativity.

"Consecrated Wafer" (*CRNH*, 21) also takes vision as its central metaphor to contemplate death. As the title suggests, the poem approaches the idea of sacramentality and faith in the context of mortality. The opening lines suggest that seeing is impaired in life and the world "withholds" its real meaning:

> The side of the world mists,
> withholds its broken-necked fruit.
> A curtain of freed light
> like silk doubled up
>
> (the shape of a woman,
> a white leaf painted
> after her breast) clouds
> the pool's gold-yellow roots. (*CRNH*, 21)

The "white leaf" referenced in the poem comes from a book written on the work of Frida Kahlo.[5] In it Ankori describes the "white leaf painted after her breast" in Kahlo's painting "My Nurse and I," and comments that Kahlo had a "white leaf painted after her breast . . . in order to balance it . . . because she could not think of anything else."[6] Kahlo's painting itself is of critical significance to this poem. The picture depicts Kahlo's native Indian nurse, breastfeeding a miniature grown-up Frida in her arms:

> Frida's mother was unable to breastfeed her because her sister Cristina was born just eleven months after her. She was therefore fed by a native Indian wet-nurse whom the family had hired for that sole purpose. The relationship between them appears distant and cold, reduced to the practical process of feeding. Because it was the adult Frida who had the memory, the baby has an adult head, and because she could not remember her wet nurse's facial features, she covered her face with a pre-Columbian funerary mask. . . . The wet nurse does not embrace or cuddle Frida . . . she displays her

> like a sacrificial offering. In this painting, Frida transformed the "*Madonna and Child*" mothering image into an expression of loss and separation from her own mother with whom she never really bonded.[7]

Kahlo mutates the nurturing, maternal image of breastfeeding into images of trauma and suffering. The painting contains a scroll on the bottom that was left empty, which suggests that she thought of it as an *ex voto* work, a painting depicting a tragedy or injury and an intervening saint, including an inscription which describes the event and gives thanks to the "divine intervention."[8] However, leaving the scroll unfilled emphasizes the lack of divine intervention, and its absence is inserted as the centerpiece of the story. Being breastfed by a wet nurse (a negative substitute for the mother) thus becomes associated with being fed by death which the funerary mask further highlights. Frida, the sacrificial offering looks away while milk dribbles into her mouth from the death-nurse's tree-like breast: the milk, and the corresponding rain in the picture, become symbols of death rather than nurturance. In addition, the plants seen in the painting morph into insects and become inseparable from them. The viewer is thus never sure whether it is a branch or a stick insect, a leaf or a caterpillar which is on show. And this is also what happens in McGuckian's poem:

> Water drips from the bark,
> the dark mannered woodland bees
> falter, as though slowed down by love.
> Voices from south of that grove
>
> divide themselves from mouth
> to flower to moth,
> their lips scoured by Lethe
> yet unharmed by the divine. (*CRNH*, 21)

The "voices" carry the message of death and permeate the nature imagery. The absence of the divine also brings into relief the spiritual perspective of the poem. The violence hinted at by the "broken-necked fruit" and by Lethe, the river of death, slowly and invisibly asserts itself in the poem, similarly to the way it happens in Kahlo's painting. Kahlo's work depicts the trauma of separation from the mother, while McGuckian seems to identify with the helplessness of the mother who inadvertently offers up her child to violence and sacrifice. Then, in the fifth stanza the "skyline," an image of open horizons, "seems to shed an eye, / a single, unpaired / violet-lidded eye" (*CRNH*, 21).

It seems that sight is focused on one thing, which is suffering and death. The injured eye, as in the previous poem, functions as a reminder of the incomprehensibility of suffering. The eye turns "outside itself" and becomes a "receiver," losing its facility to see and analyze. "Like ineffectual wings" the wounded eye cannot take the mind to a sphere of comprehension, but instead becomes a receptor. The title of the poem, "Consecrated Wafer," makes a subtle connection between the sacramental image of Christ's broken body within the Host and the injured eye. Church displays of the Eucharist encase it in an eye-like monstrance which serves as a reminder of both Christ's vulnerability and his omnipotence in this vulnerability. McGuckian observes the trauma in spiritual terms where suffering, "in its throwaway gracefulness," is "the only colour the dead can see." Ending the poem with these lines offers both hope through a Christian interpretation of suffering and also a fundamental human sadness and helplessness in having to witness trauma.

"Wood-cunning" (*CRNH*, 25) elaborates further on the traumatized mother-daughter relationship. The violent assault that injured the poet's daughter's eye takes central stage as the aftereffects of the event are observed:

> Only your eye, your silver eye,
> seems to have no sex, its deep look
> of dreamy greeting, the sense
> of a small bouquet
> in its weaker folds. (*CRNH*, 25)

The "deep look of dreamy greeting" is a quotation from *Goya: Images of Women.*[9] Goya's *Marchioness of Santa Cruz* painting depicts a supine young woman with a musical instrument in her hand, looking somewhat distractedly out of the picture. McGuckian seems to use this image as an idealized allegory for the injured daughter, outwardly still carrying the illusion of youth, together with the inheritance of feminine beauty:

> Your lips, a glass book,
> smell of the glass
> and beautiful women rest
> their weight in silver and gold
> on your acute youth. (*CRNH*, 25)

However, this stanza also contains another, somewhat more sinister reference to the Irish myth of Midhir and Éadaoin. Midhir visited his stepson, Aonghus, one day and lost his eye in an accident. Although it was replaced perfectly, he demanded restitution, asking his stepson to find for him the most beautiful maiden to marry, whom he knew to be Éadaoin. Aonghus had to work extremely hard to gain Éadaoin from her father, and one of his last tasks was to get him Éadaoin's "weight in silver and gold." McGuckian seems to symbolically equate the love-stricken Midhir with death who goes after the young woman's "acute youth." The next stanza contains a veiled reference to Éadaoin's later betrayal of the husband, whom she married in her second life. Midhir found out and visited her in disguise, later taking her to a place "on a hill near the court," gaining a kiss from her in the process,[10] referenced here as a "second begetting":

> The paths of your voice,
> plentiful and warm,
> make love a second begetting
> on a hill near the court, silver footed
> as your preference for unrest. (*CRNH*, 25)

The last two stanzas seem to explore the entwined relationship of love and death: the possibility of the young woman's death ("if your lips were to expire") accentuates the inevitability of death in life. This idea is also highlighted by the Christian symbolism of the "second begetting" mentioned in the previous stanza, which is a rebirth in love following death in Christ. The poem ends in depicting the helplessness of love:

> the echo of having known you,
> chieftain-to-be and amateur poet,
> would travel together with every
> legal and official kissing
> like a spear barely missing a plait of hair. (*CRNH*, 25)

Here the act of loving ("kissing") is associated with the murderous weapon ("spear") which could have caused so much damage. In a literal reading the poet might be referring directly to her daughter's injury, which could have turned out so much worse. Metaphorically speaking however, the poem explores the vulnerability of human love in the face of death. McGuckian said at a reading that she considers these poems written about her daughter's injury "highly political,"[11] not only in the sense of their reference to the Troubles, but also investigating the human cost of "trying to bring up kids" in this environment. As she succinctly put it: "The Troubles are never over, because people are still enduring."

However, McGuckian also claimed that *The Currach Requires No Harbours* is a "woman's book." The second part of the volume shifts the focus to (older) women and explores the metaphor of the "house" in this context. The image of the house is a powerful metaphor of ownership, belonging, and identity. In women's poetry in particular, it is often the site of containment and security, but also imprisonment. Women poets' interaction with the physical space of the house offers diverse avenues of investigation concerning their poetic constructs of identity. Gendered and ethnic subjects' narratives of domesticity will necessarily reflect the position their bodies inhabit in their given social space. The historical and conceptual connection between bodies and space is accentuated when the space in question, the house, is assigned a role in the conceptual makeup of an identity. In simple terms, if a house, and particularly the possession of a house, is seen as an essential component of a desired status and integrity, then the lack of a house necessarily becomes conceived as a physical and mental ailment hindering personal development. However, poetic constructs of identity simultaneously take into consideration personal, social, cultural, gender, and psychological manifestations of identity. This means that the inherent tensions among these facets often present themselves as the starting point of interpretation. The answer to the question "who am I" can concurrently appear as "I am the sum of my idiosyncrasies that make me unique" and "being like all these other people makes me who I am." Thus the conflict between individuation and belonging becomes the driving force of identity negotiation. Furthermore, Scott Brewster has argued that the metaphor of the house in Northern Ireland women's poetry takes on additional political undertones:

> The invitation of home ground in the North can also be readily transformed into an economy of exclusion, silence and vulnerability rather than of shelter, custom and affiliation. In this refusal of the law of the *oikos*, and its obligations of hospitality to the stranger, doors can be shut, houses can be evacuated and streets can be cleared.[12]

McGuckian's "House without Eyebrows" (*CRNH*, 27) creates, from the outset, a metonymic connection between human body and architectural structure. The house is anthropomorphized and organized into carefully delineated parts (face, throat, head, eyes, hands) that are dishevelled and fragmented, not only in and among themselves but also in relation to the narrative "I":

> I will remember, with my entire body,
> how you were torn. It was wind-still.
> A room of idols. You were light blue

> on the inside, drowning in darkness;
> the sun also spread a despairing
> light for me. Great sheaves of lightning
> stroked your neckless face, your straight
> throat, your small, smooth head,
> your yawning eyes, wide-open hands (*CRNH*, 27).

Interestingly, the body of the "I" is contrasted to the body of the house in a way that suggests wholeness within the speaking self ("my entire body") as opposed to the torn features of the house. The description of the interior of the house plays with the tension created by the meeting of light and darkness: we see "light blue," a "despairing light," and "lightning" juxtaposed with "drowning darkness," suggesting a subtle interaction between the first-person singular "I" and the "yawning eyes" of the house. The speaker, with the aid of light, is looking inside the house in a markedly tactile manner, which the building seems to reciprocate in the physical, inviting gesture of the "wide-open hands." At this point, in a subtle shift, the house becomes more anthropomorphic than the distant, ephemeral speaking "I." In McGuckian's poetry "house," the color "blue," and "darkness" are recognizable tropes denoting creativity, and the second-person singular is often associated with the reader. In this light, if we assume that the image of the house embodies the reader, the first stanza yields itself to an interpretation where the creative, writing self evokes and interacts with a constructed audience. In a typical McGuckianesque fashion, the site of creativity is placed outside the realms of the writing self or, more precisely, into the communicative vortex of writing and reading. The reader thus becomes internalized and incorporated bodily within the writing self: this is why the house takes over the corporeality of the speaking "I" and the inviting, creative blue darkness is placed within it.

This creative cooperation is developed further in the second stanza where we see the "sheaves of lightning" bringing the creative "blue" onto and out of the house. The voice (and body) of the first-person singular disappears and is swallowed up within the "blue-green aura" of the house. Creativity, which is so strenuously denied to the exterior of the house (it is "without blue, not an atom of blue, the blue well taken out"), is delivered onto it, suggesting that the reader's initial reluctance is, and has to be, overcome by the writing self's input. However, as we have seen, the boundary between writer and reader has been blurred in the visual play of the first stanza, which suggests that the creative performance necessarily has to be shared. And this is exactly what happens in the third stanza, which depicts the act of writing as an interactive event shared between the inside and the outside. In these lines the (writing) arm warms its sleeve, the hair forms sentences, and eventually words appear on the house's "skin." The metonymic connection between house and human body is complete, and the words surface from the interaction between the corporeal and the constructed, or, in other words, the writing and the reading selves. In terms of personal identity, the poem suggests that the creative self is multifaceted, fragmented, yet rooted within the interactive context of writing and reading. The poem finishes with the words "no wings," which, I suggest, simultaneously recalls a negative connotation of "lacking in a romantic notion of creativity," but, more importantly, also a positive association of corporeality and humanity. In simple words, the writer has invaded the reader's house and created a poem out of it. However, the poem also offers a reading where the second-person "you" is embodied as a woman, a female relative perhaps. The "torn" body of the house-woman invites into her creative interior the poetic self with her "wide-open hands." However, the constant tension and "dance" between the inside and the outside destabilizes a potential union. The house remains hospitable but inhabitable, a grotesque and uncanny face "without eyebrows" (*CRNH*, 27).

Body parts and architectural formations also play a crucial part in "Bright Star, I Say That Thou Art Dust" (*CRNH*, 29). The poem's journey takes place on a spatial and a corporeal dimension. The opening stanza depicts a "house door" and an "enclosed bed," signifying both a threshold and an inner space of safety. However, the presence of the raven, a bird of ill omen, forecasts worse things to come:

> this will mean before its time
> the full of the bell, lace in its proliferation,
> the deepest black that could be printed. (*CRNH*, 29)

The funerary images of "bell," "lace," and "deepest black" bring into focus trauma and suffering. The raven's call "from above an enclosed bed" forecasts a cleric's visit in Irish mythology. In the context of the poem the visitation focuses on the disoriented woman whose eyes reflect "storms":

> They will say her eyes were made
> of that water, storms that raced
>
> around the world to wear the ship
> round as the round sea-pattern brooch
> her father once gave me, damaged,
> then repaired with gold lacquer,
> making it even more valuable. (*CRNH*, 29)

Here the woman's body and the appearing objects ("ship" and "brooch") fuse together into a single corporeal metaphor to suggest somatized trauma. Although the reference to the poet's daughter's eye injury is apparent, the stormy disturbances hint at deeper internalizations of a longer-lived suffering. Indeed the next stanza expands the metaphor of the body to incorporate the poetic, writing self:

> Her hair is knotted into my five fingers.
> Every part of her clothed pupil
> has left three blotches on my cheek.
> She is the hidden space in the very book
> we are now reading. (*CRNH*, 29)

The body in pain becomes the center of poetic creativity: writing becomes impossible without her. The metaphors of the house and the ship signify this hidden space of creativity. Writing the work, however, is just as painful as experiencing bodily trauma (leaving "blotches on my cheek"). This inward journey into the center of pain invokes the language of prayer, and angels appear:

> . . . and from book into throat
> the angels kiss the soul to shape
> and feed it words directly
> along the angels' fingers. (*CRNH*, 29)

As discussed in the previous chapter, angels act as transient, misplaced figures of communication in McGuckian's poetry. The angels "lean down" and "capture" the shape of the woman (pain) in the sky, among the stars. From the poetic work prayer feeds pain back to the poet: the work becomes inseparable from the experience. It is as if the trauma was somatized not only in the body of the woman but also in the body of the work. This process is also evident in the depiction of the woman's body and space: both become "empty." The poem finishes with the portrayal of poetic misunderstandings: pain is "hearing the voice that no one else hears" but is misunderstood and misnamed ("everyone else sees as 'Lucy', but Lucy sees as 'Clare'"). The poem's title queries the legitimacy of the creative rewriting of suffering. The "bright star" of the finished work is the "dust" of the experience. Pain and trauma, whether political or psychological, are interpreted as "the darkest diamond in the universe" (*CRNH*, 29).

"Thorn Piece" (*CRNH*, 37) opens with a direct quotation from Johannes Brahms's *Notebooks*. The first line reads, "Cracked flutes close up by lying in water." Looking at the *Notebooks* the context of this quotation becomes clear: "The heart, torn up by so many years, by so many arrows, submerged itself with all its wounds in warm floods of tears, just as *cracked flutes close up by lying in water* and thereby regain their tones" (emphasis added).[13] Long-endured suffering and pain bring healing in their beauty; the experience of the sublime instigates creativity. Suffering, as in the previous poem, becomes corporeal in the female body:

> her body far, a paste of dust, a stranger
> here and there, would need shores of oak
> for the slackest pear light, moonlight of sound. (*CRNH*, 37)

Trauma experienced in the female body lingers on and does not completely heal. Instead, suffering in this poem takes on another body, which becomes the embodiment of the uncanny: "With her other face she is gazing / a woman in communion with herself, her reclining friend" (*CRNH*, 37). This fragmentation of the self is further exemplified in the striking mechanical image of her body in the last stanza: "where her arms form a basin / torn up by so many years, /off the shape of its hinges" (*CRNH*, 37). "Thorn Piece" can thus also be read as "Torn Piece": trauma which, like a thorn, is impossible to ignore yet hugely difficult to remove. The scattered female body that yearns for a "mild, continuous character" is left to carry its own brokenness. Violence thus remains meaningless and the poetic psyche's journey aimless. In the context of Northern Irish society McGuckian's rebellious avoidance of obvious political referencing has left some of her critics doubting her insistence on her political voice. However, the symbolization of the traumatic memory through the image of the fragmented, injured female body serves as an immediate, almost sensual reminder of pain and loss.

The middle part of *The Currach Requires No Harbours* is populated with poems that "write" the broken female body. "February House" (*CRNH*, 39) describes the poet's mother spending days sitting in her chair ("Because she just sits like that all day, / not showing any interest in anything / except the window sills." [*CRNH*, 39]) eventually becoming one with the house:

> . . . Hands holding cabbage roses,
> opening night roses, keep her fireplace
> filled, till the evenings stretch
> warm and comfortable through her hair
> caressed
>
> on the neck: who showed
> the other side of *her* moon only

to Endymion, her radiant, fearful
room, enamoured of the snow,
and its vapourization of the existing
rooms. (*CRNH*, 39)

The female body fuses with the house and the moon, showing her love "only to Endymion." The Greek mythological character, Endymion, was a beautiful young man who was so adored by the moon (Selena) that she asked Zeus to make him immortal. Zeus granted Selena's wish but ensured that Endymion fell asleep forever. The figure of the woman in the first stanza seems to be paralyzed by unexpressed emotions ("not showing interest in anything"). The emotional blockage experienced by the female body is metaphorically reconfigured in Endymion: both appear thwarted and fragmented. McGuckian, in this poem as well as in several others within the volume, seems to comment on the psychological cost of political violence. Political trauma becomes the writing on the female body, which, in this poem, internalizes violence as a refuge in passivity. For women, as Susie Orbach has argued, the development of a stable body image can prove problematical:

> How women see and experience their bodies refers to cultural factors outside themselves. . . . For many women the immediate feeling of a sense of self is inextricable from momentary feelings about their bodies. The body is experienced as acceptable or unacceptable, providing a foundation for self-concept.[14]

In "February House" the self-concept of the woman is destabilized and inert, causing frustration and self-doubt in the speaker ("like a ship impatient to be loaded, / I want to fuse her to the city" [*CRNH*, 39]). The "two-spirit" femininity highlights the fragile boundaries of normality in times of violence, where the female body's defense is to disappear into oblivious lifelessness.

"My Must" (*CRNH*, 40) continues the theme of the hurt female body; however, a sense of urgency also appears. The first stanza depicts the body as marked by death, alluding to the effects of silenced suffering:

An early ray of death
falls on her, my remaining
everlastingness, lime
and red, at her shoulder
the veil changes to deep blue. (*CRNH*, 40)

The visual fragmentation of the female body represents a simultaneous sense of fusion and pulling apart ("in each / occurrence of drawing near and apart").

The poem seems to broach tentatively the subject of emotional blockage, where release is envisaged as completeness, a coming together of disparate facets of self:

> Till she is more sensitive to time,
> of the same blood, a chaos
> of smaller willings, alone
> with her nowhere,
> with this "with" and "and."
>
> Reality is when it happens
> a second time, to complete people;
> summer is completely male,
> my must, he is the I
> that makes us into you. (*CRNH*, 40)

"My must" is the need, the ethical imperative, for togetherness and survival. The female bodies that have been silenced by Northern Ireland's political violence are inscribed with the pain of emotional blockage and helplessness. It is difficult to read these poems through a well-formed, analytical interpretation that unfolds the work's message, because McGuckian's central preoccupation is the meaninglessness of trauma and violence. The "currach" is floating free, without a harbor, and the readers have no choice but to watch its aimless journey.

The volume finishes with some "island" poems which return to a more familiar investigation of poetic identity, albeit still in the context of meaninglessness. McGuckian introduced these works at a reading by saying that "these island poems at the end are 'me.' I was like the artist who got into the currach and sailed away from all things."[15] "Lemon with White Jug" (*CRNH*, 67) introduces the island as a metaphor of poetic identity:

> The ghost island passes us by,
> its Greek name, meaning watchful,
> like a cloud bent back upon itself
> blown smooth by the wind. (*CRNH*, 67)

The watchful turning inwardness is a typical McGuckianesque subjectivity: inaccessible yet communicative, it bears witness to the never-ending work of deciphering and decoding that goes on between writer and reader. The second stanza elaborates on the writing process and the anxiety of reception. As often in McGuckian's work, the "unaccepted space between . . . upper eyelid and eyebrow" (*CRNH*, 67) depicts the cognitive readerly responses which inadvertently miss the meaning of her authorial intentions. (The "doors of lawless scarlet" do not lead to interpretative solutions.) However, when "a dream begins to value / the fretwork" of the poetic message or, in other words, when the reader's anticipation of decoding remains in the sphere of dreams and unarticulated intuitions, meanings can be communicated. The site of understanding, significantly, no longer resides in the cognitive faculties of the brain but in the fragmented body-parts: "in the languish / of your neck, the gospel-net / fletching of your arms" (*CRNH*, 67). The indirect message of "Lemon with White Jug" is its attention to the inward psychological processes of poetry writing. McGuckian's evading narrative voice carries a kind of "enigmatic frankness." As Anne-Lise François argues, the free, indirect style (that McGuckian also uses)

> far from affording the "closest" most exhaustive, but still secondary picture of a protagonist's secret inner life, makes available experiences that may entirely elude their subjects. Indeed . . . free indirect style unlocks a range of relations of identification and nonidentification, possession and nonpossession (between protagonist and the represented experience of which she is the ostensible subject, as between readers and protagonists, and narrative or authorial presences and the characters they often designate possessively as "my" or "our") that complicate the traditional liberal subject's claims to self-authorization in ways perhaps comparable to the expropriating action of trauma or limit-experience.[16]

Thus McGuckian's speaking voice does not offer up its secrets; rather, it opens up a space where the reader can journey and experience authorial intentions. "Regaining Control of the Night" (*CRNH*, 72) is another example of open-ended, recessive writing, where the promised resolution of the title remains an illusory gift. The first stanza sets the scene by unraveling rational thought. Dichotomies between war and peace, light and dark are blurred:

> Days that belonged to war and peace
> at the same time, they were always so:
> darkened cinemas, the strength of lamps
> reduced as low as possible. (*CRNH*, 72)

Rational thought is derailed, and the poem turns toward itself. The poetic psyche dramatizes its own creation:

> or what she might look like
> while looking—her hummingbird nature,

her maple-tree nature. Hers is the first
of many languid arms to reach out

like a lifted horizon in a landscape's
perfect swaying, her opaque red plumage,
lips and heels like patched sails
in the same damp winter's afterglows. (*CRNH*, 72)

This self-observation exemplifies the unfolding poetic identity's hesitation in offering normative definitions of itself. The polarities of the tree and the small bird, the instability of the horizon and the fragmentation of the body all serve to avoid an explanatory model of identity. Rather, the deflective mode of self-reflection invites the reader to abstain from the search for consequential meaning and become instead a passive "eye":

An eye of inshore trees and shrubs,
it has in fact got brighter,
light creeping in directly
in front of the house, a burst of light

over it. (*CRNH*, 72)

The "eye" is not seeing, but knowing, quite like Emily Dickinson's knowing eye: "The Mind is smooth—no Motion— / Contented as the eye / Opon the Forehead of a Bust— / That knows—it cannot see."[17] The light circumnavigates, never quite penetrating the "house" or meaning. The eye of the reader passively accepts this light, without judgment. Anne-Lise François talks about a particular "ethics of reading" when the reader is faced with literary works that narrate what she terms "open secrets":

> To go on . . . as if nothing had happened, leaving the event unmarked, implies an ethic of reading—of the reception of narrative experience—unintelligible to novel readers except as waste and disavowal. For even when known, the open secret continues to insist, on some level, on *not* mattering. A scene of instruction that asks us to bracket rather than give consequence to what we learn, the open secret occasions a narrative lapse in development that looks like a moral lapse of knowledge—a violation of the Enlightenment imperative that we act in light of what we know.[18]

McGuckian's poetry often conceals the type of "open secret" François discusses here. The "meaning" behind many of her poems is inconsequential (some argue irrelevant) in light of ideals of interpretative access and decoding. It is as if McGuckian was asking her reader to *be* rather than to *do*. Her insistence on "not mattering" in a cognitive sense frustrates many of McGuckian's critics who ground their readings in semantics. "Regaining Control of the Night" is therefore a double negation: there is no control to be regained to start with, and even if there was, darkness and night are fundamentally uncontrollable. The poem ends with the fragmentation of the female body familiar to this whole volume:

> . . . Puckering her shoulder,
> spreading her fingers,
> knifing along the tip
> of the beauty leaf on her breast. (*CRNH*, 72)

Read as an interaction between reader and writer, the tentative touching of the body signifies the inward-looking movement of the creative process, where authorial and readerly intentions happen simultaneously to produce the final work.

In conclusion, *The Currach Requires No Harbours* is a volume with a gentle creative journey toward the (shoreless) poetic self. The opening poems offer tender reflections on the effects of political violence. The injury to the author's daughter's eye is internalized but not analyzed. Rather, the injured "eye" becomes a passively receptive wounded "I" which accompanies these poems' self-reflexive journeys. The sensory organ of the "eye" does not see, but senses and knows what is cognitively impossible to articulate. The aimlessness and meaninglessness of suffering is received by the eye and offered to the reader as a weak gift: that which can be taken but not opened. The volume asks the readers to understand (in parentheses) what is said, without the consequential interpretative urge. The "weightless experience"[19] of these poems articulates the futility of expression in suffering. There is no morality and no didactic teaching. The poems, like hurt bodies, are just there, empty-handedly stating mortality and pain.

The Funneling Paths of *My Love Has Fared Inland*

The Currach Requires No Harbours is a volume of uncounted experience and aimless journeying. However, *My Love Has Fared Inland,* Medbh McGuckian's penultimate volume to date, promises a definite inward journey in its title.[20] Taking up familiar themes of creativity and spirituality the poems trace an introspective trajectory where the reader is not always invited to join. McGuckian returns to the language, and linguistic difficulty, of her earliest volumes. Her metaphors are self-reflexive, introvert and resistant to an easy intellectual workout. The motto of the book warns that "sound ha[s] to abandon the servile function of signification" to become "vital" and "its own excuse for being." We are not invited to interpret or paraphrase, but only to enjoy the words "freely as music." However, as often is the case with McGuckian, there is a thematic coherence in her work which points beyond this promised linguistic abandon.

Despite its consistency, it is not easy to break down this new volume into thematic units: the central ideas seem to float around dispersed among a variety of themes: death, writing, nature, and love all play a part, brought together by the recurring motif of inward movement. "Sealed Composition" offers a spiritual manifesto of this new type of writing, which is likened to the journey of the news emanating from Jesus's empty tomb, "dreaming and probing, / seeing and testing the consolation / of new gospels" (*MLFI*, 17). Poetry in this context becomes "an epiphany in black anxiety" which "smothers . . . in cold and intimate brown tones." The title, together with Goethe's motto, "One learns only from those one loves," point toward an authorial strategy which "seals" language into a spiritual tomb, becoming only accessible through and in love. Rather than enticing the reader toward an interpretation, "Sealed Composition" seems to warn him/her off, suggesting that, without love, the only thing one will find is an empty tomb and "dry lips." But what exactly is readerly love? It seems to consist less of a sympathetic ear than an attitude which allows the poem to be what it is, "its own excuse of being" (*MLFI*, 17).

"Painting a Verb Half Golden" (*MLFI*, 12) traces the authorial *modus operandi* and simultaneously reflects back on McGuckian's early work. The title echoes earlier works such as "Turning the Moon into a Verb" (*MC*, 76) where the description of the creative process focused on personalized interpretations of grammar and semantics. In "Painting a Verb Half Golden" McGuckian opens with destabilizing perspective:

> The horizon is in danger,
> just off the real land grown on.
> Thoughts rub against it and it aches
> Like a poisonous otherworldly black star. (*MLFI*, 12)

The locus of creativity, or authorial presence, is notoriously difficult to "pin down" in McGuckian's work. These lines seem to suggest that it is always "just off," slipping out of focus. "Thoughts," or cognitive interpretation and logical decoding, "rub against" this type of creativity, which aims at misdirection and a sharing of an inward journey. The second stanza further empties authorial presence of consequence and seems to suggest that writing is involuntary and closer associated with "feeling" than thinking:

> The wind blows between it
> and the steep face of the wave
> that changes the way my fingers
> are and the feel of the lines
> of my skin. (*MLFI*, 12)

The "it" of creativity becomes corporeal rather than cerebral as the writing is placed on the skin. Having established that the creative process abandons cognitive responsibilities, the poetic voice introduces one of McGuckian's best known tropes: colors. The next stanza mentions a different color in every line, creating a pictorial journey through the development of the authorial voice:

> When blue was nothing
> I let you turn my wrist white
> and scorch my tongue to living silver
> with your young gold:
> I let a pretty red hold
>
> me like salt on its side. (*MLFI*, 12)

The "you" of these lines, interpreted as the reader, offers an interesting view of the control exerted on the authorial voice. When "blue," or the creative voice, was nothing (or undeveloped), the author allowed readerly expectations form her way of writing. The "young gold" and "pretty red" of popularity "held" the voice to ransom, but the price was a loss of genuine vision:

> and when I was alone
> blue's opposite
> left a naked grey
> at the corner of my eye. (*MLFI*, 12)

Denying genuine creativity resulted in blurred sight, with "grey" in the eye. These thoughts are quite familiar to McGuckian's oeuvre, and it could be argued that many of her poems are written in defense of her *modus operandi*.

What is interesting in "Painting a Verb Half Golden" is the apparent compromise, or consensus, that the authorial voice seems to find with her readers:

> The coats of my eye
> like a red-blue couple
> recycle your shadow, mortal as words,
> blue lying on the rose,
> an inverted blue tree:
>
> and next to your mouth
> though the rain does not paint softly,
> the deepest pen-shaped groove
> would be deliberately too light
> for wine-press or pine-cone. (*MLFI*, 12)

Incorporating readerly expectations (or readerly love is probably a more fitting description) results in poetry which is an "inverted blue": a creativity that carries its opposite within. Again, in a typical McGuckianesque fashion, the reader becomes incorporated into the creative process, his/her "mouth" being "next to" the authorial voice. "Painting a Verb Half Golden" thus is a poem about what it says in the title: the color gold here could be read as a metaphor for readerly expectation and interception, and the act of "painting a verb half golden" seems to suggest a creative process which incorporates its reception, as well as its conception. Whatever way we read this poem, the relationship between reader and poet seems to stand at the center of its interpretation.

Following this line of analysis the next poem in the volume, "Unsound Ship" (*MLFI*, 18), maps out this delicate relationship between reader and writer. The poet-narrator laments having grown "so stony, so polished within," living life as "a single / act of vigil remote from praise" (*MLFI*, 18). In a defensive gesture the reader is said to have never been "held . . . as if for sale / everywhere I want you to be." In other words, both freedom and respect are given to the reader here to find their own point of attachment to the work. However, the poem seems to be riddled with authorial anxiety about the reader's "coolness" and "dubious roads," and love seems to evade interaction altogether. The poet-narrator without a reader "on love's way" seems to float free like an unsound ship, "without a beyond," ready to fall to the "sandy floor" (*MLFI*, 18).

"Bashali" (*MLFI*, 20) takes a subtle approach to discussing author-reader relationship. *Bashali* is a menstrual house of the Kalasha women, a minority religious grouping living in Pakistan. The menstrual house is a refuge or a prison—depending on the perspective of the observer. Early (male) ethnographers described it as a house where women were relegated in their state of "impurity." However, Wynne Maggi argues that the *Bashali* house enhances women's agency, and it is in fact a place which becomes a "space" for Kashala women.[21] *Bashali*s are strictly off-limits to men. Women design and maintain them, and the rules of being in the house are strict and ritualistic. Kashala women go into the house on the first day of their periods and also to give birth and for a three-week sojourn postpartum. Women bring their food, and cook and share it among one another. At the end of their stay they go through a ritualistic "wash" to cleanse themselves before their return to their own houses. For many, their stay is a respite from their ordinary chores, yet for others, particularly those who for any reason cannot get pregnant, the *Bashali* becomes a house of shame. McGuckian situates her locus of creativity in the *Bashali*, thus connecting it to femininity in a very real and corporeal sense. In her early career McGuckian often struggled with notions of impurity because of her strict Catholic upbringing and as a consequence saw the development of her poetic voice as a masculine attribute.[22] After the birth of her first child when she suffered from postnatal depression doctors told her to stop writing in order to get better. Thus writing and childbirth, creativity, impurity, and female bodily functions all appear in tandem in her work as the locus of creativity. Situating this poem in a house with such ambivalent connotations allows her to explore conflicting notions of femininity and creativity. The poem opens with a surprising appearance of the male pronoun "he," who is put into a position of paternalistic power:

> I feel he would give it to me in spirit
> as rivers carve out kingdoms,
> the boulder field near the watermill,
> my father's summer land. (*MLFI*, 20).

The mysterious "it" in the first line can be read as the gift of creativity, viewed by McGuckian for so long as a male privilege. The magnanimity of the physical landscape encapsulates the expansiveness, and also the turbulence, of this creative gift. The second stanza repeats this image in the lines ". . . a crucial terrain / anchored and perturbed," further emphasising the instability experienced in writing. McGuckian claims that *My Love Has Fared Inland* is a book "about poets and poetry."[23] "Bashali" seems to offer an *ars poetica* which explores the masculine and feminine inheritances in writing. While the gift of creativity in this poem is male ("He would give it in my children's / father's name") the resulting work is shrouded in feminine imagery:

> . . . If this clothed throat
> like a nowhere-to-be-found pool
> that shelters under the youngest mountain

could be seen the new breaths
of three hundred dark roses'
third day would tell it all,
holding a door in your arms (*MLFI*, 20)

These lines reference the *Bashali* house, as described in Wynne Maggi's work:

> The *bashali* reminds me of a pool that forms behind sheltering rocks in the river, a small, calm spot in the rushing of life. The water streams around it, making it seem separate from the river, but in the same breath, it *is* the river—made of the same water and continually circulating.[24]

Maggi's description of the menstrual/birthing house as a "continually circulating" flow of water fits neatly into McGuckian's conceptualization of creativity as a circular birthing process. Quoting from the work on Kalasha women also reinforces the feminized context of this work. The poem is full of subtle references to birth: the "third day" after giving birth is the most important day in the *Bashali*—it is when the "third-day bread" is made and given to every new mother.[25] It is easy to see the symbolic significance of this offering in the context of McGuckian's poetry: the new bread on the third day "would tell it all." In other words the result of the writing process becomes the gift of poetry. However, creative success, as often in McGuckian's work, is contingent on readerly response. It is the reader who is "holding the door" to the meaning of the poem. The poem gently places this authorial power into the "arms" of the reader, who is situated at the threshold between the inside of the *bashali* and the outside world. The intensely feminine interior of the house and the masculinized offering of the gift of creativity thus meet in the arms of the reader, who reconciles and "holds" together the disparate faculties of poetic creativity. McGuckian's insistence on readerly contribution is exceptional among contemporary poets. Although subtle and circuitous, the poem's weaving together of quotations and paraphrases from Wynne Maggi's book with McGuckian's idiosyncratic and highly symbolic use of language creates a work of art which not only reflects on its own creation but also manages to draw the reader deep into the poet's creative psyche.

Continuing the theme of poetic identity many poems in *My Love Has Fared Inland* introduce a sense of authorial anxiety. "The Cliff of Thought of Renunciation" (*MLFI*, 33), as the title suggests, depicts this anxiety in terms of the landscape. The "cliff" of anticipated rejection looms large in the poet's creative anxiety. A sense of weakness and inconsequentiality permeates the first stanza:

Slight colour from the weak, late-night sunlight,
lesser reds, like a barely broken dawn.
The ship is like a leaf at the island's ceramic rim,
moths circle the net of the wild courtyard. (*MLFI*, 33)

The imagery suggests an emptying of positivity: the "weak" light and the frail ship "circle" around without much consequence or productivity. Interpreted in terms of the creative process the first stanza sets authorial expectations extremely low. The poem here seems to suggest that change or creative action is dispensed with. Instead, like "moths" around fire, the work exposes the gift, the "open secret" of inconsequential nothingness.[26] The second stanza gives up the illusion of authorial control altogether and places creative production in the realm of unconscious—and thus uncontrollable—happenings:

As it wishes, spring fragrance may cease
summer-lidded mountains, clearing autumn skies,
an inkling of winter and golden snow
sprout four seasons, all in one sitting room. (*MLFI*, 33)

Poetry, like nature, "ceases" or "sprouts" as it pleases, without much human control. The bequest of creativity is not a gift bestowed upon the deserving poet, but an almost missable nothingness which either happens or not, "as it wishes." However, in the next stanza "desire" appears, which somewhat reconfigures the authorial position within the work:

Desire steps in, a poorwill entering the door,
his inch-wide pupils resting repeatedly
on the forest geometry of the tray landscape,
his eyes the eyes of a mountain. (*MLFI*, 33)

The "poorwill" is in fact a pertinent choice of word here. Poorwills are small nocturnal birds who spend the winter in comatose torpor.[27] Their call is a weak *poor-will, poor-will* repeated over and over. Their torpor is so deep that reportedly one bird did not react when torch light was shone directly into its pupil.[28] The weak will displayed by the bird symbolically underscores the weightlessness of experience in this poem. Desire is conceptualized as fragile and passively receptive, taking in the "landscape," rather than forming it. Its "eyes of a mountain" observe but do not organize material into coherent narrative expression. The following stanza further emphasizes the passivity, and even vulnerability, of the desire-bird:

He presents his throat like a cherrystone
carved in a hundred facets, the lyrebird

> shape of his ear, the fruits and vegetables
> that make up the river diary of his head. (*MLFI*, 33)

The lyrebird not only evokes references of classical poetry, but it is also a bird which is a master of imitation. This small Australian avian can literally imitate any sound it hears, as David Attenborough famously demonstrated in his *Life of Birds*, where sounds ranging from camera shutters to Attenborough's own commentary were flawlessly repeated by the little bird.[29] It is difficult not to think about McGuckian's writing technique of copying prodigious amounts of texts from other writers when she references the lyrebird.[30] However, it is the vulnerability of the poetic voice which is most successfully transmitted in these lines. The last stanza, itself an imitation of lines from another work, pull together the "weak" authorial voice of the early stanzas with the double-faced symbolism of desire:

> And complete in his breast, within him,
> a cloud-dream-lake, a cloud-terrace
> ladder of spaces, where we sleep together
> in the windswept glimmer of shrine lamps. (*MLFI*, 33)

Here the authorial voice becomes incorporated in the "breast" of desire, turning upside down classical notions of the poet's chest "burning with desire." Thus authorial control is given completely over to a desire which is weak ("poor-willed") and unoriginal (like the song of the "lyrebird.") However, this capitulation results in forming a creative space ("a ladder of spaces") where a seemingly peaceful harmony is reached between voice and desire. On the other hand, this peacefulness is conditioned by the "glimmer of shrine lamps," symbols of death. The weakness and powerlessness lead toward death and the extinguishing of the voice. However, as often in McGuckian's work, obliteration (or the danger of it) is the instigator of creativity, rather than its doom. Thus the "cliff" of the title poses danger only if it is approached by "thought" and anxiety. Giving the voice over to powerlessness and the arbitrariness of fate results in a defining act of inconsequential loss, which, conversely, becomes the gain of the work. In other words, the secret of this poem is that renunciation of power is at the crux of writing. In this reading authorial anxiety becomes not so much directed at audience reception, but at the inevitable surrendering of authorial control. This backward-looking movement in McGuckian's work defies critical attempts to trace the authorial intentions to a starting point and a finished result. Critics therefore who look for sources, or personal intentions as explanations of her work, often come away empty-handed and disappointed, since the journey of surrender is more often at the center of the poet's *modus operandi* than the meticulously placing together of word-pieces to make a work of art which is complete and unblemished.

Ownership of her creative style is also the subject of "Shot Angel" (*MLFI*, 38), a beautifully written account of the anxiety about McGuckian's creative methodology. The poem opens with an attempt to situate and define the source of creativity. As in many other poems in this volume, pain, suffering, and death play a crucial part in invoking the locus of inspiration. The first stanza of "Shot Angel" offers a pictorial representation of the uncertainty of this center:

> A gentle pink, close to pain,
> was making the sky follow
> the innards of the landscape. (*MLFI*, 38)

The color "pink" of course is a composite of red and white, in itself not a primary color. The "innards of the landscape" are similarly blurred and indefinable. "Close to pain" again is an approximation, an "almost-ness" which seems to reside in the center of creative expression. Colors permeate this poem, and as we shall see, the movement from "pink" to "amber," "blue," "green," and, finally "red," also underlines the poet's intention of demarcating her mode of writing in terms of pictorial crystallization. If the first stanza is read as a depiction of the creative space from where writing emerges, the following three verses continue to take a closer look at the actual process of how poems "happen." This is a significant choice of word in relation to McGuckian's poetry. Her poetic voice seems to insist on an organic way of growth and happenstance, rather than designed authorial control, despite the very articulate and exact methodology of pasting together disparate written sources. Thus the following lines describe how the sun's "amber" colour becomes "blue" in an open-ended fashion that is not constrained by consequential action:

> The sun's intense amber
> slipped a near-human warmth
> over the handleless door
>
> so that it seemed to clip
> and hinge together
> in a fan of blue zigzags
>
> like the rowlock of a gondola. (*MLFI*, 38)

"Blue" is the color that throughout McGuckian's poetry depicts creativity which is innocent and pure, somewhat childlike. Significantly, this is a primary color. The "handleless door" is also a metaphor for the reader's complicated access to her work. The poetry offers a "door" into it, but it is a door without a handle, which means that access cannot be controlled. However, the "near-human warmth" of readerly regard can make the poem happen and show its true color, "blue." These lines describe how the writing happens from the work's and the reader's perspectives. The following stanzas look at the authorial process:

> I could see, starting as though
> from a cloud, the child's green aura,
> the very essence of his head
> deep-sheltered in the open curves
> of the blankets, his split and drilled
>
> face. And a field with dark edges
> in the fusion of his mouth and ear. (*MLFI*, 38)

Interestingly, the "very essence" is characterized by "green" (a secondary color made up of blue and yellow) and images of fracture and cover. The "face" of the work is "split" and distorted, and interestingly the "mouth" and "ear" are fused together, which is suggestive of the joint processes of creation and reception in McGuckian's work. As in earlier poems, the work here is also symbolically represented by the male child, referencing the poet's dual-gendered visualization of her creative process. The final part of the poem talks more directly about the finished work and its reception:

> One might question the absence of roads,
>
> the funnelling paths
> crisscrossed with narrow tracks,
> and the stylized spires
>
> in some lesser stone
> at the hushed heart of his map. (*MLFI*, 38)

It is rare to get such an unambiguous description of the poet's view of her creative work. Many critics in fact have "questioned the absence of roads" in her work and attacked her for the "funnelling paths" she took them on, not to mention the antagonistic reviews of the genetic critics who are looking for quotations (construed in this poem as the "stylized spires // in some lesser stone"). "Shot Angel" talks back to these critics though and finishes with a craftily phrased defense which destroys the myth of cognitive appropriation and shows instead an open-ended interpretative space:

> No map, however exquisite,
>
> can ever show everything,
> the wind cherubs tinted
> just the red a woman's lips should be. (*MLFI*, 38)

The poem's process from vague inspirational idea to the innocent "blue" of creativity finally arrives at the most complex, and yet purest, expression of writing, which is symbolized by the "red" of the "woman's lips." In a feminist reading this last line seems to vie for an articulation of *écriture feminine* that prescribes how a woman "should" write. However, in the case of McGuckian the message or meaning of the work is always a bit more hesitant. The end of the poem brings into focus the title again. "Shot Angel" is an overwordly being who, despite his/her immortality is shot dead but simultaneously, in a different reading, is being immortalized in a photograph. However far-fetched this ambiguity may seem, reading the poem reinforces its deliberateness. The authorial anxiety over the work being "killed" by unsympathetic readings permeates the poem which simultaneously acknowledges the crucial part reception plays in the making of the work.

This inward journey toward authorial anxiety also appears in poems which consider the other dominant concept of the book, death. "The Sin Eater" (*MLFI*, 39), a dark and sinister poem which alludes to the tradition of eating bread over a corpse to free the deceased from sin, opens with describing the poet-narrator's unease:

> Angel of the Agony, I have found
> no name for you yet. I am trying
> to fix the sounds, but am I really
> alone in this unadorned music? (*MLFI*, 39)

Solitude and abandonment drive this poem's journey inward, toward a dead center:

> Kneeling down after three steps,
> walking backwards all the way,
>
> I . . . worked my trust in God into the floor. (*MLFI*, 39)

The poem seems to travel into and beyond death, to "swerves of fantasy" which govern this work's deadly poetic expression. "Desh: The Homeland" (*MLFI*,

69) juxtaposes an imagined living space "re-arranged" in the narrator's mind with a far more tangible graveyard: "From the house of the living I may as well go / to the house of the dead" (*MLFI*, 69). This "living" space with the "character, the mood / of an incorrect city" houses a particular grave, "a vertical tombstone, /unweathered and unadorned, blue and edgy, / its blank page blanching the skin" (*MLFI*, 69). McGuckian ponders upon the space assigned to the dead, the "naked / and proper word" of the person's name and an odd inscription which "reads / 'Caute', / . . . 'Be Careful', printed just beneath / the drawing of a rose" (*MLFI*, 69). The significance of this caution reaches far beyond the immediate fear of the living encountering the dead. The narrator seems to speak from the space of the dead, as if the warning was an invitation to hiding. The poem culminates in the wonderful image of the "quietly hidden insula," the poetic voice which has travelled into isolation, into a solitude which is no longer the starting point of expression, but its ultimate destination.

This dark inner space of death is also the subject of "Watching the Owls with You" (*MLFI*, 42–43), which describes the dark inside of "a room designed to imprison" like "an almost empty coffin." Again, this space seems to become the destination of poetic expression, a kind of black hole which fails to respond:

> just as I have burned these threads
>
> and they will not come back:
> just like a bringing-back,
> just as these names are cold,
> the names of the horses
>
> and the names of the angels
> place the world as a somewhere
> deep in this circle of sky. (*MLFI*, 42–43)

Words turn upon themselves in the realm of death and language becomes "the failure of place . . . where the beginning ends" (*MLFI*, 42–43).

A sense of failure permeates this volume, not only in poems which directly deal with the theme of death, but also in works that, innovatively for McGuckian, engage with the environment. "The Realm of Nothing Whatever" (*MLFI*, 22) (in itself a revealing title) ponders the end of the earth, on which life is like a "pearl forever irritating the oyster / with inexorable tenderness." As opposed to the Big Bang of creation, the ending is visualized as a fading away,

as if at a border crossing,
fashioning your vanishing
to end without force
in a minimum, rocking note. (*MLFI*, 22)

The poem which gave the volume its title, "My Love Has Fared Inland" (*MLFI*, 48) is a true "eco-poem," describing "the raw, scraped, / bludgeoned land" taking over "what had seemed before / an idyllic countryside." However, the bruised and dark interior of the natural landscape seems to lament a lack of connection with the creative mind, which struggles to position itself in the realm of the natural world, distantly listing the environment, "the shape of the hill, / the pent-up river, / the course of the stream," as creative props in the process of writing. Rather than finding solace in a journey taken into the natural world, it is nature which seems to have been swallowed up in the darkness of poetic creation. The "love" of this poem is less the object of out-flowing emotion and more the active subject, the "loving," which travels inward to the dark interior of the creative psyche.

This minimalistic, dark tone is at the crux of McGuckian's poetic expression in this volume, which seems to foreground ideas of passivity, failure, and futility. "South of Mars" (*MLFI*, 71) opens with a linguistic closure: "It's over now. Part of the story / has disappeared, into the void / of something that has ended forever." The poem describes loss and a "sadness that slackens electrical lines." Most tellingly it muses that "perhaps / what we thought would cast a thick shadow // will cast none at all" (*MLFI*, 71). Whether this is about leaving a poetic mark or personal anxiety, it is a recurring motif throughout the volume. "Birds, Women and Writing" (*MLFI*, 45) laments "this slack heart, this white gaze" and the "songs whose story is elsewhere," while "To My Daughter, Finding Her Weeping, Because I Would Not Consent to Her Fasting" (*MLFI*, 50) describes the poet's "drive into solitude," where the poetic voice "pushed against / the silence a bit further."

My Love Has Fared Inland is a strange collection. Its inward gaze and uninviting lines (like "my backbone pulped and I closed up / like a concertina" from the opening poem "Painting by Moonlight" [*MLFI*, 11]) simultaneously discourage and entice the reader. The vitality and music hinted at in the motto remain somewhat hard to find, and yet the gloomy atmosphere which permeates these poems exert a strange magnetic pull. Like a black hole, this collection reveals its inner core through interaction with its readers. And once the reader gets too close, they might as well allow themselves to be taken in.

The Currach Requires No Harbours and *My Love Has Fared Inland* conduct a metaphorical account of McGuckian's diverse creative methodologies. The former's symbolic meandering in the harborless seas offer insight into the personal response to political violence. The poetic psyche, an isolated island surrounded by the stormy seas, accommodates an "eye" that sees not because it is powerful, but on the contrary, because it knows suffering. The injury inflicted on the poet's daughter becomes the locus of creative expression of pain. There is a sense of spiritual wisdom in this volume which looks beyond the poet's customary erudite word-plays. The women who populate this volume carry within their bodies, and in their souls, an astuteness and sense of empathy which has come to represent McGuckian's recent poetry writing. *My Love Has Fared Inland* continues this inward journey toward the author's locus of creativity which is driven by readerly love, suffering and authorial anxiety. The meditations on death subtly complement the poet's earlier work on this subject. Inconsequential action, futility, and dead ends stand to represent a voice which exists only for itself. The reader is not enticed but simply allowed to take part in this dark journey. The spiritual optimism or "light" is represented by love, which unassumingly offers itself for the reader.

The Disintegrating Voyage of *The High Caul Cap*

McGuckian's latest volume, *The High Caul Cap*,[31] which was published in 2012, charts the progress from the helplessness of watching her mother's body deteriorate, through to mourning her death and trying to come to terms with life without her, and finishing up with imagining the already departed soul's impressions on life. The book is like a haunting and haunted gaze: it sees and shows everything, courageously accompanying the body on its journey of decline. The poems are populated by images of loss, blindness, illness, and other types of atrophy, taking ownership of that which usually the human gaze avoids. There are little or no secondary literature or reviews as yet written on this volume. However, the contextual unity and beauty of the poems makes this an exceptional volume to read.

The title of "The Nth of Marchember," the first poem under scrutiny (*HCC*, 14–15), suggests that the poem is situated in a dimension which has lost its connection to reality as we know it. It is in a time outside of time, where dying takes place and a person's grasp on reality becomes weakened. We see a woman in the first two stanzas standing lost in her surroundings, turning inward, away from the observing "I":

> The way she was standing told me
> it wasn't worth going to the trouble
> of turning on any more lights.
>
> She guards her blouse, momentarily
> holding her heart as if caressing a character
> in someone else's family romance. (*HCC*, 14–15)

The distanciation between self and body is poignantly described by the image of her heart held in her hand. In this state of illness she is already living in a state of in-betweenness, losing her connection to the outside world:

> Within her inner theatre, and seemingly borderless
> surround, she quivers across the porcelain
> of evening—the bed is certainly more
>
> than it needed to be. (*HCC*, 14–15)

Her condition is further described in the city metaphor of the following lines which portray her body and mind as perpetually locked outside the lived urban space:

> When sleep undresses
> her mind to even make peace with the city of "I will,"
> her body forewarns her
>
> she is out, out of town, I understand, thumb
> on the doorbell, outside, overflying a snowy
> border, angel and puppet coming together. (*HCC*, 14–15)

The spiritual dimension of death is coupled with the loss of control experienced by the ill body: "angel and puppet" characterize the borderland stage of dying where the body and mind are pulled in the opposing directions of living and passing. The city becomes one of the central metaphors of this collection, representing the human body and mind in their different stages and forms of development and atrophy. In the context of this poem the "city of I will" is read as the vanishing faculty of willpower and control, which has already become inaccessible for the dying woman. Thus in "The Nth of Marchember" the poetic voice focuses on the acute extremes experienced within the dying process. The next two stanzas recall birth through evoking "the lanugo of her own splendid body" juxtaposing this image with the speaker's "bloody repast" of the following line (*HCC*, 14–15). Mother-daughter roles seem to reverse here as the poetic voice observes the dying mother's skin covered in the fine downy hair of a newborn. The poem culminates in the painful yet empathetic description of the slow erosion of body and mind:

> Her undeadness, her petrified unrest
> is the ending of time within her,
>
> the alleged redemption's
> copy of a grievous gift, flinging her
> in and out of the downtown. (*HCC*, 14–15)

The dying woman is denied a smooth transit to the otherworld, passively suffering the capriciousness of the dying process. The speaker's observing helplessness is emphasized through the closing image of "flinging her / in and out of the downtown," magnifying the pain and vulnerability that watching a mother's death entails.

"A Supplement to the Withering" (*HCC*, 18) further shifts the focus from the dying body to the helpless observer. The cityscape is replaced by natural imagery that attempts to contain the pain of transition into death. The poem takes its lines from a work on the history of women botanists titled *Cultivating Women, Cultivating Science: Flora's Daughters and Botany in England, 1760–1860.*[32] Most of the poem focuses on gowns and headdresses worn by Victorian women, who had a special fondness for romanticizing botanical imagery in their attire, as well as in literary works. The title of McGuckian's poem is in fact taken from a comment written by Coleridge about Elizabeth Kent's work *Flora Domestica* which, in his opinion, was a "delightfully executed" "supplement to Withering."[33] Naturally in McGuckian's poem "withering" gains its full meaning in the interpretative context of the whole volume, signaling the slow process of dying that the poet charts in these works. In this reading "supplement" becomes the supporting participant in this process, the observing poet whose voice is taken up in the first stanza:

> The evening primrose always is,
> and always will be, a memento
> of what I will no longer enjoy on earth. (*HCC*, 18)

Although originally quoted in Shteir's work as an example of botanic moralizing and sentimentality uttered by Charlotte Elizabeth Tonna,[34] in this poem these lines reverberate with the genuine despair and helplessness of the observing poet. The rest of the poem is taken up with a detailed description of an elaborately (and botanically) dressed female figure, who is named as "not-the-daughter, not-the-wife," existing in between identities, depicted throughout in the past tense:

> And her gown was a closely detailed
> landscape scene, the bottom of her petticoat
> had brown hills covered with all sorts
>
> of weeds, many of their leaves finished
> with gold. Every breadth had an old stump
> of a tree, that ran up almost to the top,
> broken and ragged and worked
> with brown chenille. Her robings
> and facings were little green banks,
>
> her sleeves loose twining branches. (*HCC*, 18)

Her body seems to unite with the natural environment. However, far from being a bucolic representation of femininity, these images ("brown hills covered with all sorts / of weeds"; "old stump of a tree"; "broken and ragged") evoke decay and atrophy. The botanical imagery reinforces the feeling of "withering" that is evoked in the title and the closing lines of the poem reinforce the sense that this is a memento written for a woman who is passing away:

> we must build a statue of a lioness with no
> tongue, but a bag of poems, to honour her. (*HCC*, 18)

The images of the tongueless lioness and poetry locked away in a bag underline the helplessness evoked by the opening of the poem. The speaker stands speechless offering locked-away poems to "honour" the dying, or more precisely the natural process that takes the living away.

"Kaluza's Law" (*HCC*, 23) continues to ponder the speechlessness of witnessing. The title is a reference to an Old English metric speech pattern that expresses "sufficient stress." The poem relies heavily on a book written about Connemara by Tim Robinson that engages with the landscape and its mythology.[35] However, in this poem, like in the one before, the poet concentrates on decay rather than bucolic beauty:

> The lake, with its almost healed scar,
> in its blue-grey withdrawal is all arms,
> badge of white on the thigh. A foggy day
> turns white linen brown and faintly browns

> the meagre winter flowers, displaying
> this degree of wear and tear, a quality of decay
> in the sky. (*HCC*, 23)

The natural environment captures the imperceptible "quality of decay" that lingers over life. The next two stanzas evoke a "half imaginary Irish saint," a "sibyl" and "an older angel," introducing a quasi-mythological element to the poem, which fails to elevate the tone of these lines toward optimism. The closing image of the slowly eroding stone and unmoving moth capture death's unstoppable erosion of life, emphasizing our helplessness in witnessing this process:

> Then the slow chamfering of a stone's edge
> by blown sandgrains, while the still-fluttering
> goatmoth settles for stillness. (*HCC*, 23)

"Kaluza's Law" suggests that death exerts sufficient stress on life to wear it away slowly, while "Sandpaper Letters" (*HCC*, 36–37) shifts the focus to the withdrawn mental universe of the dying. The poem is based on a book called *Thinking in Pictures: My Life with Autism*, by Temple Grandin, an animal scientist who in her book attempts to explain the communicative difficulties of autism. McGuckian has always been attracted to thinking in pictures and colors, as many of her ekphrastic poems attest.[36] In "Sandpaper Letters" she examines the role of perception in communication and love. The title refers to sandpaper alphabets that children trace to help them learn to read in the Montessori system, but "letters" also introduce the communicative tool of correspondence. The first three stanzas set the tone and mood of the poem. This is a universe of pain and disenchantment that is captured in the disparate imagery and emotive words:[37]

> The post-war driftwood is stored away
> in drawers of silence, bled into the rug,
> whatever the wave might suppose.
>
> In order to remain in love,
> to see the city reshape itself
> in the dangerless September,
> the last page is written upside down.
>
> Galaxies dissipate, while the new spring
> learns tranquil abiding, recent birth
> of leaves and breeding of grass
> as if painting your hand with warmth,
> at least for the sake of spring. (*HCC*, 36–37)

The rest of the poem depicts the bewilderment of the woman who "looks out of place in a room / pulsating on and off." She is locked in an autistic universe where sounds and pictures dominate, but no communication is possible, "as if she were tuned / to a vacant television channel." The pasted-together lines from Grandin's book emphasize the claustrophobia and entrapment of the woman's mind. However, in the closing stanzas the poetic speaker appears and creates a context for the woman's presence:

> I sometimes hear her total bewilderment
> about other people's unbalanced minds
> injected suddenly without warning,
>
> the faint pure tones
> of her heartbeat in my ears. (*HCC*, 36–37)

Rather than words, it is the "faint" language of love that communicates: the heartbeat is received and held, understood over the overwhelming sensory inputs of the earlier stanzas. In the context of this collection, "Sandpaper Letters" further develops the theme of separation at the moment of death. The slow sensory decline of the poem's woman (her mother?) locks her away from linguistic encounters where the only open avenue for communication remains emphatic and emotional. Similarly to McGuckian's previous volume, love is presented here as the driving force of communication. However, the reader is not explicitly invited to partake in this communion but, rather, implicitly allowed to witness the helplessness that accompanies the slow process of death.

While the first part of *The High Caul Cap* traces the slow and painful journey of decline, the middle section addresses the moment and immediate aftermath of death. "The Mercyseat" (*HCC,* 41) is one of the few poems in the collection that explicitly addresses the mother. Mercyseat refers to the cover of the Ark of Covenant, deriving its original Hebrew name (kapporeth) from cleansing and atonement. The poem describes the way in which the mother is slipping away, her hold on reality becoming weaker and weaker:

> Though Sunday my mother begins it.
> Her fingers strike each other like wood,
> moth-sand to her ear above
> in the skymole light. For a year
> she has eaten nothing but ginger.
>
> There are large, tear-shaped areas
> in her eye viewed from side-on,
> however mousy, fin shapes and a trumpet-

> void, as though she were living
> without a heart, her merest yearning edge. (*HCC*, 41)

The "eye" is seen and ceases to see, the heart becomes external to the body. Her imminent death surrounds her and colonizes her body. The listed body parts (fingers, ear, eye, heart) are dysfunctional and uncontrolled/uncontrollable, devoid of meaning. In the dying process sensory organs become inadequate, and life lingers, but it is not contained in a living and functioning body. Baudrillard says that "death demands to be experienced immediately, in total blindness and total ambivalence."[38] Without a functioning body and mind there is only blindness and ambivalence, negating the expression of "experience." Can death ever be an experience without the possibility of processing ("living") this experience? The second part of the poem further highlights the helplessness, vulnerability, and futility of this process:

> And sometimes she revolves in bed
> like a roast before a fire.
> Her Citherean temple is a nest-scene
> on a birdlip mirror, a byway
> of tenderness, as when arms seem
>
> flung out from a centre. (*HCC*, 41)

It is impossible to comprehend what life *is* in a dying body, when the organs still function somewhat but the personality is disappearing. The impossibility of relating to this experience is captured by the closing of the poem, which describes a "sort of cobweb feeling" possessing the speaker. The only possible contact is on the level of preverbal empathy, where the speaker regresses into an embryonic symbiosis with the mother, feeling rather than understanding her: "we understand how much she wants / to be understood, hearing / the grass grow and the squirrel's heart beat." (*HCC*, 41) "The Mercyseat" brings redemption and cleansing through this primeval experience of sharing and taking part in the dying process: accompanying the mother where no one can go.

"The High Caul Cap," (*HCC*, 45) the poem that gives its title to the volume, continues to explore the subject of helplessness. High caul cap, as explained in the description of the volume, was used as a charm against drowning. Cauls are pieces of membranes from the amniotic sac, which some infants are born with, "wearing" them around their heads. Being born in a sac has always been considered to be extremely lucky, and the belief was that this piece of human tissue could offer protection against drowning. In Irish homes it was customary to display cauls over the hearths of sailors' homes, protecting them from perishing at sea. The poem's four stanzas abound in water imagery, emphasizing the threat of drowning:

> The October rains set an all-time record:
> all arrivals and departures were in doubt;
> the airlines were on strike, it seems, in honour
> of the water; in raining mountains, bad, sweet smells. (*HCC*, 45)

These first few lines set a scene where everything is out of balance and "in doubt." Most of the images are taken from a book called *The Snow Leopard*, by Peter Matthiessen, who in 1973 set out to Nepal with a friend to study Himalayan sheep and possibly to set eyes on the snow leopard. Significantly, this journey was more of a spiritual quest for Matthiessen, who wrote passionately about his pilgrimage and "journey of the heart."[39] For McGuckian, these images of weather disturbances also signify a kind of spiritual journeying toward the acceptance of death. The title of the poem, the charm of the caul, fails to protect, and death is experienced as a disruption in the natural order of things:

> Calm spiders in the morning rivers,
> gusts of birds, melody of bells.
> When the heavens duly open
> dead leaves explode underfoot. (*HCC*, 45)

Rain, just like death, is uncontrollable and unstoppable. As an unnatural side effect of climate change (setting an "all-time record") this rain also brings with it the threat of global destruction where animals, humans, and plants lose their bearings. Several of McGuckian's later poems contain references to global warming and human pollution, often commenting on the helpless gaze of the observing (and polluting) human. In "The High Caul Cap" the poet draws a parallel between the "unaccountable" weather and the unaccountability of experiencing death: both are cognitive clichés and yet emotional black holes, causing a "vague melancholy" to overtake the psyche:

> This cold rain, from a cloud that had
> unaccountably overslept, overtakes us
> every afternoon like a vague
> melancholy from some other autumn.
>
> An immense red blossom, whose name
> stops just in time, is the last candidate
> for light; she pulls herself along like a broken
> cricket, past the lifeless houses. (*HCC*, 45)

The striking image of the last two lines is taken directly from Matthiessen's book, describing a poor and unkempt little girl walking on the street. In the poem, the appearance of the female pronoun could reference the mother, whose journey is represented as a slow and painful passage toward death. If the house, as in previous poems, is a repository of the poetic psyche, its lifelessness might indicate the emotional apathy that follows intense grief. The high caul cap fails to protect, the unstoppable water of death takes its victim. However, the caul also evokes the unbreakable birth bond between mother and daughter that promises psychological acceptance of loss. Maybe the power of this charm resides not in its capacity to change unstoppable events but in emphasizing the emotional continuity that reaches beyond death.

"Master of the Female Half-lengths" (*HCC*, 49) also considers the mother-daughter relationship. The title references a Netherlandish painter from the first half of the sixteenth century who was called the master of the female "half-lengths." McGuckian takes this title to indicate the severance between mother and daughter, as both are only "halves" without the other:

> Mother and daughter, you orbit them both
> in their tight widowhood. Her bleak indispositions
> whistled up my veins as though they were vacating
> houses into which we never moved. (*HCC*, 49)

The "never moved into" houses, following on from the previous poem's interpretations, hint at psychological loss and severance. The mother lives in her daughter corporally, carrying on the inheritance of "indispositions." The poem's middle section describes the mother's gradual decline, her "prolonged endurance of drowning." Things fall apart around her and her body is depicted as unstable, a "ship not made of flesh" that "began / to remove its more delicate sails." Although the reader understands the sense of decay and flux that characterizes the figure of the mother, her body is not described in pictorial terms, despite the title's promise of ekphrastic representation. Instead, the speaker receives more pictorial attention, and her actions are described in great visual detail:

> I went about my stilling, dressed
> the chamber, set up the green velvet bed,
> and made an end of my Irish-stitch cushion.

> I came to keep my fish days,
> sent cordials and conserves, a slat-powder
> to put in her beer. (*HCC*, 49)

Although these lines are taken from *Women Writers in Renaissance England*[40] their function is less the referencing of literary predecessors than to bring the reader's attention to the visible acts of kindness of the speaker. There is something about the small acts of feminine care that surpasses time and becomes intelligible through the centuries. Nevertheless, the body of the speaker, as well as that of the mother, remain invisible and assumed only. The historical references to Renaissance half-representations that only hint at corporeal presence match the poetic intention of expressing, in this poem as well as in the previous ones, the emotional difficulty of having to witness a mother's passing. The violence of grief and the lived experience of helplessness permeate the last lines of the poem that describe death's colonization of the mother's body:

> Since her throat
> quakes from time to time
>
> as dark tendrils of her brain snowbud
> the growth of that violet sunset. (*HCC*, 49)

"Dormition: Madonna with Trees" (*HCC*, 52–54) is arguably the centerpiece of this collection. A beautiful elegy written to her mother, it charts the body's slow decline toward death, pondering the very human questions of what happens to the soul of the dead and those who are left behind. Dormition is a word for a peaceful, painless death, and "Madonna with Trees" is a painting by the renaissance painter Giovanni Bellini. Interestingly, Julia Kristeva wrote extensively about Bellini's paintings[41] in relation to psychoanalytical interpretations of motherhood. In this particular painting the standing figure of baby Jesus and Mary behind him are flanked by two trees and a vista of space behind them. Mary Bittner Wiseman, paraphrasing Kristeva, argues that

> Bellini's early Madonna paintings take charge of the necessary and impossible bond between mother and child by putting it into signs, *assigning a form to what can be suffered but not spoken.* He painted its strength and its fragility: for the bond with the mother, like the thread of the spider, is at the same time most strong and most fine. (emphasis added)[42]

McGuckian's focus is exactly this form that "can be suffered but not spoken," which explains the abundance of pictorial references, as well as linguistic obscurity, in this collection. "Dormition: Madonna with Trees" opens with a voice of the first-person singular, addressing an undefined "you":

> I suppose today is more or less your birthday:
> I pray you, send one word
> Whether I shall maintain your taper in the chapel. (*HCC*, 52)

"Suppose" and "more or less" destabilize the speaker's point of view, and although the following two lines are verbatim quotations from a letter by Lord Lisle,[43] which could offer an intertextual grounding for this poem, their content hints at uncertainty and expectation. From the second stanza onward the focus shifts to the figure of the mother and her collapse into death:

> Our mother, who never seemed to sit down,
> takes nothing but broth;
> she has crazed eyes, her singing voice out of tune
>
> in any case—how did this one find
> her speaking voice? She leaves her next thought
> unknown, the unshared thoughts
>
> fall through her upper arms
> and through my left arm runs
> a flood of striped silk. (*HCC*, 52)

The mother's voice is stripped of its communicative faculties, remaining locked away in her disintegrating mind. However, the blood ties of mother and daughter ("the flood of striped silk" that runs in the daughter's arm) remain in place, strengthening the sense of empathy that permeates this poem (*HCC*, 52). The failing of the mother's body is accompanied by the breakdown of communication:

> the next breathing movement
> is a halt in breathing: the throttling sentence
> pulls itself together and stops. (*HCC*, 52)

These lines subtly express a sense of frustration with the unaccountability of the dying process, where nobody, not the dying, or the observing witnesses, can be in control. Life slips away, unaccountably but unstoppably, "almost not to move and not to end / but only to dissolve / in an elsewhere that racks her." (*HCC*, 52). Dying dissolves the body of the mother and she becomes "full of clouds, broken, refashioned, / and infinite" (*HCC*, 52), stressing the helplessness of the observing daughter. Witnessing the death of a parent regresses the observing child into infancy, since the realization, as in the Bellini painting, that mother and child are the two branches of the same tree, brings with it the recognition of the child's own mortality. As the speaker of this poem puts it, the dying body of the mother is "reminding us there are limits / to how long we can follow her" (*HCC*, 52). Like the separation at birth, which in McGuckian's earlier poetry is often represented as traumatic severance from the child, the death of the mother brings with it a distressing split from the mother's body. However, the middle section of the poem calls attention to the spiritual perspective of this coming apart, by acknowledging the otherworldly place that the mother now occupies. Here the mother becomes depicted as an angel figure, outlined by an otherworldly "jubilation" of the afterlife:

> We fear her not to be
> of our world at all, her winged breasts
>
> pleated and yellow:
> time to ripen up to him.
> I turn my microphone then
>
> a little over the yew trees,
> the willows old as from the middle ages,
> all forming a sort of chalice.
>
> She liked to have a line
> around her—the line seems guided
> by a sweet jubilation where she is not. (*HCC*, 53)

"Where she is not" is the incomprehensible loss, the place where no language can follow. This abyss of death is the moment of annihilation, after life has finished but no certainty has taken over. Love does not allow the child to follow the mother here, because this is a journey of disintegration, a point of no return which does not support life:

> It is she who appears
> ready to leave—we mainly lose
> a music, or a boat sunk
>
> containing her as music.
> All of this, her searching odyssey,
> her disintegrating voyage
>
> must be slipped into silk herbs
> by the tips of fingers only. (*HCC*, 53–54)

Death cannot be comprehended "head-on" by language; it can only be circumnavigated by the light touch of art, which leaves things unsaid. This pre-, or rather, postverbal terrain is the subject of Bellini's painting as well, which only hints at, by pictorial references, the baby Jesus's impending death. The central question that interests McGuckian is the impossibility of relating to a loved one's journey towards oblivion. The process of dying has significance only for the living, as Maurice Blanchot explains:

> To die well is to die in one's own life, turned towards one's life and away from death; and this good death shows more consideration for the world than regard for the depth of the abyss.[44]

At the closing of this poem the dying mother stands alone, "anchored" in her life, while her loved ones hold on and "go beyond her," into the abyss of death:

> Now all of the bodies
>
> stand to one edge of the drapery,
> without releasing, go beyond her,
> so that she may stall and anchor there. (*HCC*, 54)

The mother dies as she lived, quietly slipping away from her loved ones, just as she has done in life. What is changing is her child's encounter with oblivion, which alters her relationship with the mother. As McGuckian describes in an interview,

> I imply that even an ordinary death in natural circumstances is a heroic deed and, certainly, I want to honour my mother for her behaviour, her acceptance, her refinement, and her dignity at this time. I find ordinary life so extraordinary; images from war help a little to explain it. . . . She went into a sort of amnesia or depression once the Troubles began here in earnest in the 1970s and 1980s, which affected her whole outlook and her ability to cope with life. She became virtually a prisoner in her own house, as many did although eventually, by the time she reached old age, she had adjusted to never going out and we all accepted that. Her religion was her main and possibly only raft. . . . I try in my poetry to distil something lasting and precious out of all the anguish. I find poetry is one way of dealing with all this inherited fear and violence. It is something dark and menacing that never goes away. Despite all the ways I myself am included and welcomed in my environment as my mother never was, I still am aware of resentment and segregation. . . . I am after truth and justice—I try to deal with all the complexities. I am glad my mother survived the Second World War or I would

> not have been born, but I would have preferred to see her doing something more positive with her excellent mind and body rather than retreating into social paralysis and eking out a rather joyless existence on the margins of society.[45]

"Dormition: Madonna with Trees" attempts to accompany the mother on her "disintegrating voyage." The dying process is also a process of love that embraces oblivion, rather than turns away from it. This is why evoking the Madonna in the title is significant. Her *pietà* gives example to the way love can make sense of death, an idea that stands at the center of this collection.

The High Caul Cap is a volume about death and loss. It charts the body's slow disintegration and love's struggle to come to terms with grief. The poems seem to "touch death" (*HCC*, 76) and ask questions about the transitory process from life to death. Looking for a safe place in the abyss these works explore ideas of spirituality, interiority, and love, inviting the reader to be touched by what Blanchot termed the "sordid intimacy of the abyss." McGuckian concludes her latest works by subtly positioning together her ideas on aesthetics, politics, gender, and spirituality. It remains to be seen what direction her future volumes will take, and she will certainly have readers who eagerly await any such work. In the meantime the inward journeys of her last three volumes offer a unique insight into McGuckian's poetic self and unite the creative methodologies of this truly exceptional poet.

Notes

1. Medbh McGuckian, "Interview with McGuckian," by Shane Alcobia-Murphy and Richard Kirkland, in *The Poetry of Medbh McGuckian: The Interior of Words*, ed. Shane Alcobia-Murphy and Richard Kirkland (Cork: Cork University Press, 2010), 205.

2. "A Book of Rains" might in fact be a direct allusion to G. Levi della Vida's translation of *Book of Rains and Wind*, an obscure, ancient Arabic weather forecasting by Masaallah. Although the similarity in the titles might be accidental, the intentional or unintentional reference is interesting. The Arabic work contemplates control in connection with astrological definitions of the weather. See Giorgio Levi della Vida, "Un opuscolo astrologico di Mâšâ'allâh" [A Small Astrological Work of Mâšâ'allâh], *Rivista degli studi orientali* [Review of Oriental Studies] 14 (1934): 270–81.

3. Alcobia-Murphy and Kirkland, *Poetry of Medbh McGuckian*, 13.

4. Sean Hand, ed., *Emmanuel Levinas: The Levinas Reader* (Oxford: Blackwell, 1989), 83.

5. Gannit Ankori, *Imaging Her Selves: Frida Kahlo's Poetics of Identity and Fragmentation* (Westport, CT: Greenwood Press, 2002), 64.

6. Ibid.

7. See quoted from memorial website of Frida Kahlo, "My Nurse and I," (n.p., n.d., c. 1937), http://www.fridakahlofans.com/c0190.html (accessed November 30, 2010).

8. For more information on the influence of Mexican votive art on Kahlo's work see Andrea Kettenmann, *Frida Kahlo, 1907–1954: Pain and Passion*, trans. Karen Williams (Köln, Germany: Benedikt Taschen, 2003), 35.

9. Janis A. Tomlinson, ed., *Goya: Images of Women* (New Haven, CT: Yale University Press, 2002), 195.

10. For a detailed recount of the story see Dáithí Ó hÓgáin *Myth, Legend and Romance: An Encyclopedia of the Irish Folk Tradition* (New York: Prentice Hall Press, 1991), 173.

11. An audio version of Medbh McGuckian's reading from *CRNH* can be downloaded from: http://www.qub.ac.uk/schools/SeamusHeaneyCentreforPoetry/pal/medbhmcguckian/

12. Scott Brewster. "The Space That Cleaves: The House and Hospitality in Medbh McGuckian's Work," in *The Poetry of Medbh McGuckian: The Interior of Words*, ed. Shane Alcobia-Murphy and Richard Kirkland (Cork: Cork University Press, 2010), 105.

13. Johannes Brahms, *The Brahms Notebooks: Little Treasure Chest of the Young Kreisler*, ed. Carl Krebs, trans. Agnes Eisenberger (Hillsdale, NY: Pendragon Press, 2003), 53.

14. Susie Orbach, *Hunger Strike: The Anorectic's Struggle as a Metaphor for Our Age* (London: Faber and Faber, 1986), 51.

15. Launch of the Medbh McGuckian symposium at the University of Ulster, Magee, Derry on January 26, 2007, personal notes.

16. Anne-Lise François, *Open Secrets: The Literature of Uncounted Experience* (Stanford, CA: Stanford University Press, 2008), 19.

17. Emily Dickinson, "The Difference between Despair," quoted and exquisitely analyzed in François, *Open Secrets,* 173–75.

18. Ibid., 135.

19. Ibid., 133.

20. Medbh McGuckian, *My Love Has Fared Inland* (Oldcastle, Ireland: Gallery Press, 2008) (hereafter cited as *MLFI*).

21. Wynne Maggi, *Our Women Are Free: Gender and Ethnicity in the Hindukush* (Ann Arbor: University of Michigan Press, 2001), 160.

22. See an interview quoted in chapter 2 where she discussed her desire to become a priest. Laura O'Connor, "*Comhrá*: Conversation between Medbh McGuckian and Nuala Ní Dhomhnaill," with foreword and afterword by Laura O'Connor, *Southern Review* 31, no. 3 (Summer 1995): 596.

23. Alcobia-Murphy and Kirkland, *Poetry of Medbh McGuckian*, 207.

24. Maggi, *Our Women Are Free,* 121.

25. Ibid., 147.

26. See François's concept of the "open secret." François, *Open Secrets*, 65.

27. Edmund C. Jaeger, *Desert Wildlife* (Stanford, CA: Stanford University Press, 1950), 246.

28. Ibid., 247.

29. BBC nature documentary series, *Life of Birds*, written and presented by David Attenborough, first transmitted in the UK from October 21, 1998. David Attenborough, Mike Salisbury, Fergus Beeley, Nigel Marven, Peter Bassett, Miles Barton, and Joanna Sarsby, *The Life of Birds* ([S.l.]: BBC Video, 2002).

30. This poem is itself partly "inspired" by another text, with several phrases in the last stanza copied from it. The book is Minna Törmä, *Landscape Experience as Visual Narrative: Northern Song Dynasty Landscape Handscrolls in the Li Cheng-Yan Wengui Tradition* (Helsinki: Tiedekirja, University of Michigan Press, 2002).

31. Medbh McGuckian, *The High Caul Cap* (Oldcastle, Ireland: Gallery Press, 2012) (hereafter cited as *HCC*).

32. Ann B. Shteir, *Cultivating Women, Cultivating Science: Flora's Daughters and Botany in England, 1760–1860* (Baltimore: Johns Hopkins University Press, 1996).

33. Ibid., 139. "Withering" is a reference to William Withering, who published his botanical work in 1776.

34. Ibid., 158.

35. Tim Robinson, *Connemara: Listening to the Wind* (London: Penguin Books, 2007).

36. For more on this subject see Shane Alcobia-Murphy, *Medbh McGuckian: The Poetics of Exemplarity* (Aberdeen Introductions to Irish and Scottish Culture, Aberdeen: AHRC Centre for Irish and Scottish Studies, 2012).

37. It is also interesting to note that some of these lines were taken from Sylvia Plath's journal and also from Assia, Ted Hughes's later lover. The emotional turmoil of Plath comes across for example in "drawers of silence, bled into the rug" (*HCC*, 36–37).

38. Jean Baudrillard, *Symbolic Exchange and Death* (Thousand Oaks, CA: Sage Publications, 2004), 186–87.

39. Peter Matthiessen, *The Snow Leopard* (New York: Penguin Nature Classics, 1996).

40. Randall Martin, *Women Writers in Renaissance England* (London: Longman, 1997).

41. Julia Kristeva, "Motherhood According to Giovanni Bellini," in *20th Century Theories of Art*, ed. James M. Thompson (Ottawa: Carleton University Press, 1999), 441–66.

42. Mary Bittner Wiseman, "Renaissance Paintings and Psychoanalysis: Julia Kristeva and the Function of the Mother," in *Ethics, Politics and Difference in Julia Kristeva's Writings*, ed. Kelly Oliver (New York: Routledge, 1993), 105.

43. Muriel St. Clare Byrne, ed., *The Lisle Letters: An Abridgement*, selected and arranged by Bridget Boland (Chicago: University of Chicago Press, 1983), 258.

44. Maurice Blanchot, *The Space of Literature*, trans. Ann Smock (Lincoln: University of Nebraska Press, 1982), 100.

45. Medbh McGuckian, interview by John Hoppenthaler, *Connotation Press Online* 4, no. 4 (February 2013), http://www.connotationpress.com/a-poetry-congeries-with-john-hoppenthaler/415 (accessed October 18, 2013).

5

Thematic Readings of Medbh McGuckian's Work

As noted in the introduction there is a creative lack of consensus among critics about the best way to interpret Medbh McGuckian's poetry. Some argue for philosophical readings, some for political, and yet others for feminist methodologies. To help readers orientate themselves within McGuckian's oeuvre, this chapter offers an outline of four major themes and reading strategies within the poet's work. The first of these considers McGuckian's poetry in terms of literary performance. In this strand the poet's creative methodology comes under scrutiny, whether the precise focus centers on her intertextual sources or her self-reflective *modus operandi*. The common theme in these readings is creativity and the poet's diverse attitude to poetic methodology. The second strategy looks at gendered readings of McGuckian's work and discusses the figure of the mother in particular. McGuckian is a somewhat reluctant feminist, who claims to write for women and yet often espouses masculinist vocabulary when discussing her poems. The section investigates to what extent gendered readings are possible within her work. The third reading strategy discusses McGuckian's politicized aesthetic and asks how far the Northern Irish conflict influences her poetry. Finally, I will look at spirituality and the potential of spiritual readings of McGuckian's poetry, discussing religious and, in particular, Catholic influences within her work.

Literary Performance: Creativity and Intertextuality

The methodology of reading McGuckian is intimately and centrally connected to her methodology of writing. The poet's fascination with her creative process(es) begets a critical approach that explores the exegesis of creativity and inspiration. Critical perspectives of this discussion are varied, however.

Some scholars conduct a meaning-based inquiry which prioritizes the finished textual product to explain McGuckian's literary performance, while others, as discussed in the introduction, use source-based, genetic criticism to unearth textual origins as their starting point.

Meaning-based readings of McGuckian's work primarily investigate the published textual product, and not its method of creation, as the source for interpretation. The current study can certainly be situated within this broad "family" of critical approach. However, one of the central focuses of my own research has been the attempt to explore the performative aspect of the creative process in McGuckian's poetry, and since this informs much of the current study it is necessary to sketch in more detail what "creativity" signifies in the context of her work.

How is a poem written? How does McGuckian conceptualize the process of creation, and what is the reader's role in this "performance"? Examining the concept of performance with regard to Medbh McGuckian's poetry, I argue that the creative process is often portrayed in her work as the performative tension between communicative interaction and subjectivity. This translates as a fundamental ambiguity between the desire to communicate with others and the desire to express the self. McGuckian recognizes the anxiety which this interface creates. If a means of self-articulation, poetry is in danger of losing its "function" as sociopolitical reflection, while, if the focus of writing is to reach out and communicate, self-expression may become jeopardized. Naturally, this division of public and private concerns is neither simple nor unproblematic. Much of McGuckian's poetry, however, focuses on the compositional effort to incorporate poetry's double bind as expression and communication, and her poems reflect on the poet's effort to formulate an aesthetic, which articulates its own performance as ambiguous.

In the context of Medbh McGuckian's work, the question of creativity is intricate and ambiguous. Close to incomprehensible on a surface level, her poems do not invite the reader for an easy intellectual workout. Although often criticized for incommunicability, her work also aspires to be a reflection on sociopolitical issues. A deep-seated ethical awareness runs through her often secretive language, and the reader, as a result, is given the opportunity to take part in her singular poetic performance. Critical work on her poetry has so far focused largely on her linguistic and political peculiarities. Yet, the mostly uncharted territory of her performance of creativity within her work offers invaluable insight into her poetic methodology. Many of McGuckian's poems, particularly in the first four collections, investigate the creation of self through the prism of poetry writing. Given that offering a precise definition of creation seems futile (since all its elements, the individual, society, culture, cognitive process, and emotion are questionable and unstable) it seems best to consider it as the cohort of all constituents and concentrate consequently on its methodology. The first chapter set out to do this in the context of McGuckian's development of her writing self in her early volumes. The close reading of the poems traced a subtle progress and growing awareness of woman as poet and argued that the performance of creativity was intricately connected to a conscious shaping of McGuckian's creative self.

The desire of the human mind to apprehend divinity was the driving force behind most of the articulations of creativity in antiquity. Because desire plays such a fundamental role in human creativity, it is not surprising that there is often a phantom participant in the performance of inspiration. Whether functioning as a subject or as an object of desire, the spectre of another person usually accompanies poetic expression, and this is particularly true of Medbh McGuckian's work. She says:

> Nuala Ní Dhomhnaill and I would talk about this muse figure. The first thing I would say when I meet her is "How is your muse?." We might not always have this figure that we need to encounter, but certainly it's a very big advantage to have one, or at least one, and then one to fall back on when the major one dies or ceases to attract. It is a lodestone. . . . I would have this colloquy, often with a male, sometimes a female, and often with a dead person, for example with the young boy that I didn't know, who suddenly became the muse for the period of the poem. It is a funny process, that there is this other person, who you can't actually speak to in real life, but you can in this space that you create. They come into it, or you pull them into it, and sometimes they pull you into it, and it's not something you can control.[1]

This "other person" in her poetry is not only recognizable as someone of personal significance to the poet, but also as a modern-day manifestation of both a pre-Platonic and post-Romantic figure of the muse. What differentiates it from other subjects appearing in her poems is its direct influence on the creation of the work. Whether passive or active, male or female, divine or human, visible or invisible, these figures unequivocally participate in the performance of poetry-making.

Thus the muse, the most enigmatic participant in the performance of creativity is the imaginary subject who, in one way or another, exerts authorial influence on the completion of the work. Whether imagined or real, this person functions as the created projection of the work's singularity. In simpler terms, he or she becomes an essential participant in the performance of creativity. The ancient, pre-Platonic (and plural) muses embodied the power of language, which was their gift to humans. Because the human mind at that time was conceptualized as a receptor, rather than as the originator of language, the muses were credited with creativity and expression. They had authorial power, which they exercised through love. They metaphorically represented the ambiguity inherent in desire, in that they were situated at the threshold of the unattainable divine and the empirical human spheres. Then, with Plato, their function underwent a fundamental change. The Platonic muses' gift becomes the arousal of the poet by their divine power. Socrates says, "The god takes their intellect away from them when he uses them as his servants."[2] An individual muse, therefore, takes possession of an individual poet, thus forming the beginning of the magnetic chain. The muse becomes a facilitating metaphor for describing an altered state of mind, which puts the poet into a state of desiring or "giving birth in beauty." The metamorphosis of a mortal into a true poet, sane into insane, is named as possession by the muse. Socrates claims that "beautiful poems" are the "invention of the muses." However, if one accepts that the muses represent the process that enables a human to become pregnant with creative expression, it follows that authorial responsibility can only rest with the poet himself. From this moment on, consequently, inspiration (possession by the muses), self-expression, and madness become inseparable concepts. The author as subject was born and for almost two millennia his (and much less often her) creative ego has dominated discourses on poetic creativity. The muse also took up her new position within the male imagination. Because she was no longer expected to communicate or form a relationship, she was talked at and talked about, but never spoken to. She became what Irigaray calls a "commodity," which is passed between men. To put it simply, she becomes the empty vessel the poet used to be and quietly swallows whatever comes her way.

What the work of Medbh McGuckian demonstrates is a drastic rejection of this romanticized stereotype. However, as mentioned earlier on, this rejection does not mean disregard for the muse as possible subject of poetic discourse. Rather, McGuckian's conceptualization of the source of inspiration as a contingent power of communication between author, text, and reader arguably sees its antecedent in the figure of the ancient muse. I do not want to assume that for this poet the ancients were models of representation, but merely suggest that rather than casting the idiom of the muse aside as an irrelevant and romantic cliché, it is possible to interpret their reemergence in contemporary poetry as a reiteration of their original function as manifestations of language and desire. The pre-Platonic muses have created a blueprint where the authorial voice is conceptualized as a distinct and distant entity from the self, whereas the Platonic and post-Platonic model allows for a variable, gendered subjectivity to emerge within the poetic imagination. With the prestige of the individual gone, theory has given the text dominance over the author. When Medbh McGuckian engages with the ancient imagery of the muses (whichever "model" she follows) or when she personifies the source of origin in any other form, she fundamentally subverts the dominance of both text and author. McGuckian's poetry develops a theoretical connection between the metaphor of the muse and the metaphor of the text: both disclaim the individual as responsible author, thus creating in themselves that "oblique space" which comfortably describes a voice of origin. This voice, crucially, communicates but refuses to be captured as singular. This phenomenon also has a precursor in Plato. As Judith Butler comments on the Symposium: "So who speaks here? Plato, Socrates, Diotima, the gods? Is there a singular speaker at all? What has love done to the singularity of the subject of speech?" Contemporary representations of the source of origin conceptualize the lost singularity of the subject in metaphorical images, which range from the concrete to the abstract and from the ancient to the postmodern. What they have in common with the Greek muses is their power over language and desire. Whatever forms the voice of origin takes, it is endowed with the divine privilege of telling lies and truth, of materializing as something concrete and yet evading interpretation. The contemporary muse has the vanishing face of Eurydice, as Simon Critchley describes in his analysis of the story of Orpheus:

> Orpheus' gaze is fascinated by something which its desire cannot resist and over which it has no power. . . . The fascinated gaze does not perceive any real object or form, it is like seeing with eyes open in the insomniac night, when familiar objects take on strange and terrible contours in the darkness, where they seem to attract the gaze to the extent that they continue to evade it—the experience of the uncanny.[3]

Thus the familiar shape and form of the muse attract and evade the glance of poets and critics alike, enticing further flirtation and inquiry.

In summary, Medbh McGuckian's poems reflect upon their source, their creative process, and also the reading strategies employed to decode them. Uniquely, McGuckian challenges the reader to trace all these elements in her writing. In McGuckian's earlier poetry the creative performance is intrinsically linked to the formation of the poetic self, while in the later volumes of her considerable oeuvre sociopolitical concerns become enmeshed with aesthetic inquiry. In the reading methodology outlined above McGuckian's creative processes come to the fore. The reader is thus alerted to metaphorical representations of writing and also to personified manifestations of the figure of the muse. Because literary performance is central to McGuckian's poetry, and one of the most prevalent themes in her work is poetic creativity, the various reading methodologies of focusing on how her poems are written—whether through the theory of creativity or through genetic criticism—yields, I believe, the most diverse and interesting interpretative results. And because of her perceived obscurity, looking at her *modus operandi* also represents one of the most common critical approaches to her work.

Gender, Motherhood

This thematic review concerns itself with tracing Medbh McGuckian's writing through the complex metaphorical representations of gender. Medbh McGuckian has always been considered as a somewhat reluctant feminist, who, in her interviews, is keen to confound inquiries concerning her gender politics. Unlike Eavan Boland, for example, whose literary career has been centered around an accessible politicization of female authority, McGuckian upsets readings that search for a liberation of the silenced woman. Her poetry demonstrates an apparent lack of interest in feminist strategies of emancipation, and yet, many of her poems, and the female muses in them, reflect on the (formidable) self of the woman writer. It seems that her aim is to challenge and reject narrowly defined identities and offer instead a conceptual feminization of poetic identity. This is achieved within her peculiar aesthetic, which poeticizes the politicized gestures of contemporary feminism.

The representation of motherhood takes center stage in McGuckian's poetic expressions of gender. The most commonly referenced critical apparatus in the interpretation of "the mother" in her work is psychoanalysis. McGuckian herself often talks about motherhood as one of the most significant driving forces behind her writing. She was heavily pregnant when in 1979 she won the prestigious National Poetry Competition, and in subsequent interviews she often referred back to this as a pivotal moment in her life. Her early volumes are suffused with birthing and pregnancy images, which are probably the most prevalent themes throughout her early work. Motherhood as a concept has been approached from several directions by critics utilizing mainly psychoanalytic theories as their interpretative tool. Pregnancy is often discussed as metaphorically representing burden and expectation, both applied not only to childbearing but also to writing. Michaela Schrage-Früh talks about the motif of pregnancy as "linking or contrasting the processes occurring in her body to phenomena of the natural and cultural world around her."[4] There are critics who investigate the prenatal embryo as symbolic of the locus of McGuckianesque language, and who also analyze the strange bind between mother and fetus as a prelinguistic representation of the creative process.[5] Language in fact takes center stage in these discussions, and McGuckian's obscurity is often approached from the point of view of feminist readings of mother tongue, redeploying and reinterpreting Héléne Cixous's *écriture feminine*.[6] When critics look at early childhood in McGuckian's poetry, they often highlight the poet's personal postnatal depression as a creative driving force behind her writing and also, connected to this point, the sense of entrapment which permeates some of her early work. However, from a linguistic point of view the special preverbal bond between mother and child also takes center stage. At the center of all these readings is an investigation of ownership within McGuckian's work, which is of course intricately connected to her consideration of literary performance. McGuckian, like many of her contemporaries, evidently seeks to take ownership of her feminine creativity in a male-dominated poetry scene. The starting point for this is often the site of the pregnant female body and the child it contains. Acknowledgment of possession of the embryo empowers McGuckian to acknowledge ownership of her poetic creativity.[7] This, however, is not an unambiguous relationship: her poems, just like her children, are distinct and separate identities taking up residence in her imagination, and the language that expresses this bond is also often fraught with ambivalence and uncertainty. On the one hand this uncertainty refers to a conflict all women writers confront when faced with balancing maternal and artistic duties, but on the other this is very specific to McGuckian and betrays a commitment to containing, rather than resolving, ambivalence. This is highlighted by her concentration on the birthing process in many of her poems. Parturition is an act of simultaneous creation and severance—the mother gives life but also severs the intrauterine bond with her offspring. Similarly, poetic creation contains this ambiguity of giving and letting go, where the end product becomes a distinct entity with only metaphorical bonds to its creator.[8] In McGuckian's later volumes, less often analyzed from this perspective, a different approach emerges to motherhood which sees the poet positioning herself intergenerationally: her focus turns less toward mothering a child and more toward her personal position as mother and daughter simultaneously. It is interesting to note that parallel to this development McGuckian's examination of her creative process also changes, as she becomes more interested in contextualizing her work in a public sphere than describing the progress of the development of her poetic self.

There is, significantly, also a spiritual dimension to motherhood in McGuckian's work: she often describes in interviews how in the early stages of her career she compared her poetic vocation to a vatic one. She claimed in 1995 for example that she had a "priestly" vocation: "I realised I had some kind of message to hand on and that I was in some degree a priest."[9] The vocational aspect of her profession is imbued with maternal responsibilities, where she sees herself as a mother giving birth to words and readers alike. McGuckian's tendency to reconstruct, rather than simply obliterate, masculinized symbolism is evidently at play here. The culturally embedded image of the priestly, protecting father figure (problematic as it is) becomes replaced by a nurturing, albeit ambiguous mother figure whose spiritual maternity presides over her poetic progenies. A similar rewriting tendency can be observed in McGuckian's approach to the figure of the Virgin Mary. Deeply entrenched in the mythological vocabulary of Catholic Ireland, the Virgin Mary is for many an icon of purity, sublime goodness, maternal perfection, and also feminine submissiveness. For McGuckian, a Northern Irish Catholic woman poet, the idealization of these female characteristics causes necessary rupture and conflict: emulating the Virgin is not only an unattainable goal but also something which conflicts deeply with her aspirations toward independence and authenticity. However, interestingly, the Virgin Mother (similarly to the muse) does not disappear from McGuckian's poetry but, rather, becomes a central driving force behind her writings. She explains this in an interview:

> So at first I wrote in order to get rid of all stale and false notions about religion that were imposed on me. . . . But then through the writing I'm exploring my own idea of her [Virgin Mary]. What I feel is important to me is the beauty of the whole image, especially in Renaissance paintings and in sculpture. . . . In my deepest consciousness, whatever she means to me is that she must have been a real person sometime. She must have existed and she must have had some qualities that made her a valuable, sacred being. I try very hard when I'm writing—not writing about her exactly because

> I think she's very remote—to strip away all the accretions of heresy and the accretion of losing whatever was human. Even though she's been so twisted, torn and manipulated by men for their own purposes, she still for me has an identity that I'm drawn to. . . . To me, as an artist, if beauty is your inspiration, then why could she be not that, for a woman as well?[10]

It is very interesting to observe how the figure of the Virgin Mary becomes subliminal in McGuckian's thoughts. The psychological qualities of "realness" transform the Virgin into a humanized source of the aesthetic sublime: for McGuckian she is no longer simply an icon of purity but, rather, that of the sublime. McGuckian's conceptualization of the Virgin Mary is inherently tinged with a Burkean sense of the positive sublime: the primary aesthetic response to her is experienced through "love" (she talks about a "nonpredatory love" when describing her relationship to Mary[11]). This devotional love expresses the tension that McGuckian faces in relation to her religion when she acknowledges the contrary pulls of her religion's oppressive forces and its simultaneous invitation to unconditional love. Interestingly, in many of her poems she embodies these concepts in gendered terms, depicting masculine awe-inspiring powers alongside feminine love, perhaps subconsciously following in the footsteps of Edmund Burke.[12] The Virgin's creative inspiration in McGuckian's poetry is a maternal one, where Mary "fuses into [an] idea of God" for the poet.[13] McGuckian describes God as the "writer of the joke"[14] (humor being the representation of love), and Mary is an extension of that concept. Marian and spiritual motherhood therefore contain, rather than simplify, McGuckian's vocational and maternal ambiguities.

The poet's conceptualization of motherhood is of course greatly influenced not only by religious but also political iconography. Mother Ireland is a highly symbolic, and easily recognizable, trope in Irish nationalist discourse, which emphasizes her unambiguous, submissive, charitable, and most of all desexualized maternal qualities. The dominant relationship within this narrative is between mother and son, which leaves little space for the development of a woman's voice. McGuckian and her contemporaries have put major emphasis on the poetical rewriting of this myth. Subverting the iconography from within, McGuckian positions the female body in the center of her attention and, significantly, claims it as her own. Many critics have misinterpreted this technique as a kind of domesticization of the political; however, a closer look betrays its complexity.[15] McGuckian on several occasions takes up and seemingly endorses the myth of Mother Ireland when portraying Northern

Ireland as passive and vulnerable (as for example in the cover image of her *Selected Poems,* which depicts a sleeping woman).[16] Elsewhere she addresses the feminine stereotype by reimagining her country as an organic, physical part of the body of Ireland. When asked about colonial gender stereotypes in an interview she commented:

> I was always perplexed by Heaney's analogy [England as the imperial male] which worked with 1801 but not with 1921 and the division of Ireland. So here the head of the woman i.e. the North is detached from her shoulders and in a way her body—the South—is liberated but her mind is still a colonial subject.[17]

Unlike her contemporaries, most of whom strive to reinterpret or subvert this stereotype, McGuckian views these maternal images in visual terms. She reconciles her feminine and national identities by internalizing, rather than critiquing, the gendered myth of Mother Ireland.

In conclusion, McGuckian's poetry offers itself up to psychoanalytical readings in relation to motherhood: her inscrutable language, complex creative process, and ambiguous relationship with childbirth (and death) are all aspects of her work which yield to this type of reading methodology. In addition, the national and religious iconography of the mother further influence McGuckian's poetic reinterpretation of childbirth and maternity, delving deeper into the poet's complex approach to this subject. As Schrage-Früh remarks: "in a culture so dependent on religious and national images of the mother, the subject of female sexuality and motherhood can never be purely private and 'nonpolitical.'"[18]

Politics and Poetics

Politics is one of the most divisive issues in relation to McGuckian's poetry. In the early years of her career her reviewers often accused her of not engaging with the Northern Irish situation.[19] This was partly because of the perceived "domestic" obscurity of her poetry, but McGuckian herself seemed reluctant to explore the subject. In one of her early interviews in 1990 she says:

> Poetry is not a servant of politics. The "Troubles" affect my life and enter my poetry that way, but I avoid them as a subject as I avoid taking arms up against the sea. The crisis informs my work,

> naturally, but I can't confront it there, it is too complex. . . . One could argue that I don't deal with or solve anything. I just suggest an attitude of compassion in what is part of a universal tragedy.[20]

Three years later she talks about the emotional difficulty of engaging with this subject:

> I think when it's over [the Troubles] maybe you can comment. But our violence was such an inbred thing, and so ongoing, it wasn't like a war. For years, the bloodshed was chaotic. Here it was like a person killed every night, like just a drip. I've never been able to write about it; I'm very squeamish about it.[21]

And later on she comments, "You see, I would be political in a very homely way."[22] In her confessional essay "Drawing Ballerinas," which was written in 1995 after the first IRA ceasefire, McGuckian discusses in great detail the intended political undertone of all her volumes written up to that date. She describes how, in 1970, in the year of Bloody Sunday, Seamus Heaney showed her how to turn the Troubles into art: "There was a kind of complicity that many things were wrong in the State of Denmark, but that the way to redress them was through the non-violence of poetry."[23] Retrospectively McGuckian claims to have been affected very deeply by the widespread violence but lacking the "tools" to write about it:

> A girl who had been in my class at school and lived a few doors from us was one of the Saturday afternoon victims of the Abercorn Café explosion. My father was asked to go to the morgue and identify her, as her own family were too shocked, and he said he could only go by the blue fur of her anorak—she always wore this very pretty mini-jacket. I would have wanted to write about that in some way, but had not the tools at the time.[24]

It is interesting to note that in her 1988 collection *On Ballycastle Beach* she included a poem titled "The Blue She Brings with Her," which was written for a friend of hers who lost a son in the Troubles, with covert reference to the "blue" her friend brought with her into death. Also, her 2001 poem "Drawing Ballerinas" includes a footnote explaining it was written to commemorate Frances Ann Owens, the schoolfellow who lost her life in the explosion. This example seems to demonstrate the subtle growth of confidence, or outspokenness, in relation to the theme of political violence in McGuckian's poetry. However, it is important not to disregard as domestic escapism the poet's earlier attempts at addressing the Troubles. Although the relationship between literature and politics is explicitly commented on in Medbh McGuckian's later poetry, a case can be made that her earlier volumes also address the complex links between political and poetical consciousness. McGuckian's work seems to reconfigure the division between these two spheres, with the effect that they deconstruct and reconstruct one another.

Clair Wills, one of the first critics to take notice of McGuckian's political aesthetic, has argued that McGuckian's intimate, private sphere is never separated from the public, political world.[25] In her informative study she argues that McGuckian's radicalism lies in her secrecy and resistance to interpretation:

> It is only because of the elements of representation in her work that McGuckian can hope to engage fruitfully with the particular construction of public and political discourse in Ireland. . . . What is at stake in her work is not the investigation and protection of interior space, it is not even the *addition* of that interior or private story to the public narrative. Instead this kind of aesthetic representation has an interventionist function. While engaging with the construction of political discourse in Ireland, it is saying to an iniquitous system of political representation, to, if you like, an unrepresentative bureaucracy—the normal processes of political negotiation have failed, and I will take no part in them.[26]

When Clair Wills wrote this in 1993, only the first four of McGuckian's volumes had appeared. In these collections, as mentioned previously, the focus is largely directed toward the creation of self and the negotiations of the private. Wills's argument, therefore, concerns the political interpretations of what she terms the "intimate sphere" of McGuckian, rather than her later, more overtly political poetry. Nevertheless, strategies of "not taking part" in the political discourse of Ireland are strongly discernible in the later volumes as well. As argued earlier, McGuckian's involvement in politics does not amount to an explicit articulation of a political viewpoint. Rather, as Leontia Flynn puts it:

> Medbh McGuckian's poetry is largely self-conscious in its attitudes to history and public life; her "readerliness" and her focus on language continue to foreground the interpretation of these political narratives rather than engaging with the narratives themselves.[27]

What the later volumes show is a growing political consciousness and an increased acknowledgement of poetry's cultural embeddedness. This means that the literary performance within these poems suggests an amplified sensitivity to contemporary political debate, but not an expression of dogmatic viewpoints. McGuckian's approach to politics is subtle, circuitous, and inseparable from her aesthetic interests. It is important therefore to remain aware of the political undercurrents informing her work.

It can be further argued that as a result of her sustained exposure to Northern Irish politics, the representation of violence is symptomatic in Medbh McGuckian's poetry. This violence, however, does not appear exclusively in a political context, but also within language and composition, as was discussed in the chapters focusing on the poet's most openly political volumes. McGuckian's Northern Irish background predisposes her to creating a "symbiotic relationship" (as Fran Brearton calls it) between poetry and violence.[28] This relationship, however, is fraught with tension. McGuckian demonstrates reluctance toward entering into poetical witnessing. Instead, her poetry looks at violence "sideways," never confronting its manifestations but yet testifying to its reality. As Peter McDonald explains:

> Poetry facing events in the troubles tends to avoid the elegiac, and is more closely attuned to bewilderment than consolation, insisting on the integrity of specifics at the same time as the individuality of the poetic voice. Successful poetry "about" violence is always aware that it is apart from that violence, just as all good poetry understands its own linguistic medium as something which, while in a comprehensible (and thus finally accountable) relation to reality, is not the same thing as the reality it addresses.[29]

McGuckian's poetry thus is "not the same thing" as its political referent. It is almost as if the poet deemed poetry an insufficient means to comment on her personal experiences of the Troubles. Shane Alcobia-Murphy argues that rather than avoiding political references McGuckian is employing a kind of code language that allows her to speak about the Troubles and its victims. In Alcobia-Murphy's reading the poet "uses the words of other writers—the biographers or their subjects—to set up analogies for the Troubles, detailing experiences of oppression or societal turmoil." He further argues that McGuckian, like Heaney, "looks towards Eastern Europe for precursors."[30] Alcobia-Murphy believes that the poet's "secret embedding of quotations"[31] testifies to a strategy of political reflection. The most interesting question in this debate concerns poetry's ethical responsibility in times of turmoil. Does McGuckian owe it to her compatriots to be more directly involved in political narratives? Eastern European poets certainly believed in their duty to report, reflect, and proclaim. However, the context in which they wrote was somewhat different in one important aspect: freedom of expression. While the level of experienced personal violence is difficult to measure and judge, the censorship and brutal silencing of poets and other artists were an integral part of Eastern European experience. In contrast, the Northern Irish situation created an atmosphere of physical threat and intimidation where proclaiming one's religious identity could be construed as more dangerous than the actual content of artistic expression. Medbh McGuckian claimed that it was just as dangerous for her to be outspoken in her voice as it was for Mandelstam.[32] However, much of the ethical imperative in Mandelstam's work originated from the very real threat (and later reality) of Siberian exile and silencing imposed by Stalin. As Mandelstam says, "Only in Russia is poetry respected, it gets people killed. Is there anywhere else where poetry is so common a motive for murder?"[33] It is easy to see how Mandelstam's circumstances do not equate with McGuckian's experiences. It is arguable therefore that McGuckian articulates her ethical empathy toward the Russian poet and in particular his wife, Nadezhda Mandelstam, who was his long-suffering companion, rather than creating a metaphorical analogy between their differing societal circumstances.

Alcobia-Murphy attempts to demonstrate the way in which McGuckian circumnavigates societal expectations for "talking about" the Troubles by using an elaborate code language through referencing (and indeed utilizing quotes from) Mandelstam in her poetry. However, this narrative still believes in an underlying ethical imperative which should report on political events. Alcobia-Murphy sets out to reveal "just how directly political much of her [McGuckian's] poetry is."[34] Although immensely more helpful than her early critics' dismissal of her as a writer concerned exclusively with a "feminine point of view,"[35] it can be argued that Alcobia-Murphy still contrives to miss the point. In my view it is more helpful to view McGuckian's work as a reflection on interpreting this ethical imperative and responding to it in a distinctively unique way.

Spirituality and Religion

Just as she is often labeled a reluctant feminist, many argue that McGuckian's relationship with religion is also fraught with tension. She has often claimed in interviews that Catholicism is one of the most important identity markers in her life, both politically and spiritually. In her essay "Drawing Ballerinas: How Being Irish Has Influenced Me as a Writer" she speaks candidly about her relationship with the church. Describing her identity as a Northern Irish teenager she claims that "What I most categorically was, was a Roman Catholic, first and foremost."[36] This strong sense of belonging was of course politically demarcated by the sectarian society of the time and was coterminous with a nationalist and republican identity. However, as McGuckian describes, the idea of the church as "shelter and emotional or spiritual refuge, was in fact highly inimical to me, as a woman."[37] Very soon McGuckian experienced that within the church she could only be a second-class citizen:

> So being excluded from one's society on the grounds of being Catholic resulted in an ultimate exclusion from the heart of the Catholic rituals themselves, on the grounds of sex. My mother was in the third order of the Carmelites, and on dismal Sunday afternoons I would attend long meetings with her. But I could not be an altar boy, although I learned Latin. I could sing in the choir but I could not walk on the altar. It was still the days when you had to keep your head covered with a mantilla because St Paul said women's hair was a temptation. Also my mother went through the churching ceremony after her babies, and related a story of how she was once refused Communion because she was wearing lipstick. We would pass perfume from our handbags up and down the pew until elderly gentlemen behind us would complain. Eventually with developing sexuality I came to a painful rejection of much of what had been inculcated.[38]

This "painful rejection" manifested itself in a turning away from the institutional church and instead turning to writing poetry as a spiritual "substitute." Although McGuckian recounts how at this point in her life she "hated Christianity for its divisiveness and the sectarian nature of the violence,"[39] religion continued to play a significant part in her creative imagination. As noted previously, in the early stages of her career she often compared her poetic vocation to a vatic one, and described in interviews how she saw herself as "in some degree a priest."[40] In her early volumes spirituality appears in the form of birthing imagery; however, explicit religious references are scarce. Instead, quasi-superstitious beliefs handed down by the poet's grandmother occupy her imagination:

> My grandmother was a strong and influential figure who had her own vital brand of superstition, her own adherences to the old rural faith with its penances and its indulgences, which lived side by side in her with a zest for physicality, the vanity of a marketswoman who adored hats and hatpins.[41]

Religion thus seems to be relegated to the realm of the private in these books. However, as with politics in her work, "private" does not mean disregard for wider cultural relevance. While the representation of more explicitly political themes were accompanied by the relaxing of political sectarianism, the change in writing about religious and spiritual issues stemmed from personal experience. After the birth of her first child McGuckian suffered serious postpartum depression and was hospitalized for several weeks. At this time she experienced hallucinations and epiphanies about the Virgin Mary and was hearing "celestial" voices. These cathartic experiences left a fundamental mark on the way McGuckian viewed religion:

> The other thing was that one Sunday in the mental home, when I was coming out of it, I said I'd like to go to Mass. I hadn't been to Mass or confession since before my marriage, but because of this praying and Virgin Mary thing I went to Mass, and the experience was exactly like it had been with my grandmother a long time ago. The preconceptual, when the words were Latin, and everything there was slow motion. Because of the slowness I heard the creed like a poem. All the words of the Mass came through to me as poetry. I felt this is the most beautiful poetry in the world. It is just because we have got used to it. That was when I realised what poetry could be. I realised I had some kind of message to hand on and that I was in some degree a priest, from having been through this awful sacrificial thing.[42]

This most private of experiences has led the poet to engage again with the profundity of her religious heritage, albeit in a circuitous fashion.

In her later poetry, McGuckian introduces more overt religious symbolism. One of the most striking of these is the figure of the angel in her poems, who becomes an agent of poetic perception. Angels are arcane spiritual beings, whose personalities hover between celestial perfection and human frailty. Similarly to the muses, their characters inhabit our literary and religious consciousness. In literature, whether considered as messengers of God or translators of human prayer, their main role is to mediate the eternal discourse between humans and the other world. McGuckian has remarked that "Catholicism is simply a part of the way my mind thinks . . . there is a spiritual dimension with Catholicism which sometimes influences the way you see things like nature."[43] This explains the complexity in appearance and attitude of her angels. The attraction of these creatures for McGuckian seems to be their position as perpetual outsiders to both human and divine realms. Their purpose in "life" is analogous to poetry's function in McGuckian's view. They are not there to take sides; they are there to assist communication and mediate between segregated facets of the divide, whether this is political, religious, or personal. One could argue that McGuckian, by reviving the figure of the angel in her work, reverts to romantic notions of affinity between poetry and religion.[44] However, in most cases her poems are devoid of prophetic urges.

Another significant characteristic of the angels of McGuckian is their speech, or, on occasion, the lack of it. Linguistic indeterminacy is a well-known feature of McGuckian's work. However, the ambivalence of the speaking subject in most of the angel poems further complicates a straightforward resolution of meaning. Eléanor Kuykendall argues that "the existential challenge to win meaning from existence can be interpreted linguistically as the subject's challenge to win an understanding of the ambiguous sign—to attach meaning to a word."[45] By contrast, McGuckian's speaking subjects seem to strive for exactly the opposite: to challenge meaning and establish ambiguity as a means of communication. Problematizing their integrity as subjects, McGuckian allows her angels the freedom of incoherence. Or, in other words, she focuses on the processes of linguistic exchange, rather than its outcome.

Religion and spirituality thus have become expressions of mutability where slippage and transition can be freely expressed within McGuckian's oeuvre. Poetry, a world of near magic realism in McGuckian's imagination, presents a forum where the poet's voice cannot be held accountable but still has the freedom of expression. McGuckian sees a similarity between poetry and prayer which raises the question whether her entire oeuvre can be considered spiritualized even in the absence of obvious references.

The four overarching themes within Medbh McGuckian's poetry offer a window into her work and also help orientate scholars within the maze of literary criticism concerning her oeuvre. Literary performance is perhaps the most wide ranging theme that is under scrutiny in this study, as it is in many others. McGuckian is a poet whose *modus operandi* fascinates readers and critics alike. She is revolutionary in her linguistic expression and yet she is portrayed by some as a kind of "literary magpie" who hoards other people's words and puts them together with spectacular effect. Her originality and innovativeness are under constant scrutiny, as are her inventive vocabulary and rebellious grammar. Gender and motherhood form a different, yet similarly rich source of critical inquiry within her work. McGuckian defies stereotypes and one-dimensional symbolisms. Among the often conflicting female representations within her work critics can freely navigate with the help of psychoanalysis or feminist theories, unearthing new and exciting meanings and metaphorical connections. Political readings of her work are possibly more constrained by historical limitations that define her position within Northern Ireland. However, her linguistic inventiveness extends to her politicized aesthetics that avoids sectarian straight-jacketing. Spirituality remains the least explored (and probably most prevalent) aspect of her work, offering a rich source material for future scholars.

Notes

1. Elim Holmsten, "Double Doors: An Interview with Medbh McGuckian," *Nordic Irish Studies*, 3.1 (2004): 96.

2. Plato, *Complete Works*, ed. John M. Cooper and D. S. Hutchinson (Indianapolis, Cambridge: Hackett Publishing, 2007) Ion 534c; 942.

3. Simon Critchley, *Very Little . . . Almost Nothing: Death, Philosophy, Literature* (London: Routledge, 1997), 44.

4. Michaela Schrage-Früh, *Emerging Identities: Myth, Nation and Gender in the Poetry of Eavan Boland, Nuala Ni Dhomhnaill and Medbh McGuckian* (Trier: WVT, Wissenshaftlicher Verlag Trier, 2004), 145.

5. Moynagh Sullivan, "The Woman Poet and the Matter of Representation in Modern and Postmodern Poetics," PhD diss., University College of Dublin, 2001.

6. The works of Luce Irigaray and Jacques Lacan are also often invoked for this purpose. See for example Eileen Cahill, "'Because I Never Garden': Medbh McGuckian's Solitary Way," *Irish University Review: Journal of Irish Studies* 24, no. 2 (Fall–Winter 1994): 264–71; or Helen Blakeman, "Metaphor and Metonymy in Medbh McGuckian's Poetry," *Critical Survey* 14, no. 2 (2002): 61–74.

7. On this point see Patricia Boyle Haberstroh, *Women Creating Women: Contemporary Irish Women Poets* (Dublin: Attic Press, 1996), 132.

8. It is not accidental that Plato also chose to refer to poetic creation through birthing imagery. See "Symposium" and Diotima's definition of poets as being "pregnant in soul," "giving birth in beauty" (Plato, "Symposium," lines 206–7).

9. Laura O'Connor, "*Comhrá*: Conversation between Medbh McGuckian and Nuala Ní Dhomhnaill," *Southern Review* 31, no. 3 (Summer 1995): 596.

10. Medbh McGuckian, "Double Doors: An Interview with Medbh McGuckian," by Elin Holmsten. *Nordic Irish Studies* 3, no. 1 (2004): 96–97.

11. Ibid., 97.

12. On the gendering of the sublime in Edmund Burke's work see Jefferson Holdridge, *Those Mingled Seas: The Poetry of W. B. Yeats, the Beautiful and the Sublime* (Dublin: University College Dublin Press, 2000), 19–21.

13. Holmsten, "Double Doors," 98.

14. Ibid.

15. On this subject see Schrage-Früh, *Emerging Identities*, 201–7.

16. "I suppose the sleeping woman on the cover of my *Selected* is one way I could visualise the North. Passive, unconscious, undeveloped, sheltered, vulnerable, exposed all at once," quoted in Ibid., 200.

17. Michaela Schrage-Früh, unpublished interview with Medbh McGuckian, 2004.

18. Schrage-Früh, *Emerging Identities*, 139.

19. Patrick Williams for example, in his notoriously scathing review of *On Ballycastle Beach*, laments that "even if one allowed that the assembled imagery constitutes a personal lyric vision, there is the question of how that vision relates to the wider social and political world we all live in. Surely no writer's personal vision . . . is so inward that it will not at times be seen to inform an attitude towards the more commonly shared world around him [*sic*]? I doubt whether a writer whose work does not do this at all can be said to have a valid way of seeing, and I believe this applies here." Patrick Williams, "Spare That Tree," review of *On Ballycastle Beach*, by Medbh McGuckian, *Honest Ulsterman* 86 (Spring–Summer 1989): 51. Neil Corcoran also states that McGuckian's poetry "does not address itself, even obliquely, to the social and political circumstances of the North; it does not speak about 'the Troubles.'" Neil Corcoran, "Medbh McGuckian," in *Poets of Great Britain and Ireland since 1960, Dictionary of Literary Biography*, ed. Vincent B. Sherry, Jr., vol. 40, pt. 1 (Detroit: Gale Group, 1985), 353.

20. Medbh McGuckian, "An Attitude of Compassions: Q and A with Medbh McGuckian," by Kathleen McCracken, *Irish Literary Supplement: Review of Irish Books* 9, no. 2 (Fall 1990): 21.

21. Medbh McGuckian, "An Interview with Medbh McGuckian," by Susan Shaw Sailer, *Michigan Quarterly Review* 32, no. 1 (Winter 1993): 117.

22. Ibid., 123.

23. Medbh McGuckian, "Drawing Ballerinas: How Being Irish Has Influenced Me as a Writer," in *Wee Girls: Women Writing from an Irish Perspective*, ed. Lizz Murphy (North Melbourne, Vic, Australia: Spinifex Press, 1996), 194.

24. Ibid., 194.

25. Clair Wills, *Improprieties, Politics and Sexuality in Northern Irish Poetry* (Oxford: Clarendon Press, 1993), 17–18.

26. Ibid., 77.

27. Leontia Flynn, "Reading Medbh McGuckian," PhD diss., Queens University Belfast, 2004, 204.

28. Fran Brearton, *Reading Michael Longley* (Tarset, Northumberland: Bloodaxe Books, 2006), 54.

29. Peter McDonald, *Mistaken Identities: Poetry and Northern Ireland* (Oxford: Oxford University Press, 1997), 80.

30. Shane Alcobia-Murphy, *Sympathetic Ink: Intertextual Relations in Northern Irish Poetry* (Liverpool: Liverpool University Press, 2006), 117.

31. Ibid., 96.

32. Interview with Medbh McGuckian in Alcobia-Murphy, *Sympathetic Ink*, 117.

33. Nadezhda Mandelstam, *Hope against Hope: A Memoir*, trans. Max Hayward (New York: Atheneum, 1972) 167.

34. Alcobia-Murphy, *Sympathetic Ink,* 116.

35. Michael Allen "Barbaric Yawp, Gibbous Voice," review of *Venus and the Rain*, by Medbh McGuckian, *Honest Ulsterman* 77 (Winter 1984): 63.

36. McGuckian, "Drawing Ballerinas," 186.

37. Ibid., 188.

38. Ibid.

39. Medbh McGuckian, e-mail message to author, November 11, 2011.

40. O'Connor, "*Comhrá*," 596.

41. McGuckian, "Drawing Ballerinas," 188.

42. O'Connor, "*Comhrá*," 596.

43. Medbh McGuckian, "Interview with Medbh McGuckian," by John Brown, in *In the Chair: Interviews with Poets from the North of Ireland* (Cliffs of Moher, Ireland: Salmon, 2002), 174.

44. For a detailed discussion of this topic see David Fuller, "Poetry, Music, and the Sacred," in *The Arts and Sciences of Criticism*, ed. David Fuller and Patricia Waugh (Oxford: Oxford University Press, 1999), 180–99.

45. Eléanor H. Kuykendall, "Simone de Beauvoir and Two Kinds of Ambivalence in Action," in *The Thinking Muse: Feminism and Modern French Philosophy*, ed. Jeffner Allen and Iris Marion Young (Bloomington: Indiana University Press, 1989), 36.

AFTERWORD: HOW TO END IT ALL

"The authentic answer is always the question's vitality."

—Blanchot[1]

In her essay "How to End it All" Hermione Lee ponders a biographer's psychological difficulty in completing a book on her subject: "But we have still not reached a point, in the writing and reading of life-stories, where 'end of story' is a neutral or simple moment."[2]

Hermione Lee concludes that eventually it is the life, work, and personality of the subject which will determine the ultimate shape and structure of the book written. The current study is of course not a biography; however, there is still a necessary sense of letting go when a monograph on a single poet is completed. But along with the need to conclude and summarize, to tie the loose ends, this book must end in searching. As Tsvetaeva famously proclaimed in one of her letters: "All my doors are entrances, with no exits."[3] In a similar vein this research should stand as an invitation to enter the peculiar and fascinating poetic world of Medbh McGuckian, without offering a way to escape, following in the spirit of the poet's statement that "my words are traps / Through which you pick your way."[4] Throughout her volumes McGuckian positions small clues within large poetic strokes. These clues lead to a set of understandings that are as diverse and contradictory as the work itself. Even for the most devoted McGuckian scholars areas of obscurity, absence, and sheer bafflement remain. However, this uncertainty also gives encouragement for McGuckian's readers. Not only are there vast numbers of poems that await scrutiny, but the wide palette of critical approaches also leaves space for any number of new readings of this poet's work. All kinds of interpretations can be written and rewritten. Thus this book, rather than offering the ultimate key to McGuckian's poetry, was written with the purpose of introducing the major themes that occur in the poet's work and also to present a critical reading that can act as one potential entryway into this fascinating writer's oeuvre.

The aesthetic development of the creative voice alongside with the poet's conceptualization of the writing process emerges as the major theme of this study. For the most part the reading methodology offered in this book considers the writing processes and the formation of the creative self. This aesthetic approach offers a coherent reading through the majority of the volumes, allowing McGuckian's work to crystallize in terms of the joint processes of creation and reception. Although her poetic voice has gone through significant transformations since the early years, the poet's insistence on reflecting on the reading, as well as on the writing processes, has ensured that aesthetic analyses are always germane to her criticism. In the early work McGuckian's main aesthetic concern was the development and formation of an authentic writing self, one recognizably feminine and yet free from a feminist agenda. In her middle volumes her attention shifts more toward society, reflecting on the political situation of Northern Ireland and also introducing a historical dimension to her work. Arising from this concern is her consideration of violence in some of the later volumes, which, in turn, leads to a deep-seated meditation on spirituality in her most recent work. As a new departure, some of her latest poems consider environmental issues, offering scholars an opportunity to investigate her work in a novel critical context.

Apart from the aesthetic, the second main theme that this research has discussed is McGuckian's consideration of gender within her work. Part of this concerns the poet's reimagining of the figure of the muse, which is traditionally, and quite uselessly for women writers, conceptualized as a passive female backdrop to male creativity. Many feminist critics of McGuckian rightfully identify a sensitivity to this dichotomy in her work, highlighting the poet's subversive and innovative response to the patriarchal delegitimization of female authorship in the sexist and outdated image of the muse. However, as this book demonstrates, the subversive strategies of McGuckian transcends the sexual polarity justly rejected by feminism and presents her readers with a model of artistic creation that, arguably, reaches back to pre-Platonic times and beyond romanticized notions of creativity. In that context the muse is not necessarily entangled in the battle of the sexes but, rather, is represented as a sometimes regendered, and at other times de-gendered, figure, who participates in, and occasionally dictates, literary performance.

In an Irish feminist context this is a genuinely innovative approach. Medbh McGuckian has consistently resisted conscription into feminist ranks, and in her interviews she proves keen to confound inquiries concerning her gender politics. As noted previously, in contrast to figures such as Eavan Boland, McGuckian disrupts readings that search for a feminist liberation politics in her work. Her poetry demonstrates an apparent lack of interest in feminist strategies of emancipation, and yet, as I have pointed out in this book, many of her poems reflect on the self of the woman writer. This is also true with regard to the figure of the mother in her poetry. In her earliest volumes childbirth and motherhood are portrayed as traumatizing life events that shape the creation of the writing self. McGuckian, quite exceptionally among her peers, articulates some of the psychological processes that she experienced during pregnancy and childbirth. Thus many of her earlier poems recreate a sense of unconscious birthing and severance, with the work on the page emerging as the loved progeny, who nevertheless traumatizes its maker. In the middle volumes motherhood, just as her other themes, becomes more markedly politicized. Figures like Mother Ireland and the Virgin Mary inhabit the poems, hinting at an increased sense of abstraction in the poet's mind. As a result maternity becomes less corporeal and more cognitive, reflecting on the historical and political significance of the mother figure in an Irish context. In the final volumes intergenerationality appears and alongside with it a reinterpretation of maternal roles. However, the subconscious link between corporeal mothering and poetic creation never leaves the poet: many of these later poems return to the idea of letting go, albeit transported into the context of adulthood and grieving for a lost parent. Thus, several works ponder mothering adult children, and, similarly, the poems' creative process reflect on the poet's meditations on letting them go to their readers. In terms of gender then it seems that McGuckian's primary aim is to challenge and reject narrowly defined identities and offer instead a conceptual feminization of poetic identity, whether through the figure of the muse or the mother or other feminine markers within her work. This is wonderfully achieved within her peculiar aesthetic, which poeticizes the politicized gestures of contemporary feminism.

The same strategy characterizes Medbh McGuckian's exploration of Irish history and political ideology. In her efforts to detach her poetry from sectarianism and overt political commentary, she often divorces meaning from the historical referents she enlists within her work. Thus, for example, Robert Emmet and Orpheus—two of her male muses—metamorphose into poeticized signifiers, who thematize but do not articulate, her political ideology. Tracing McGuckian's politicized aesthetic highlights her unique strategy in dealing with her social and ideological environment. In these political volumes

McGuckian thematically approaches significant historical moments and offers covert commentary on current political situations. However, the real strength of her poems emanates from what is left unsaid. Violence, the most disturbing aspect of living in Northern Ireland, takes center stage in these works. There are direct references to horrific sectarian events, but there are also more covert ways of meditating on the meaning of this violence. Aesthetically many of the poems reflect on their own violent beginnings and also on the violence experienced by their exposure to readers, a concept that frequently occupies the poet's mind. In addition, violence appears in many guises, both as corporeal and mental injuries in historical and current events. McGuckian does not document violence but, rather, finds poetic ways to recreate its process, as well as effects. This results in a poetry which is meditative but also commemorative and reflective. Unlike her fellow Northern Irish poets, such as Seamus Heaney or Michael Longley, she chooses abstraction rather than narration to comment on the lived experience of violence within her home country.

Spirituality, the fourth and final major theme considered in this book, has perhaps the greatest potentiality in opening up new avenues of research in the future. McGuckian was often pressed about her Catholicism in the early years of her career. Many critics were interested in this subject because of the sectarian identity politics of Northern Ireland, while others were keen to position McGuckian within the context of a more secularized feminist ideology. As always, the poet has remained enigmatic in relation to this subject. On the one hand she stated to less than popular acclaim among feminist readers that she had thought of her vocation as a poet in terms of becoming a priest. Yet, on the other hand she discussed a sense of oppression that she experienced in her upbringing in a religious catholic environment. Interestingly, in her early volumes she presents a kind of feminized spirituality which considers birth and rebirth in this context. However, there are few direct references to her religion in her early work, despite the sporadically surfacing Catholic iconography in the poems. The middle volumes, on the other hand, introduce a more robust articulation of a catholic identity, albeit more in political than in religious terms. An identification with a catholic heritage takes center stage, with frequent references to well-known saints and Catholic political figures. Spirituality becomes increasingly central to some of her later volumes, particularly *The Book of the Angel.* These works reevoke the spirituality of the early volumes, but interestingly with a more overt use of Catholic imagery and references to Christ, angels, and saints. It seems that the poet's Catholic identity is becoming increasingly articulated in religious as well as political terms. This may be traced partly to the more relaxed political atmosphere within Northern Ireland but also to the poet's amplified interest in matters religious.

To conclude, McGuckian's peculiar aesthetic of poeticization reveals her as a poet of major importance. Her considerable poetical output and diverse thematic approaches open up many avenues for further research, most obviously, perhaps, in terms of her political intertexts, her identity politics within a wider context of feminist scholarship, and her spiritual and environmental concerns. However, as this book has sought to demonstrate, tracing her creative processes produces an opportunity to explore previously neglected aspects of her poetry. Applying the notion of creativity as performance allows the inner mechanisms of her compositional process to be brought to light. Combining the metaphorical with the performative has also proved a viable reading technique in a contemporary context. Thus the book has provided a reading of the poems of Medbh McGuckian which considered them in their entirety as literary performances that offer metaphorical interpretations of their own production. In this way both the theory and methodology presented in this book offer productive ways to examine the work of this exciting poet. It is my hope, however, that the questions raised in this book remain open to further interpretation and that they can serve as testimony to the vitality and exceptional quality of the poetry of Medbh McGuckian.

Notes

1. Maurice Blanchot, *The Space of Literature*, trans. Ann Smock (Lincoln: University of Nebraska Press, 1982), 9.
2. Hermione Lee, *Virginia Woolf's Nose: Essays on Biography* (Princeton, NJ: Princeton University Press, 2007), 105.
3. Marina Tsvetaeva, "Letter to Boris Pasternak," in *Letters Summer 1926: Correspondence between Pasternak, Tsvetaeva, Rilke*, quoted in Clair Wills, *Improprieties, Politics and Sexuality in Northern Irish Poetry* (Oxford: Clarendon Press, 1993), 169.
4. "On Ballycastle Beach," in Medbh McGuckian, *OBB* (Loughcrew: Gallery Press, 1995), 61.

AWARDS

2002	Forward Poetry Prize (Best Single Poem), "She is in the Past, She Has This Grace"
1992	Irish Times Irish Literature Prize for Poetry, *Marconi's Cottage*, shortlist
1989	The Cheltenham Prize, *On Ballycastle Beach*
1983	Alice Hunt Bartlett Award, *The Flower Master*
1982	Rooney Prize for Irish Literature, *The Flower Master*
1982	Ireland Arts Council Award, *The Flower Master*
1980	Eric Gregory Award
1979	National Poetry Competition, "The Flitting"

BIBLIOGRAPHY

Primary Sources

POETRY COLLECTIONS

The Book of the Angel. Oldcastle, Ireland: Gallery Press, 2004.
Captain Lavender. Oldcastle, Ireland: Gallery Press, 1994.
The Currach Requires No Harbours. Oldcastle, Ireland: Gallery Press, 2006.
Drawing Ballerinas. Oldcastle, Ireland: Gallery Press, 2001.
The Face of the Earth. Oldcastle, Ireland: Gallery Press, 2002.
The Flower Master. Oxford: Oxford University Press, 1982.
The Flower Master and Other Poems. Oldcastle, Ireland: Gallery Press, 1993.
Had I a Thousand Lives. Oldcastle, Ireland: Gallery Press, 2003.
The High Caul Cap. Oldcastle, Ireland: Gallery Press, 2012.
Marconi's Cottage. Oldcastle, Ireland: Gallery Press, 1991.
My Love Has Fared Inland. Oldcastle, Ireland: Gallery Press, 2008.
On Ballycastle Beach. Oxford: Oxford University Press, 1988. Reprint, Oldcastle, Ireland: Gallery Press, 1995, 2000.
Portrait of Joanna. Belfast: Ulsterman Publications, 1980.
Selected Poems. Oldcastle, Ireland: Gallery Press, 1991. Reprint, *Selected Poems: 1978–1994,* selected and edited by Peter Fallon, 1997.
Shelmalier. Oldcastle, Ireland: Gallery Press, 1994. Reprint 1998.
Single Ladies. Budleigh Salterton, Devon: Interim Press, 1980.
The Soldiers of the Year II. Winston-Salem, NC: Wake Forest University Press, 2002.
Two Women, Two Shores, Poems by Medbh McGuckian and Nuala Archer. Galway: Salmon Poetry, 1989.
Venus and the Rain. Oxford: Oxford University Press, 1984. Reprint, Oldcastle, Ireland: Gallery Press, 1994.

DISCOGRAPHY

Medbh McGuckian, Paul Durcan, Brendan Kennelly, and Michael Longley. "Four Irish Poets Reading and Talking about Their Work." Poetry Quartets Series, vol. 4. London: British Council [with] Bloodaxe Books, 1999. Audiobook on cassette. Durcan and Kennelly recorded at Trinity College, Dublin, on June 23, 1999; Longley and McGuckian recorded in Belfast on June 24, 1999.

SELECTED ARTICLES, REVIEWS, AND TRANSLATIONS

"Author Statement." British Council Literature, n.d. http://literature.britishcouncil.org/medbh-mcguckian (accessed October 19, 2013).

The Big Striped Golfing Umbrella: An Anthology of Children's Poetry from Northern Ireland, edited by Medbh McGuckian. Belfast: Arts Council of Northern Ireland, 1985.

"Birds and Their Masters." *Irish University Review: Journal of Irish Studies* 23, no. 1 (Spring–Summer 1993): 29–33.

"Death Withstood." Review of *The Redress of Poetry: Oxford Lectures*, by Seamus Heaney. *Fortnight Review* 344 (November 1995): 36.

"Don't Talk to Me About Dance." Review of *Philomena's Revenge*, by Rita Ann Higgins. *Poetry Ireland Review* 35 (Summer 1992): 98–100.

"Drawing Ballerinas: How Being Irish Has Influenced Me as a Writer." In *Wee Girls: Women Writing from an Irish Perspective*, edited by Lizz Murphy, 185–203. North Melbourne, Vic, Australia: Spinifex Press, 1996.

"Emotion Recollected in Tranquillity." In *Delighting the Heart: A Notebook by Women Writers*, edited by Susan Sellers, 59–60. London: Women's Press, 1989.

"An Eye on the Everyday." Review of *Faber Poetry Introduction 5* [with Hugh Haughton]. *Times Literary Supplement,* August 13, 1982, 876.

"Horsepower Pass By!: A Study of the Car in the Poetry of Seamus Heaney." *Metre* 3 (Autumn 1997): 70–83.

"How Precious Are Thy Thoughts Unto Me." Review of *Art in the Light of Conscience: Eight Essays on Poetry*, by Marina Tsvetaeva, *Common Knowledge* 2, no. 1 (Spring 1993): 132–41.

"How to Write a Prize-Winning Poem Every Quarter Century." *Rialto* 52 (2002): 5–7.

"If Poetry Come Not as Naturally as the Leaves to a Tree." In *Delighting the Heart: A Notebook by Women Writers*, edited by Susan Sellers, 142–47. London: Women's Press, 1989.

"Michael Longley as a Metaphysical." *Colby Quarterly*, 39, no. 3 (September 2003): 215–20.

"Mystical Island in a Dusky Bay." Review of *Real Ireland: People and Landscape,* by Liam Blake. *Fortnight,* 211 (December 1984), 23.

"Rescuers and White Cloaks: Diary, 1968–69." In *My Self, My Muse: Irish Women Poets Reflect on Life and Art*, edited by Patricia Boyle Haberstroh, 137–54. Syracuse, NY: Syracuse University Press, 2001.

Review of *The Harper of the Only God, Selected Poems of Alice Milligan*, by editor Sheila Turner Johnston. *Fortnight Review* 328 (May 1994): 47.

Review of *Irish Arts Review*, by editor Homan Potterton. *Fortnight* 339 (May 1995): 34–35.

"Room of Calm, Room of Thunder . . ." In *Delighting the Heart: A Notebook by Women Writers*, edited by Susan Sellers, 25–26. London: Women's Press, 1989.

"There is No Feminine in Eternity." In *Delighting the Heart: A Notebook by Women Writers*, edited by Susan Sellers, 177–79. London: Women's Press, 1989.

"The Timely Clapper." Contributory short piece in "The State of Poetry" special issue, edited by Gerald Dawe and Jonathan Williams. *Krino* 14 (Winter 1993): 45–46.

The Water Horse: Poems in Irish, by Nuala Ní Dhomhnail. Translations into English by Medbh McGuckian and Eiléan Ní Chuilleanáin. Oldcastle, Ireland: Gallery Press, 1999.

"Women Are Trousers." In *Border Crossings: Irish Women Writers and National Identities*, edited by Kathryn Kirkpatrick, 157–89. Tuscaloosa: University of Alabama Press, 2000.

"Visiting Poet." *Irish Review* 11 (Winter 1991–1992): 47–49.

INTERVIEWS

"An Attitude of Compassions: Q and A with Medbh McGuckian." By Kathleen McCracken. *Irish Literary Supplement: Review of Irish Books* 9, no. 2 (Fall 1990): 20–21.

"A Dialogue with Medbh McGuckian, Winter 1996–1997." By Rand Brandes. *Studies in the Literary Imagination* 30, no. 2 (Fall 1997), 37–62.

"Double Doors: An Interview with Medbh McGuckian." By Elin Holmsten. *Nordic Irish Studies* 3, no. 1 (2004): 93–100.

"A Hinge Into Something Larger: Meetings with Medbh McGuckian." By Helen Kidd. *Oxford Poetry* 8, no. 2 (Winter 1994–1995): 53–57.

"'I Am Listening in Black and White to What Speaks to Me in Blue': Medbh McGuckian." By Helen Blakeman. *Irish Studies Review* 11, no. 1 (April 2003): 61–69.

"In the Country of Comparative Peace: Interview with Medbh McGuckian." By Philip Harvey. *Encounter*, ABC Radio National, December 12, 2004. Transcript at: http://www.abc.net.au/radionational/programs/encounter/in-the-country-of-comparative-peace/3427894 (accessed October 18, 2013).

"Interview with Medbh McGuckian." By Shane Alcobia-Murphy and Richard Kirkland. In *The Poetry of Medbh McGuckian: The Interior of Words*, edited by Shane Alcobia-Murphy and Richard Kirkland, 194–207. Cork: Cork University Press, 2010.

"An Interview with Medbh McGuckian." By Rand Brandes. *Chattahoochee Review* 16, no. 3 (Spring 1996): 56–65.

"Interview with Medbh McGuckian." By John Brown. In *In the Chair: Interviews with Poets from the North of Ireland*, by John Brown, 169–84. Cliffs of Moher, Ireland: Salmon, 2002.

"Interview with Medbh McGuckian." By Gerald Dawe. *The Poetry Programme*, RTE Radio 1, December 6, 2008.

"Interview with Medbh McGuckian." By Vona Groarke. In *The VERSE Book of Interviews: 27 Poets on Language, Craft, and Culture*, edited by Brian Henry and Andrew Zawacki, 106–17. Amherst, MA: Verse, 2005.

"Interview with Medbh McGuckian." By John Hoppenthaler. *Connotation Press Online* 4, no. 4 (February 2013). http://www.connotationpress.com/a-poetry-congeries-with-john-hoppenthaler/415 (accessed October 18, 2013).

"An Interview with Medbh McGuckian." By María Jesús Lorenzo-Modia. *European English Messenger* 13, no. 2 (Autumn 2004): 35–43.

"Interview with Medbh McGuckian." By Deirdre Murphy. *Irish Literary Supplement* 16, no. 1 (1997): 21–23.

"An Interview with Medbh McGuckian." By Susan Shaw Sailer. *Michigan Quarterly Review* 32, no. 1 (Winter 1993): 111–27.

"An Interview with Medbh McGuckian." By Michaela Schrage-Früh. *Contemporary Literature* 46, no. 1 (Spring 2005): 1–17.

"An Interview with Medbh McGuckian." By Danielle Sered. *Nua: Studies in Contemporary Irish Writing* 2, nos.1–2 (Autumn–Spring 1998–1999): 151–62.

"Interview with Medbh McGuckian." By Rebecca Wilson. In *Sleeping with Monsters: Conversations with Scottish and Irish Women Poets*, edited by Rebecca Wilson and Gillean Somerville-Arjat, 1–7. Dublin: Wolfhound Press, 1990.

"Interview with Michael Longley, Edna Longley, Medbh McGuckian, and Ciaran Carson." By Simon Armitage, BBC STANZA. Radio broadcast recorded at John Hewitt International School, July 28, 1995. Excerpt printed in *Sympathetic Ink: Intertextual Relations in Northern Irish Poetry*, by Shane Alcobia-Murphy, 116–17, 139. Liverpool: Liverpool University Press, 2006.

"Medhb McGuckian—Telling Men about the Feminine Experience." By Anne Langford. *Queen's Letter* 2, no. 6 (April 1986), 3.

"The Mutiny of Selves: An Interview with Medbh McGuckian." By Rebecca Wilson. *Cencrastus* 29 (Spring 1988): 17–21.

"'My Words Are Traps': An Interview with Medbh McGuckian." By John Hobbs. *New Hibernia Review/Iris Éireannach Nua: A Quarterly Record of Irish Studies* 2, no. 1 (Spring 1998): 111–20.

"The Resolution of Opposites: Part One. Interview with Medbh McGuckian." By Sarah Broom. *Poetry and Audience* 37, no. 1 (1995): 39–44.

"The Resolution of Opposites: Part Two. Interview with Medbh McGuckian." By Sarah Broom. *Poetry and Audience* 37, no. 2 (Summer 1996): 10–17.

"Surfacing: An Interview with Medbh McGuckian." By Kimberly S. Bohman. *Irish Review* 16 (Autumn–Winter 1994): 95–108.

"Under the North Window: An Interview with Medbh McGuckian." By Sawnie Morris. *Kenyon Review* 23, nos. 3–4 (Summer–Fall 2001): 64–74.

Secondary Sources

Alcobia-Murphy, Shane. "'If I Prolonged the Look to Rediscover Your Face': Medbh McGuckian's Ekphrastic Elegies." In *The Enclave of My Nation: Crosscurrents in Irish and Scottish Culture*, edited by Cross-currents Conference, Shane Alcobia-Murphy, and Margaret Maxwell, 1–17. Aberdeen: AHRC Centre for Irish and Scottish Studies, 2008.

———. *Medbh McGuckian: The Poetics of Exemplarity.* Aberdeen Introductions to Irish and Scottish Culture, Aberdeen: AHRC Centre for Irish and Scottish Studies, 2012.

———. "'The Name Flows from the Naming': The Key to Understanding Medbh McGuckian's Poetry." *Estudios Irlandeses: Journal of Irish Studies* 3 (March 2008): 1–9. http://estudiosirlandeses.org/2008/03/the-name-flows-from-the-naming-the-key-to-understanding-medbh-mcguckians-poetry/ (accessed October 10, 2013).

———. "'Not Forgotten or Passed Over at the Proper Time': The Representation of Violent Events in Contemporary Culture." *Cultura, Lenguaje y Representación* [*Culture, Language and Representation*] 2 (2005): 19–40.

———. "'Re-Reading Five, Ten Times, the Simplest Letters': Detecting Voices in the Poetry of Medbh McGuckian." *Nordic Irish Studies* 5, no. 1 (2006): 123–47.

———. ed. "'The Same Seed That Carried Me Till It Saw Itself as Fruit': Medbh McGuckian's Exemplars." In *What Rough Beasts? Irish and Scottish Studies in the New Millennium*, 12–24. Newcastle-upon Tyne: Cambridge Scholars Publishing, 2008.

———. *Sympathetic Ink: Intertextual Relations in Northern Irish Poetry*. Liverpool: Liverpool University Press, 2006.

———. "'That Now Historical Ground': Memory and Atrocity in the Poetry of Medbh McGuckian." In *The Poetry of Medbh McGuckian: The Interior of Words*, edited by Shane Alcobia-Murphy and Richard Kirkland, 130–46. Cork: Cork University Press, 2010.

Alcobia-Murphy, Shane, and Richard Kirkland, eds. *The Poetry of Medbh McGuckian: The Interior of Words*. Cork: Cork University Press, 2010.

Allen, Michael. "Barbaric Yawp, Gibbous Voice." Review of *Venus and the Rain*, by Medbh McGuckian. *Honest Ulsterman* 77 (Winter 1984): 59–64.

———. "The Poetry of Medbh McGuckian." In *Contemporary Irish Poetry: A Collection of Critical Essays*, edited by Elmer Andrews, 286–309. London: Macmillan, 1992.

Andrews, Elmer, ed. *Contemporary Irish Poetry: A Collection of Critical Essays*. Basingstoke: Macmillan, 1992.

———. "'Some Sweet Disorder': The Poetry of Subversion: Paul Muldoon, Tom Paulin, and Medbh McGuckian." In *British Poetry from the 1950s to the 1990s: Politics and Art*, edited by Gary Day and Brian Docherty, 118–42. London: Macmillan; New York: St. Martin's Press, 1997.

Ankori, Gannit. *Imaging Her Selvei: Frida Kahlo's Poetics of Identity and Fragmentation*. Westport, CT: Greenwood Press, 2002.

Archer, Nuala. "Preface." In *Two Women, Two Shores: Poems,* by Medbh McGuckian and Nuala Archer. Galway: Salmon Press; Baltimore: New Poet Series, 1989.

Arthur, Paul. "Republicanism and the Implementation of the Agreement—An Academic Perspective," Working Paper in British-Irish Studies, no. 44. Dublin: Institute for British-Irish Studies, University College of Dublin, 2005. http://www.ucd.ie/ibis/filestore/wp2005/44/44_mmpa.pdf (accessed October 23, 2013).

Attridge, Derek. *The Singularity of Literature*. London: Routledge, 2004.

Batten, Guinn. "Boland, McGuckian, Ní Chuilleanáin and the Body of the Nation." In *The Cambridge Companion to Contemporary Irish Poetry*, edited by Matthew Campbell, 169–88. Cambridge: Cambridge University Press, 2003.

———. "'The More with Which We Are Connected': The Muse of the Minus in the Poetry of McGuckian and Kinsella." In *Gender and Sexuality in Modern Ireland*, edited by Anthony Bradley and Maryann Gialanella Valiulis, 212–44. Amherst: University of Massachusetts Press, 1997.

Baudrillard, Jean. *Symbolic Exchange and Death*. Thousand Oaks, CA: Sage Publications, 2004.

Beer, Ann. "Medbh McGuckian's Poetry: Maternal Thinking and a Politics of Peace." *Canadian Journal of Irish Studies* 18, no. 1 (July 1992): 192–203.

Beistle, Bronwyn S. "Honeyed Secrets: Authority, Sexuality, and Flower Imagery in Women's Literature from Wollstonecraft to McGuckian." PhD diss., University of Pennsylvania, 2004. http://repository.upenn.edu/dissertations/AAI3152014 (accessed October 10, 2013).

Bendall, Molly. "Flower Logic: The Poems of Medbh McGuckian." *Antioch Review* 48, no. 3 (Summer 1990): 367–71.

Benfey, Christopher. "A Venusian Sends a Postcard Home." Review of *Venus and the Rain*, by Medbh McGuckian. *Parnassus: Poetry in Review* 12–13, nos. 1–2 (1985): 500–512.

Bernard-Donals, Michael. "Governing the Tongue: Seamus Heaney's (A)Political Aesthetic." *Canadian Journal of Irish Studies* 20, no. 2 (December 1994): 75–88

Bew, Paul, and Gordon Gillespie. *Northern Ireland: A Chronology of the Troubles 1968–1999*. 2nd ed. Dublin: Gill and MacMillan, 1999.

Blakeman, Helen. "Medbh McGuckian and the Poetics of Mourning." In *The Body and Desire in Contemporary Irish Poetry*, edited by Irene Gilsenan Nordin, 197–212. Dublin: Irish Academic Press, 2006.

———. "Metaphor and Metonymy in Medbh McGuckian's Poetry." *Critical Survey* 14, no. 2 (2002): 61–74.

———. "'Poetry Must Almost Dismantle the Letters': McGuckian, Mallarmé and Polysemantic Play." In *The Poetry of Medbh McGuckian: The Interior of Words*, edited by Shane Alcobia-Murphy and Richard Kirkland, 68–83. Cork: Cork University Press, 2010.

Blanchot, Maurice. *The Space of Literature*. Translated by Ann Smock. Lincoln: University of Nebraska Press, 1982.

Blyth, Stephen. "Gift Rapt." Review of *Venus and the Rain*, by Medbh McGuckian. *PN Review 106* 22, no. 2 (November–December 1995): 59.

Bohman, Kimberly S. "Borders or Frontiers?: Gender Roles and Gender Politics in McGuckian's Unconscious Realm." *Irish Journal of Feminist Studies* 1, no. 1 (March 1996): 119–32.

———. Primordial Voices: Culture and Consciousness in the Poetry of Medbh McGuckian." PhD diss., Queen's University Belfast, 1994.

Booth, Martin. Review of *Venus and the Rain*, by Medbh McGuckian. *British Book News* (October 1984): 624.

Brahms, Johannes. *The Brahms Notebooks: Little Treasure Chest of the Young Kreisler*. Edited by Carl Krebs. Translated by Agnes Eisenberger (Hillsdale, NY: Pendragon Press, 2003.

Brazeau, Robert. "Troubling Language: Avant-Garde Strategies in the Poetry of Medbh McGuckian." *Mosaic: Journal for the Interdisciplinary Study of Literature* 37, no. 2 (June 2004): 127–44.

Brearton, Fran. *Reading Michael Longley*. Tarset, Northumberland: Bloodaxe Books, 2006.

Brewster, Scott. "The Space That Cleaves: The House and Hospitality in Medbh McGuckian's Work." In *The Poetry of Medbh McGuckian: The Interior of Words*, edited by Shane Alcobia-Murphy and Richard Kirkland, 105–16. Cork: Cork University Press, 2010.

Bristow, Joseph. Review of *The Flower Master*, by Medbh McGuckian. *Outposts Poetry Quarterly* 136 (Spring 1983): 29–30.

Broom, Sarah. "McGuckian's Conversations with Rilke in *Marconi's Cottage*." *Irish University Review: Journal of Irish Studies* 28, no. 1 (Spring–Summer 1998): 133–50.

Brown, Anne E., and Marjanne E. Goozé. *International Women's Writing: New Landscapes of Identity*. Westport, CT: Greenwood Press, 1995.

Burgoyne-Johnson, Jolanta. *Bleeding the Boundaries: The Poetry of Medbh McGuckian*. Coleraine: Cranagh Press, 1999.

Burt, Stephen. "A Wave Gone West." Review of *Selected Poems*, by Medbh McGuckian. *Times Literary Supplement*, February 13, 1998, 1.

Butler, Judith. *Precarious Life: The Powers of Mourning and Violence*. London: Verso, 2004.

Byrne, Muriel St. Clare, ed. *The Lisle Letters: An Abridgement*. Selected and arranged by Bridget Boland. Chicago: University of Chicago Press, 1983.

Byron, Catherine. "A House of One's Own: Three Contemporary Irish Women Poets." *Women's Review* 19 (May 1987): 32–33.

———. "Such Declarations Are Routine in the McGuckian Household—A Response to Patrick Williams's Review of *On Ballycastle Beach*." *Honest Ulsterman* 87 (Summer–Autumn 1989): 89.

———. "'This Room Is a Kind of Travel Also': An Appreciation of the Poetry of Medbh McGuckian." *Linen Hall Review* 5, no. 1 (Spring 1988): 16–17.

Cahill, Eileen. "'Because I Never Garden': Medbh McGuckian's Solitary Way." *Irish University Review: Journal of Irish Studies* 24, no. 2 (Fall–Winter 1994): 264–71.

Cahoone, Lawrence E., ed. *From Modernism to Postmodernism: An Anthology*. Oxford: Blackwell, 2003.

Campion, Peter. Review of *The Soldiers of Year II*, by Medbh McGuckian. *Poetry* 183, no. 2 (November 2003): 96–98.

Carson, Ciaran. "This Great Estrangement." Review of *Shelmalier*, by Medbh McGuckian. *Verse* 16, no. 2 (Spring 1999): 31.

Carville, Conor. "'Warding Off an Epitaph': Had I a Thousand Lives." In *The Poetry of Medbh McGuckian: The Interior of Words*, edited by Shane Alcobia-Murphy and Richard Kirkland, 117–29. Cork: Cork University Press, 2010.

Chapman, Sandra. "A Lot of My Work at the Moment Is a Cry from the Heart—Medbh McGuckian." *Belfast Telegraph*, February 1, 1984.

Clark, Timothy. *The Theory of Inspiration: Composition as a Crisis of Subjectivity in Romantic and Post-Romantic Writing*. Manchester: Manchester University Press, 1997.

Clutterbuck, Catriona M. "Gender and Self-Representation in Irish Poetry: The Critical Debate. *Bullán: An Irish Studies Journal* 4, no. 1 (Autumn 1998): 43–58.

———. "A Gibbous Voice: The Poetics of Subjectivity in the Early Poetry of Medbh McGuckian." In *The Poetry of Medbh McGuckian: The Interior of Words*, edited by Shane Alcobia-Murphy and Richard Kirkland, 41–67. Cork: Cork University Press, 2010.

———. "Irish Women's Poetry and the Republic of Ireland." In *Writing in the Irish Republic: Literature, Culture, Politics 1949–1999*, edited by Ray Ryan, 17–43. Basingstoke: Macmillan, 2000.

———. "Self-Representation and the Politics of Authority in Contemporary Irish Poetry: Eavan Boland and Medbh McGuckian." PhD diss., University of Oxford, 1996.

Clyde, Tom "An Ulster Twilight: Poetry in the North of Ireland." *Krino* 5 (Spring 1988): 95–102.

Collins, Lucy. "Here, More Than Anywhere." Review of *The Tree House*, by Kathleen Jamie and *The Book of the Angel*, by Medbh McGuckian. *Metre* 17 (2005): 95–99.

———. "Joyful Mysteries: Language and Spirituality in Medbh McGuckian's Recent Poetry." In *Irish Women Writers: New Critical Perspectives*, edited by Elke D'hoker, Raphaël Ingelbien, and Hedwig Schwall, 41–55. Oxford: Peter Lang, 2011.

Conboy, Katie. "The Join Between Centuries." Review of *Shelmalier*, by Medbh McGuckian. *Poetry Ireland Review* 62 (Autumn 1999): 30–33.

Cook, Jim. "New Found Land." Review of *Venus and the Rain*, by Medbh McGuckian. *New Statesman*, August 31, 1984, 26.

Corcoran, Neil, ed. *The Chosen Ground: Essays on the Contemporary Poetry of Northern Ireland*. Bridgend: Seren Books; Chester Springs; PA: Dufour Editions, 1992.

———. "Medbh McGuckian." In *Poets of Great Britain and Ireland since 1960, Dictionary of Literary Biography*, edited by Vincent B. Sherry, Jr., vol. 40, pt. 1, 352–55. Detroit: Gale Group, 1985.

———. "A Pen Mislaid: Some Varieties of Women's Poetry: Medbh McGuckian, Anne Stevenson, Carol Rumens, and Denise Riley." In *English Poetry Since 1940*, edited by Neil Corcoran, David Carroll, and Michael Wheeler, 221–34. Harlow, Essex: Longman Publishing Group, 1995.

Critchley, Simon. *Very Little . . . Almost Nothing: Death, Philosophy, Literature*. London: Routledge, 1997.

Cunningham, Francine. Review of *Marconi's Cottage*, by Medbh McGuckian. *Fortnight* 310 (October 1992): 52.

Cunningham, Valentine. *Reading after Theory*. Oxford, MA: Blackwell, 2002.

Daniels, Kate. "Ireland's Best." *Southern Review* 35, no. 2 (Spring 1999): 387–402.

———. "Poet to Poet: A Look at Medbh McGuckian's Language." *Shenandoah: Washington and Lee University Review* 51, nos. 2–3 (Summer–Fall 2001): 46–54.

Davis, Dick. "Private Poems." *Listener* 108, no. 2791, December 16, 1982, 23–24.

Dawe, Gerald. "Notion of Perfection." *Fortnight* 190 (January 1983): 20.

de Fréine, Celia. "Translator's Licence—A Look at Translation in Relation to the Poetry of Nuala Ní Dhomhnaill." *Honest Ulsterman* 103 (Spring 1997): 25–29.

Denman, Peter. "Ways of Saying: Boland, Carson, McGuckian." In *Poetry in Contemporary Irish Literature*, edited by Michael Kenneally, 158–73. Gerrards Cross, UK: Colin Smythe, 1995.

Derrida, Jacques. "Deconstruction and the Other: An Interview with Jacques Derrida." In *Dialogues with Contemporary Continental Thinkers*, edited by Richard Kearney, 105–26. Manchester, UK: Manchester University Press, 1984.

Docherty, Thomas. *Alterities: Criticism, History, Representation*. Oxford: Clarendon Press, 1996.

———. "Initiations, Tempers, Seductions: Postmodern McGuckian." In *The Chosen Ground: Essays on the Contemporary Poetry of Northern Ireland*, edited by Neil Corcoran, 189–210. Bridgend: Seren Books; Chester Springs, PA: Dufour Editions, 1992.

Dooley, Tim. "Soft Cushionings." Review of *The Flower Master*, by Medbh McGuckian. *Times Literary Supplement*, October 29, 1982, 1200.

Drexel, John. "Threaders of Double-Stranded Words: News from the North of Ireland." Review of *On Ballycastle Beach*, by Medbh McGuckian. *New England Review and Bread Loaf Quarterly* 12, no. 2 (Winter 1989): 179–92.

Duffy, Michael, ed. "Dug-Out," *FirstWorldWar.Com: The War to End All Wars*, May 25, 2006, http://www.firstworldwar.com/atoz/dugout.htm (accessed October 22, 2013).

Eberle, Wendy J. "Painting a Pictographic Language, beyond Sound Boundaries: Medbh McGuckian's Poetic Making." *Canadian Journal of Irish Studies* 22, no. 1 (July 1996): 61–70.

Eco, Umberto. *Interpretation and Overinterpretation*. Cambridge: Cambridge University Press, 1992.

Elliott, Andrew. "Poetry." Review of *Venus and the Rain*, by Medbh McGuckian. *Linen Hall Review* 1, no. 3 (Autumn 1984): 20–21.

Elliott, Marianne. *Wolfe Tone: Prophet of Irish Independence*. New Haven, CT: Yale University Press, 1990.

Emmitt, Helen V. "Rhyming Hope and History: Medbh McGuckian's Recent Poetry." *Shenandoah: Washington and Lee University Review* 51, nos. 2–3 (Summer–Fall 2001): 55–67.

Faragó, Borbála. "Artfully Placed Mirrors: The Poetry of Medbh McGuckian." *Ana ChronisT* 3 (1997): 166–84.

———. "Medbh McGuckian: The Angel in Two Parts." *European English Messenger* 13, no. 2 (Autumn 2004): 47–55.

———. "'The Meeting of Two Tidal Roads': Tradition and Identity in Medbh McGuckian's *The Face of the Earth* and Eiléan Ní Chuilleanáin's *The Girl Who Married the Reindeer*." *Hungarian Journal of English and American Studies* 10, nos. 1–2 (Spring–Fall 2004): 331–41.

———. "Origin and Oblivion: Representations of Death in the Poetry of Medbh McGuckian and Eiléan Ní Chuilleanáin." In *Ireland: Space, Text, Time*, edited by Yvonne Whelan, Liam Harte, and Patrick Crotty, 67–76. Dublin: Liffey Press, 2005.

———. "Other People's Houses in Contemporary Irish Women's Poetry." In *The Binding Strength of Irish Studies: Festschrift in Honour of Csilla Bertha and Donald E. Morse*, edited by Marianna Gula, Mária Kurdi, and István D Rácz, 179–91. Debrecen, Hungary: Debrecen University Press, 2011.

———. "'Self-Portrait in the Act of Painting a Self-Portrait': Tropes of Inspiration in Medbh McGuckian's Shelmalier." *Études Britanniques Contemporaines* 25 (December 2003): 31–45.

———. "'They Come Into It': The Muses of Medbh McGuckian." In *The Poetry of Medbh McGuckian: The Interior of Words*, edited by Shane Alcobia-Murphy and Richard Kirkland, 162–77. Cork: Cork University Press, 2010.

Fine, Ellen S. "Witness of the Night." In *Bloom's Modern Critical Interpretations: Night.* New York: Chelsea House, 2001.

Flam, Jack. *Matisse: The Man and His Art, 1869–1918.* Ithaca, NY: Cornell University Press, 1986.

———. *Matisse on Art.* Berkeley: University of California Press, 1995.

Flanagan, Joseph. "A Review Essay of Ciaran Carson's *The Twelfth of Never*, Medbh McGuckian's *Shelmalier*, and Michael Longley's *The Weather in Japan.*" *Nua: Studies in Contemporary Irish Writing* 3, nos. 1–2 (2002): 171–78.

Fleming, Deborah, ed. *Learning the Trade: Essays on W. B. Yeats and Contemporary Poetry.* West Cornwall, CT: Locust Hill Press, 1993.

Flynn, Leontia. "Domestic Violences: Medbh McGuckian and Irish Women's Writing in the 1980s." In *The Oxford Handbook of Modern Irish Poetry*, edited by Fran Brearton and Alan Gillis, 419–34. Oxford: Oxford University Press, 2012.

———. "'No Misprints in This Work': The Poetic 'Translations' of Medbh McGuckian and Frank Kuppner." In *Modern Irish and Scottish Poetry*, edited by Peter Mackay, Edna Longley, and Fran Brearton, 280–93. Cambridge: Cambridge University Press, 2011.

———. "Reading Medbh McGuckian" PhD diss., Queen's University Belfast, 2004.

———. "Re-Assembling the Atom: Reading Medbh McGuckian's Intertextual Materials." In *The Poetry of Medbh McGuckian: The Interior of Words*, edited by Shane Alcobia-Murphy and Richard Kirkland, 177–92. Cork: Cork University Press, 2010.

Fogarty, Anne. "Fault Lines." *Graph* 2, no. 1 (1995): 18–25.

———. "'A Noise of Myth': Speaking (as) Woman in the Poetry of Eavan Boland and Medbh McGuckian." *Paragraph: Journal of Modern Critical Theory*, 17, no. 1 (March 1994): 92–102.

Foley, Imelda. "Girls in the Big Picture." *Women's Tongues*. Special Issue, *Fortnight* 393 (March 2001): 17–19.

François, Anne-Lise. *Open Secrets: The Literature of Uncounted Experience.* Stanford, CA: Stanford University Press, 2008.

French, Mikela. "Resurrecting the Live Body: Medbh McGuckian, Marina Carr and Felim Egan." Master's thesis, Queen's University Belfast, 2001.

Fulford, Sarah. *Gendered Spaces in Contemporary Irish Poetry.* Oxford: Peter Lang, 2002.

———. "Lyric Flight." Review of *Had I a Thousand Lives*, by Medbh McGuckian. *Poetry Review* 93, no 4. (Winter 2003–2004), 84. http://www.poetrysociety.org.uk/content/publications/poetrynews/922to951/pr93no4/ (accessed October 16, 2013).

Fuller, David. "Poetry, Music, and the Sacred." In *The Arts and Sciences of Criticism*, edited by David Fuller and Patricia Waugh, 180–99. Oxford: Oxford University Press, 1999.

Gilsenan Nordin, Irene, ed. *The Body and Desire in Contemporary Irish Poetry.* Dublin: Irish Academic Press, 2006.

Gonzalez, Alexander G. "Celebrating the Richness of Medbh McGuckian's Poetry: Close Analysis of Six Poems from *The Flower Master*." In *Contemporary Irish Women Poets: Some Male Perspectives*, edited by Alexander G. Gonzalez, 43–64. Westport, CT: Greenwood Press, 1999.

———. "An Introduction to Reading Medbh McGuckian's Poetry: Close Analysis of 'The Chain Sleeper.'" *Notes on Modern Irish Literature* 9 (1997): 44–47.

———. "Older Women, Younger Men: Different Perspectives on the Use of Power in Nuala Ní Dhomhnaill's 'Flowers' and Mebdh McGuckian's 'From the Dressing-Room.'" *Notes on Modern Irish Literature* 12 (2000): 22–26.

Goodby, John. *Irish Poetry since 1950: From Stillness into History.* Manchester: Manchester University Press, 2000.

Grant, Patrick. *Breaking Enmities: Religion, Literature and Culture in Northern Ireland, 1967–1997.* Basingstoke: Macmillan, 1999.

———. *Literature, Rhetoric and Violence in Northern Ireland, 1968–98: Hardened to Death.* Houndmills, Basingstoke: Palgrave, 2001.

Gray, Cecile. "Medbh McGuckian: Imagery Wrought to Its Uttermost." In *Learning the Trade: Essays on W. B. Yeats and Contemporary Poetry*, edited by Deborah Fleming, 165–77. West Cornwall, CT: Locust Hill Press, 1993.

Guiccioli, Byron, and Teresa Guiccioli. *The Last Attachment: The Story of Byron and Teresa Guiccioli as Told in Their Unpublished Letters and Other Family Papers.* Edited by Iris Origo. New York: C. Schribner's Sons, 1949.

Haberstroh, Patricia Boyle. *Women Creating Women: Contemporary Irish Women Poets.* Dublin: Attic Press, 1996.

Hall, Linda Biesele. *Mary, Mother and Warrior: The Virgin in Spain and the Americas.* Austin: University of Texas Press, 2004.

Han, Eunwon. "A Possibility of Women's Writings: A Study on Medbh McGuckian's Poems in the Context of J. Kristeva's Theory." *Journal of English Language and Literature/Yongo Yongmunhak* 42, no. 4 (Winter 1996): 791–811.

Hand, Sean, ed. *Emmanuel Levinas: The Levinas Reader.* Oxford: Blackwell, 1989.

Hannan, Dennis J., and Nancy Means Wright. "Irish Women Poets, Breaking the Silence." *Canadian Journal of Irish Studies* 16, no. 2 (December 1990): 57–65.

Haughton, Hugh. "An Eye on the Everyday." *Times Literary Supplement*, August, 13, 1982, 876.

Heaney, Seamus. *The Cure at Troy, A Version of Sophocles' Philoctetes.* London: Faber and Faber, 1990.

Henigan, Robert H. "Contemporary Women Poets in Ireland." *Concerning Poetry* 18, nos. 1–2 (1985): 103–15.

Hipp, Shannon. "'Things of the Same Kind That Are Separated Only by Time': Reading the Notebooks of Medbh McGuckian," *Irish University Review: Journal of Irish Studies* 39, no. 1 (Spring–Summer 2009): 130–48.

Holden, James. *In Search of Vinteuil: Music, Literature and a Self Regained.* Eastbourne: Sussex Academic Press, 2010.

Holdridge, Jefferson. *Those Mingled Seas: The Poetry of W. B. Yeats, the Beautiful and the Sublime.* Dublin: University College Dublin Press, 2000.

Holmsten, Elin. "The Hermeneutics of Otherness in Medbh McGuckian's Poetry." PhD diss., Uppsala University, 2006.

———. "'Like a Wished-For Body': Dialogues of Desire in the Poetry of Medbh McGuckian." In *The Body and Desire in Contemporary Irish Poetry*, edited by Irene Gilsenan Nordin, 163–81. Dublin: Irish Academic Press, 2006.

———. "Signs of Encounters in Medbh McGuckian's Poetry." In *The Poetry of Medbh McGuckian: The Interior of Words*, edited by Shane Alcobia-Murphy and Richard Kirkland, 84–107. Cork: Cork University Press, 2010.

———. "'Those Deeply Carnal Moments': The Hermeneutics of Flesh in Medbh McGuckian's Poetry." *Nordic Irish Studies* 2, no. 1 (2003): 29–45.

Homem, Rui Carvalho. "Looking for Clues: McGuckian, Poems and Portraits." In *Writing and Seeing: Essays on Word and Image*, edited by Rui Carvalho Homem and Maria de Fátima Lambert, 187–98. Amsterdam, Netherlands: Rodopi, 2006.

Hooley, Ruth, ed. *The Female Line: Northern Irish Women Writers*. Belfast: Northern Ireland Women's Rights Movement, 1985.

Hope, Christopher. "Meaty Flavours." Review of *The Flower Master*, by Medbh McGuckian. *London Magazine* 22, nos. 9–10 (December 1982–January 1983): 106–11.

Hufstader, Jonathan. *Tongue of Water, Teeth of Stones: Northern Irish Poetry and Social Violence.* Lexington, KY: University of Kentucky Press, 1999.

Iser, Wolfgang. "The Reading Process: A Phenomenological Approach." In *Modern Criticism and Theory: A Reader*, edited by David Lodge, 211–28. London: Longman, 1994.

———. "Towards a Literary Anthropology." In *The Future of Literary Theory*, edited by Ralph Cohen, 208–28. London: Routledge, 1989.

Jaeger, Edmund C. *Desert Wildlife*. Stanford, CA: Stanford University Press, 1950.

Jenkins, Alan. "Private and Public Languages." Review of *The Flower Master*, by Medbh McGuckian. *Encounter* 59, no. 5 (November 1982): 56–63.

Jones, Noragh. *Power of Raven, Wisdom of Serpent: Celtic Women's Spirituality*. Edinburgh: Floris Books, 1994.

Joyce, James. *The Portrait of the Artist as a Young Man*, edited by Richard Ellmann, rev. ed. London: Jonathan Cape, 1956.

Kahlo, Frida. "My Nurse and I," n.p., n.d. c. 1937. http://www.fridakahlofans.com/c0190.html (accessed November 30, 2010).

Kay, Magdalena. "Review of *The Currach Requires No Harbours*, by Medbh McGuckian." *World Literature Today* 82, no. 3 (May–June 2008): 72.

Kearney, Richard. ed. *Modern Movements in European Philosophy*. Manchester: Manchester University Press, 1994.

Kenneally, Michael. *Cultural Contexts and Literary Idioms in Contemporary Irish Literature*. Gerrards Cross: Smythe, 1988.

———. ed. *Poetry in Contemporary Irish Literature*. Gerrards Cross, UK: Colin Smythe, 1995.

———. "Preface." In *Map-Maker's Colours: New Poets of Northern Ireland*, edited by Todd Swift and Martin Mooney, 10. Montreal, Quebec: Nu-Age Editions, 1988.

Kennedy-Andrews, Elmer. "Medbh McGuckian, the Lyric of Gendered Space." In *Writing Home: Poetry and Place in Northern Ireland, 1968–2008*, 225–48. Cambridge: D. S. Brewer, 2008.

Keogan, Kate. "Questioning Faith." Review of *Collected Poems*, by Sally Purcell, *Portrait of My Lover as a Horse*, by Selima Hill, and *The Face of the Earth*, by Medbh McGuckian. *PN Review 152* 29, no. 6 (July–August 2003): 77–78.

Keogh, Dáire, and Nicholas Furlong. *The Mighty Wave: The 1798 Revolution in Wexford.* Dublin: Four Courts Press, 1996.

Kettenmann, Andrea. *Frida Kahlo, 1907–1954: Pain and Passion.* Translated by Karen Williams. Köln, Germany: Benedikt Taschen, 2003.

Kiberd, Declan. *Irish Classics.* London: Granta Books, 2000.

Kirkland, Richard. "Medbh McGuckian and the Politics of Minority Discourse." In *The Poetry of Medbh McGuckian: The Interior of Words*, edited by Shane Alcobia-Murphy and Richard Kirkland, 147–61. Cork: Cork University Press, 2010.

Krauss, Rosalind. "The Future of an Illusion." In *The Future of Literary Theory*, edited by Ralph Cohen, 280–90. London: Routledge, 1989.

Kristeva, Julia. "Motherhood According to Giovanni Bellini." In *20th Century Theories of Art*, edited by James M. Thompson, 441–66. Ottawa: Carleton University Press, 1999.

———. *Powers of Horror: An Essay on Abjection.* New York: Columbia University Press, 1982.

Kuykendall, Eléanor H. "Simone de Beauvoir and Two Kinds of Ambivalence in Action." In *The Thinking Muse: Feminism and Modern French Philosophy*, edited by Jeffner Allen and Iris Marion Young, 35–50. Bloomington: Indiana University Press, 1989.

Lee, Hermione. *Virginia Woolf's Nose: Essays on Biography.* Princeton, NJ: Princeton University Press, 2007.

Lorenzo-Modia, María Jesús, and Cristina Fernández-Méndez. "'Longer and Longer Sentences Prove Me Wholly Female': Medbh McGuckian and Feminism(s)." In *Writing Bonds: Irish and Galician Contemporary Women Poets*, edited by Manuela Palacios and Laura Lojo, 33–56. Bern: Peter Lang, 2009.

Lowry, Elizabeth. "Dream On." Review of *Selected Poems*, by Medbh McGuckian. *Metre* 4 (Spring–Summer 1998): 46–53.

Lucas, John. "Pleading for the Authenticity of the Spirit." Review of *The Flower Master*, by Medbh McGuckian. *New Statesman*, August 13, 1982, 20–21.

———. "A Rose for the Betrayed World." Review of *The Flower Master*, by Medbh McGuckian. *New Statesman and Society Master,* August 26, 1988, 38.

Maggi, Wynne. *Our Women Are Free: Gender and Ethnicity in the Hindukush.* Ann Arbor: University of Michigan Press, 2001.

Mallot, J. Edward. "Medbh McGuckian's Poetic Tectonics." *Éire-Ireland: Journal of Irish Studies* 40, nos. 3–4 (Fall-Winter 2005): 240–55.

Mandelstam, Nadezhda. *Hope against Hope: A Memoir.* Translated by Max Hayward. New York: Atheneum, 1972.

Maron, Meva. "The Stamps Had Squirrels on Them." *Honest Ulsterman* 88 (Winter 1989–1990): 33–34.

Martin, Randall. *Women Writers in Renaissance England.* London: Longman: 1997.

Masson, Georgina. "The Navicella." In "The Companion Guide to Rome." St. Peters Basilica website http://saintpetersbasilica.org/Interior/Navicella/Navicella.htm (accessed January 17, 2012).

Matthews, Steven. *Irish Poetry: Politics, History, Negotiation.* London: Macmillan Press, 1997.

Matthiessen, Peter. *The Snow Leopard*. New York: Penguin Nature Classics, 1996.

McAlpine, Katherine, and Gail White. *The Muse Strikes Back: A Poetic Response by Women to Men*. Brownsville, OR: Story Line Press 1997.

McAuley, Leon. "Wuthering Depths." Review of *Marconi's Cottage*, by Medbh McGuckian. *Honest Ulsterman* 93 (1992): 63–65.

McCarthy, Gerard. Review of *On Ballycastle Beach*, by Medbh McGuckian. *Irish University Review: Journal of Irish Studies* 19, no. 1 (Spring 1989): 175–77.

McDonald, Peter. *Mistaken Identities: Poetry and Northern Ireland*. Oxford: Oxford University Press, 1997.

McElroy, James. "Night Feed: An Overview of Ireland's Women Poets." *American Poetry Review* 14, no. 1 (January–February 1985): 32–39.

McGuiness, Arthur E. "Hearth and History: Poetry by Contemporary Irish Women." In *Cultural Contexts and Literary Idioms in Contemporary Irish Literature*, edited by Michael Kenneally, 197–220. Gerrards Cross: Colin Smythe, 1988.

Meaney, Gerardine. "Myth, History and the Politics of Subjectivity: Eavan Boland and Irish Women's Writing." *Women: A Cultural Review* 4, no. 2 (Autumn 1993): 136–53.

———. "Sex and Nation: Women in Irish Culture and Politics." In *A Dozen Lips*, edited by Eavan Boland et al., 188–204. Dublin: Attic Press, 1994.

Melander, Ingrid. "Two Poems by Medbh McGuckian: Symbol and Interpretation." In *Anglo-Irish and Irish Literature: Aspects of Language and Culture. Proceedings of the Ninth International Congress of the International Association for the Study of Anglo-Irish Literature Held at Uppsala University, 4–7 August 1986*, edited by Birgit Bramsbäck and Martin Croghan, 237–41. Uppsala, Sweden: Uppsala University Press,1988.

———. "The Use of Traditional Symbols in Three Poems by Medbh McGuckian." *Moderna språk* 83, no. 4 (1989): 298–303.

Meredith, Fionola. "Like Reading in the Dark." Review of *The Face of the Earth*, by Medbh McGuckian. *Fortnight* (February 2003): 25–29.

Michelis, Angelica. "A Country of One's Own? Gender and National Identity in Contemporary Women's Poetry." *European Journal of English Studies* 6, no. 1 (April 2002): 61–70.

Mitchell, Erin C. "Slippage at the Threshold: Postmodern Hospitality in Medbh McGuckian's Poetry." *LIT: Literature Interpretation Theory* 17, no. 2 (April–June 2006): 137–55.

Moi, Toril. *What Is a Woman?: And Other Essays*. Oxford: Oxford University Press, 1999.

Mole, John. "From Wave to Cave." Review of *Venus and the Rain*, by Medbh McGuckian. *Encounter* 63, no. 5 (December 1984): 56–63.

Moloney, Ed. *A Secret History of the IRA*. New York: W. W. Norton, 2002.

de Montaigne, Michel. "That to Study Philosophy Is to Learn to Die." In *The Complete Workes of Michel de Montaigne*, edited by William Hazlitt. London: J. Templeman, 1842.

Morrison, Blake. "Tropical Storms." Review of *Venus and the Rain*, by Medbh McGuckian. *London Review of Books* 6, no. 16 (September 1984): 22–23.

Murphy [a.k.a. Alcobia-Murphy], Shane. "A Code of Images: Northern Irish Centos." *Irish Studies Review* 10, no. 2 (August 2002): 193–203.

———. "Don't Mention the War: The Trouble(s) in Northern Irish Poetry." In *The Aesthetics and Pragmatics of Violence*, edited by Michael Hensen and Annette Pankratz, 89–102. Passau, Germany: Verlag Karl Stutz, 2001.

———. "'A Dove Involving A Whole Nation': Politics in the Poetry of Medbh McGuckian." *Études Irlandaises* 24, no.1 (Spring 1999): 91–108.

———. "'The Eye that Scanned It': The Picture Poems of Heaney, Muldoon, and McGuckian." *New Hibernia Review/Iris Éireannach Nua* 4, no.4 (Winter 2000): 85–115.

———. "Intertextual Relations in the Poetry of Medbh McGuckian." In *Back to the Present Forward to the Past: Irish Writing and History since 1798*, edited by Patricia A. Lynch, Joachim Fischer, and Brian Coates, vol. 2, 271–85. Amsterdam, Netherlands: Rodopi, 2006.

———. "Obliquity in the Poetry of Paul Muldoon and Medbh McGuckian." *Éire-Ireland: Journal of Irish Studies* 31, nos. 3–4 (Fall–Winter 1996): 76–101.

———. "Roaming Root of Multiple Meanings: Intertextual Relations in Medbh McGuckian's Poetry." *Metre* 4. (Winter 1998): 99–109.

———. "Sonnets, Centos and Long Lines: Muldoon, Paulin, McGuckian and Carson." In *The Cambridge Companion to Contemporary Irish Poetry*, edited by Matthew Campbell, 189–208. Cambridge: Cambridge University Press, 2003.

———. "Writing in the Shit: The Northern Irish Poet and Authority." *Canadian Journal of Irish Studies* 24, no. 1 (July 1998): 1–21.

———. "'You Took Away My Biography': The Poetry of Medbh McGuckian." *Irish University Review: Journal of Irish Studies* 28, no. 1 (Spring–Summer 1998): 110–32.

Newmann, Kate. "All Sorts of Untils." Review of *Marconi's Cottage*, by Medbh McGuckian; *The Man Who Was Marked*, by Paula Meehan. *Irish Review* 12 (Spring–Summer 1992): 173–75.

O'Brien, Peggy. "Reading Medbh McGuckian: Admiring What We Cannot Understand." *Colby Quarterly* 28, no. 4 (December 1992): 239–50.

O'Connor, Laura. "*Combrá*: Conversation between Medbh McGuckian and Nuala Ní Dhomhnaill." *Southern Review* 31, no. 3 (Summer 1995): 581–614.

O'Connor, Mary. "'Rising Out': Medbh McGuckian's Destabilizing Poetics." *Eire-Ireland: Journal of Irish Studies* 30, no. 4 (Winter 1996): 154–72.

O'Donnell, Mary. "Responsibility and Narcosis." Review of *What's What*, by Julie O'Callaghan; *Marconi's Cottage*, by Medbh McGuckian. *Poetry Ireland Review* 35 (Summer 1992): 108–12.

Ó hÓgáin, Dáithí. *Myth, Legend and Romance: An Encyclopedia of the Irish Folk Tradition*. New York: Prentice Hall Press, 1991.

O'Loughlin, Michael. "Twenty One Today." Review of *The Younger Irish Poets*, by Gerald Dawe; *Behind the Garden Gnomes*, by Conleth O'Connor; *The Flower Master*, by Medbh McGuckian; *Saturday Night in York Street*, by John Campbell." *Books Ireland* 66 (September 1982): 148.

O'Mahony, John. "Troubles in Mind." *Guardian*, July 7, 1993, 4.

O'Neill, Charles L. "Medbh McGuckian's Poetry: Inhabiting the Image." In *Contemporary Irish Women Poets: Some Male Perspectives*, Alexander G Gonzalez, 65–78. Westport, CT: Greenwood Press, 1999.

O'Rawe, Des. Review of *Captain Lavender*, by Medbh McGuckian. *Irish Review* 19 (Spring–Summer 1996): 123.

Orbach, Susie. *Hunger Strike: The Anorectic's Struggle as a Metaphor for Our Age*. London: Faber and Faber, 1986.

O'Reilly, Catriona. "Afloat on the Sea of Language." Review of *Selected Poems*, by Medbh McGuckian. *Irish Times*, November 22, 1997, weekend edition, 9.

Pasternak, Yevgeny, et al. *Pasternak, Tsvetaeva, Rilke. Letters: Summer 1926*. Translated by Margaret Wettlin and Walter Arndt. Oxford: Oxford University Press. 1988.

Plato. *Collected Works*. Edited by John M. Cooper and D. S. Hutchinson. Indianapolis, IN: Hackett Publishing, 1999. *Ion* 534c; 942.

Porter, Susan. "The 'Imaginative Space' of Medbh McGuckian." *Canadian Journal of Irish Studies* 15, no. 2 (December 1989): 93–104.

Potts, Donna L. *Contemporary Irish Poetry and the Pastoral Tradition*. Columbia: University of Missouri Press, 2011.

Pratt, William. Review of *Selected Poems, 1978–1994,* by Medbh McGuckian. *World Literature Today* 72, no. 4. (Autumn 1998): 836.

———. Review of *Shelmalier*, by Medbh McGuckian. *World Literature Today* 73, no. 4 (Autumn 1999): 744–45.

Purbrick, Louise. "The Last Murals of Long Kesh: Fragments of Political Imprisonment at the Maze Prison, Northern Ireland." In *Archaeologies of Internment*, edited by Adrian Myers and Gabriel Moshenska, 263–83. New York: Springer, 2011.

Pybus, Rodney. "Matters of Ireland: Recent Irish Poetry." *Stand* 22, no. 3 (1981): 72–78.

Quinn, Justin. "The Weather of Irish Poetry." *Sewanee Review* 111, no. 3 (Summer 2003): 486–92.

Rafferty, Clodagh. "'*Breaking the Blue*': A Study of Female Voices in Contemporary Irish Poetry," PhD diss., Vassar College, 2006.

Rees-Jones, Deryn. "Motherlands and Mothertongues: Writing the Poetry of Nation." In *Consorting with Angels: Essays on Modern Women Poets*, 174–214. Newcastle: Bloodaxe Books, 2005.

Ricoeur, Paul. *Hermeneutics and the Social Sciences*. Translated by John B. Thompson. Paris: Éditions de la Maison des Sciences de l'homme; Cambridge: Cambridge University Press, 1998.

Robinson, Alan. "Declarations of Independence: Some Responses to Feminism." In *Instabilities in Contemporary British Poetry*, 202–8. Basingstoke: Macmillan, 1988.

Robinson, Tim. *Connemara: Listening to the Wind*. London: Penguin Books, 2007.

Sailer, Susan Shaw. "Women in Rooms, Women in History." In *Pedagogy, Praxis, Ulysses: Using Joyce's Text to Transform the Classroom*, edited by Robert Newman, 97–120. Ann Arbor: University of Michigan Press, 1996.

Sansom, Ian. "Savours." Review of *On Ballycastle Beach*, by Medbh McGuckian. *PN Review 105* 22, no. 2 (November–December 1995).

Schrage-Früh, Michaela. *Emerging Identities: Myth, Nation and Gender in the Poetry of Eavan Boland, Nuala Ni Dhomhnaill and Medbh McGuckian.* Trier: WVT, Wissenschaftlicher Verlag Trier, 2004.

———. "'My Being Cries Out to Be Incarnate': The Virgin Mary and Female Sexuality in Contemporary Irish Women's Poetry." In *The Body and Desire in Contemporary Irish Poetry*, edited by Irene Gilsenan Nordin, 123–44. Dublin: Irish Academic Press, 2006.

———. "Speaking as the North: Self and Place in the Early Poetry of Medbh McGuckian." In *The Poetry of Medbh McGuckian: The Interior of Words*, edited by Shane Alcobia-Murphy and Richard Kirkland, 22–40. Cork: Cork University Press, 2010.

Sealy, Douglas. "Review of *The Flower Master*, by Medbh McGuckian." *Poetry Ireland Review* 5–6 (1982): 57–63.

Sered, Danielle. "'By Escaping and [Leaving] a Mark': Authority and the Writing Subject of the Poetry of Medbh McGuckian." *Irish University Review: Journal of Irish Studies* 32, no. 2 (Autumn–Winter 2002): 273–85.

———. *The Destination of a Rhyme: Elusiveness and Theft in the Poetry of Medbh McGuckian.* Ft. Lauderdale, FL: Dept. of Liberal Arts, Nova Southeastern University, 2001.

Shenandoah. "A Medbh McGuckian Feature." Shenandoah: *Washington and Lee University Review* 51, nos. 2–3 (Summer–Fall 2001): 39–67.

Shteir, Ann B. *Cultivating Women, Cultivating Science: Flora's Daughters and Botany in England, 1760–1860.* Baltimore: Johns Hopkins University Press, 1996.

Sirr, Peter. "'How Things Begin to Happen': Notes on Eiléan Ní Chuilleanáin and Medbh McGuckian." *Southern Review* 31, no. 3 (Summer 1995): 450–67.

Smith, Michael. "Seeing the World through Metaphors." Review of *On Ballycastle Beach*, by Medbh McGuckian. *Irish Times,* June 24, 1995, 41.

Spike, John T. *Masaccio.* New York: Abbeville Press, 1995.

Starnino, Carmine. "Five from Ireland." Review of *The Currach Requires No Harbours*, by Medbh McGuckian. *Poetry* 193, no. 2 (November 2008): 149–61.

Stewart, A. T. Q. The Summer Soldiers: *The 1798 Rebellion in Antrim and Down.* Belfast: Blaxkstaff Press, 1995.

Sullivan, Moynagh. "The In-formal Poetics of Medbh McGuckian." *Nordic Irish Studies* 3 (2004): 75–92.

———. "A Poetic Self in Progress." Review of *Selected Poems*, by Medbh McGuckian. *Irish Literary Supplement* 17, no. 1 (Spring 1998).

———. Review of *The Face of the Earth*, by Medbh McGuckian. *Irish University Review: Journal of Irish Studies* 33, no. 1 (Spring–Summer 2003): 237–40.

———. "The Woman Poet and the Matter of Representation in Modern and Postmodern Poetics." PhD diss., University College Dublin, 2001.

Summers-Bremner, Eluned. "History's Impasse: Journey, Haunt and Trace in the Poetry of Medbh McGuckian." In *The Body and Desire in Contemporary Irish Poetry*, edited by Irene Gilsenan Nordin, 40–54. Dublin: Irish Academic Press, 2006.

Thomas, Michael. Review of *Selected Poems*, by Medbh McGuckian. *Irish Studies Review* 6, no. 3 (December 1998): 347–50.

Tillinghast, Richard. "Comedy, Interiority, History." Review of *Marconi's Cottage*, by Medbh McGuckian. *New York Times Book Review* 97 (August 30, 1992): 12.

Todd, Jennifer. "The Changing Structure of Conflict in Northern Ireland and the Good Friday Agreement." Working Papers in British-Irish Studies, no. 26. Dublin: Institute for British-Irish Studies, University College of Dublin, 2003. http://www.ucd.ie/ibis/filestore/wp2003/26_todd.pdf (accessed January 20, 2012).

Tomlinson, Janis A., ed. *Goya: Images of Women*. New Haven, CT: Yale University Press, 2002.

Törmä, Minna. *Landscape Experience as Visual Narrative: Northern Song Dynasty Landscape Handscrolls in the Li Cheng-Yan Wengui Tradition*. Helsinki: Tiedekirja, University of Michigan Press, 2002.

Townshend, Charles. *Easter 1916: The Irish Rebellion*. London: Penguin Bodes, 2006.

Vida, Giorgio Levi della. "Un opuscolo astrologico di Mâŝâ'allâh." *Rivista degli studi orientali* 14 (1934): 270–81.

Volsik, Paul. "Engendering the Feminine: Two Irish Poets—Eavan Boland and Medbh McGuckian." *Études Anglaises* 56, no. 2 (April–June 2003): 148–61.

Wheeler, Lesley. "Both Flower and Flower Gatherer: Medbh McGuckian's *The Flower Master* and H. D.'s *Sea Garden*." *Twentieth Century Literature* 49, no. 4 (Winter 2003): 494–519.

Welsch, Camille-Yvette. "New Irish Poets." Review of *The Soldiers of the Year II*, by Medbh McGuckian. *Women's Review of Books* 20, no. 9 (June 2003): 17.

Williams, Patrick. "Spare That Tree!" Review of *On Ballycastle Beach*, by Medbh McGuckian. *Honest Ulsterman* 86 (Spring–Summer 1989): 49–52.

Wills, Clair. "Contemporary Irish Women Poets: The Privatisation of Myth." In *Diverse Voices: Essays on Twentieth-Century Women Writers in English*, edited by Harriet Devine Jump, 248–72. New York: St Martin's Press, 1991.

———. *Improprieties, Politics and Sexuality in Northern Irish Poetry*. Oxford: Clarendon Press, 1993.

———. "Modes of Redress: The Elegy in Recent Irish Poetry." *Princeton University Library Chronicle* 59, no. 3 (Spring 1998): 594–620.

———. "The Perfect Mother: Authority in the Poetry of Medbh McGuckian." *Text and Context: Journal of Interdisciplinary Studies* 3 (Autumn 1988): 91–111.

———. "Upsetting the Public: Carnival, Hysteria and Women's Texts." In *Bakhtin and Cultural Theory*, edited by Ken Hirschkop and David Shepherd, 85–108. Manchester: Manchester University Press, 2001.

———. "Voices from the Nursery: Medbh McGuckian's Plantation." In *Poetry in Contemporary Irish Literature*, edited by Michael Kenneally, 373–99. Gerrards Cross, UK: Colin Smythe, 1995.

Wilson, William A. "A Dream—without the Pronoun 'I.'" Review of *On Ballycastle Beach*, by Medbh McGuckian. *Irish Literary Supplement* (Spring 1989): 17.

Wiseman, Mary Bittner. "Renaissance Paintings and Psychoanalysis: Julia Kristeva and the Function of the Mother." In *Ethics, Politics and Difference in Julia Kristeva's Writings*, edited by Kelly Oliver, 92–115. New York: Routledge, 1993.

Woolf, Virginia. *The Diary of Virginia Woolf 1920–1924*. Edited by Anne Olivier Bell. Vol. 2. New York: Harcourt, Brace, Jovanovich, 1980.

Zeiger, Melissa F. *Beyond Consolation: Death, Sexuality, and the Changing Shapes of Elegy*. Ithaca, NY: Cornell University Press, 1997.

Žižek, Slavoj. *Violence: Six Sideways Reflections*. London: Profile Books, 2008.

INDEX

ABOUT THE AUTHOR

Borbála Faragó is currently a Marie Curie Intra-European Fellow in the Central European University Budapest, Department of Gender Studies. She holds a PhD from University College Dublin and is the author of a number of articles on contemporary Irish poetry. A coedited collection of essays, titled *Facing the Other: Interdisciplinary Studies on Race, Gender and Social Justice in Ireland,* was published in 2008. Together with Eva Bourke she has also edited an anthology of Irish immigrant poetry titled *Landing Places: Immigrant Poets in Ireland* in 2010.